So Unimaginable a Price

So Unimaginable a Price

Baldwin and the Black Atlantic

✦

John E. Drabinski

NORTHWESTERN UNIVERSITY PRESS
EVANSTON, ILLINOIS

Northwestern University Press
www.nupress.northwestern.edu

Printed in the United States of America

10 9 8 7 6 5 4 3 2 1

Library of Congress Cataloging-in-Publication Data

Names: Drabinski, John E., 1968– author
Title: So unimaginable a price : Baldwin and the Black Atlantic / John E. Drabinski.
Description: Evanston, Illinois : Northwestern University Press, 2025. | Includes index.
Identifiers: LCCN 2025030203 | ISBN 9780810149557 paperback | ISBN 9780810149564 cloth | ISBN 9780810149571 ebook
Subjects: LCSH: Baldwin, James, 1924–1987—Criticism and interpretation | Black people—Atlantic Ocean Region—Philosophy | Black people—Atlantic Ocean Region—Intellectual life | African Americans—Intellectual life—20th century | Black people—Race identity | African American philosophy—20th century | African diaspora | Critical theory
Classification: LCC PS3552.A45 Z647 2026 | DDC 818.5409—dc23
LC record available at https://lccn.loc.gov/2025030203

for Jeff Ferguson, in memory

CONTENTS

PREFATORY NOTES

Why write about James Baldwin now?

Perhaps more than any other intellectual, Baldwin's nonfiction seems like a kind of cultural and political Rorschach test. Baldwin was really made for an age of memes and social media.[1] His snippet quotations are camera ready for an age of mass consumption and, in times of justice-based desperation, for the need of a synoptic take on the varieties of racial and political violence that have animated the United States since before its founding. This place, now the United States and prior to that an English colony, has been a site of racial violence—the conquest and genocide of indigenous people and its aftermaths, enslavement of Africans and its aftermaths—since the moment of English and European arrival. The need for a diagnosis and expression of outrage has been here from the beginning. A beginning, it is always worth underscoring, that, while transformed, seems to have no interest in or prospect for disappearing into history's rearview mirror. Like most beginnings, racial violence is less a mythic origin story and more a cruel recurrence. This is who we are. What it means to live in the long, immovable shadow cast by the moment of arrival, the moment of conquest and settlement and enslavement, and how we ought to live in relation to pasts and presences of racial violence (perpetrator and victim classes share inheritances, whatever the lived differences) are questions that do not close. The questions reshape themselves and repropose themselves to our conscience. We live in gruesome witness. We are seemingly set forever in front of outrageous and singular, yet reproducible at all levels of being and polis, racial injustice. This is the unimaginable price of being here, of being who we are. But when we live (or perhaps *because* we live) in the modality of witnessing, there is an obstinacy about time that opens up at least the *possibility* of another horizon. Another way of living. Another order of being that is not recurrence and cruel repetition, but something *otherwise*.

Perhaps this is the reason that we can find a Baldwin for any moment: rage, reconciliation, aloof perspective, historical purview, the view from nowhere, and so on. I have always thought that Baldwin, whether consciously or subconsciously, wrote in order to be quoted. It is part of what makes him such a compelling figure. Baldwin can capture, with pithy, quick words, just about any form of injustice we see in the United States. Perhaps injustice elsewhere too, but, in the end, he was always a thinker of *his* place: the United States, and perhaps more specifically the United States of the Northeast. Baldwin and the South is its own kind of question. At each turn, he is witness to his moment. Witness to the long, extended moment from emancipation to the Movement for Black Lives and everything in between.[2] Witness in his moment and witness, in his quotability, for decades after his death, which in the end is less about his prophetic voice than it is about his eye for what never changes. The recurrence of our beginning.[3] And so, I suspect, Baldwin will have been a certain kind of witness to and for everything to come in our foreseeable future. His words sit in a strange, alienated, and melancholic sense of time. Baldwin sees, describes, and witnesses what has been, what is, and, at his most ambitious, what we can conceive along the lines of the possible. That possible is never particularly edifying, even if Baldwin will posit himself at key points in interviews, and also in essays and fiction, as an optimist who engages in the rhetorical play and soul work of hope. All of this indicates real philosophical depth to his claims, many of which are at stake in the pages that follow. While antiblack racism is not metaphysical in the strict sense—that is, it is not *actually* an immovable structure of reality—it is pretty damn close. There is so little evidence to the contrary. That is the pain of time and the recurrence of our beginning.

No one wants that to be the case. Or at least no decent and better person does. But if there is a single lesson to be learned about the long history of antiblackness in the Americas, it is that that history is less a story of overcoming and more a story of transformation and reiteration. Transformation and reiteration come with diminishing violence, for sure. Our contemporary moment is not the horror of plantation slavery. It also comes without seriously diminishing returns because recurrence is terrible, terrifying, and persistent. The unimaginable price of antiblack racism continues to animate white people's deepest desires while also underpinning senses of rage, revolutionary consciousness, and refusal in African American identity formation.

At the same time, and this is the enigmatic kernel of his thinking, Baldwin's nonfiction is also *anything but* a Rorschach test and a ready-made quotation machine. The essays are also and first long meditations of the most serious and sincere order, meditations that a discerning reader can track with strong threads of continuity, philosophical depth, and nuanced distinctions that revolutionize and confound our thinking about race, identity, world making, and senses of home and belonging. Any serious reader of Baldwin, by which I mean anyone who reads and rereads his nonfiction in sequence and with an eye toward continuities and ruptures in thinking, also knows that Baldwin is forever an evasive read. He absolutely escapes our boldest projections of interests onto his text. Whatever the sound-bite, there is always more, and it resists easy characterization. Our critical discipline, patience, and attentiveness as readers is therefore paramount. Perhaps we see what we want in his work, as in the nature of the hermeneutic event, the event of reading and interpreting that discovers the reader in what is read. By the hermeneutic event I mean simply how we always read with *interests* and how those interests form what the critical essay says to us. We discover ourselves in acts of reading and interpretation; interest, concern, and conviction are just that strong, inserting themselves into the experience of readerly life. But Baldwin's essays are also in every case their own kind of journey and they take us there. Dragging and kicking or cheering and joyful, they take us there. Indeed, one thing that always strikes me about Baldwin's nonfiction style is how he draws us out in multiple directions, producing a swirl of attention and highlight, shifting across provocative tangents, and then he interrupts and surprises with some of the most incisive observations one can imagine about race and racism in the United States. That surprise and the jolt to our understanding is as transformative as it is thrilling. Baldwin's easy style and casual prose lure us into identification and confirmations of our habits of thinking, but from inside that intimacy he issues moments of productive alienation: familiar resonance, and then surprising twists of new insight. We move from affirming nod to bewilderment. This is writing at its best. In that way, we as readers are invited to think *with* and *alongside* Baldwin. Rather than an argument or exposition, Baldwin thinks out loud on the page, working with words and sentences that function as invitations and commentary on shared experiences, embedding his thinking in our anxieties and vexations, all of which fundamentally upend a reader-centered hermeneutic event of the text. Yes, we as interpreters—playing Hermes the messenger god as inside the very term "hermeneutics"—carry a message from the text to our intellect, then back to the page with our curiosities and interests, but the text also captivates, guides, and shapes our discovery of the message to be carried. Baldwin interprets us as he interpolates us, returning readers to themselves with a suddenly fractured sense of self. A readerly, thoughtful self, awash in the paradoxes of racial life in the United States. This is reading Baldwin's nonfiction: to be led by a text while also discovering ourselves—to the point of confounding our sense of self—in the act of reading.

As a matter of generalized principle, the hermeneutic event is the event of reading in which the text gives to us and we assimilate what it gives (knowledge, feeling, value, insight), but, in that assimilation, we also make interpretation happen, bringing our own conceptions and anticipations to bear on the writer's words. In other words, we read with a purpose, seeking and finding with intention what will be taken or consumed in the act of reading, learning, and knowing. No digestion without digestive aid. There is no pure reportage version of reading, nor should we want there to be. We are never blank slates onto which the text projects its meaning. Who would be excited about or interested in such a positivist, and frankly authoritarian, idea of the literary and intellectual event? Discovering ourselves in the text and the text *also* alienating what we thought we knew in the chiasma of interpretation is what makes intellectual life vital. It is what makes ideas vibrant and compelling. Our approach to the text as readers (critical framing, focused lens, theory, ideology) is what draws out the finer, often hidden grain in a text and, because our approach to it is interrupted and disrupted by the text's resistance to what we might want it to say, the text speaks against our framing of it. Resistance, refusal. For example, we might want Baldwin to be radical and find that he is moderate, even conservative, but what does our desire for radicalism lift out of the text despite its push in the other direction, what does that desire for radicalism allow us to see that would otherwise remain hidden were we to anticipate otherwise? Baldwin might tailor his philosophical imagination to the United States, but what does a reading that seeks the south Atlantic elements of the text—present and absent, read in implication and under erasure—reveal as hidden discourses, counternarratives, internal unraveling and reraveling of concepts, values, visions, and moral and cultural claims? Ideas happen in the irruption between anticipation and textual gifts. Interpretative reading, especially when soberly and deliberately undertaken, tells us both about the author's prerogative(s) and how the text modifies that author—me, in this case—as a thinker. That is, purposive interpretative reading tells us what the text is able to prompt in the reader, how it lives and bequeaths the life of new, unexpected, and impactful ideas to the readerly gaze.

I say all of this because it goes to the heart of the aim of *So Unimaginable a Price*. Like any scholar of his work, I am interested in what Baldwin has to say in his nonfiction, and I find it to be among the most compelling writing of the twentieth century. What is he telling us? How does he demonstrate his claims? And what is the significance of those claims? How do they speak to his moment in history and also to the present moment, or even the future? We all ask these questions when we read provocative work on race and meaning. But the interpretative moment of *assessing significance* is where the hermeneutic event becomes so immensely important. What is Baldwin telling us, and how and why is it important for us to contemplate? The text is not the entire story. There is also the story of the reader. I come to Baldwin's nonfiction after years of philosophical study of the south Atlantic world, with particular emphasis on the anglophone and francophone Caribbean and elements of both in western Africa. How does Baldwin fit in the Black Atlantic context? How do his texts signify inside *that* frame? The mid-century, Baldwin's moment, produced an incredible cluster of ideas in the south Atlantic world. Black writing exploded in a moment of independence struggle and postcolonial anxieties around world- and nation building. What is race? What is identity? What is home? How is there hope or hopelessness after centuries of catastrophic violence? How does that violence live both in institutions and in the psyche? These are mid-century Black Atlantic questions that swirl around central themes in Baldwin's work, but often with important, compelling differences. What does it mean that these ideas emerged simultaneously? How did Baldwin work to distinguish himself from these ideas, these other emerging traditions, as well as the imperatives that flowed from them? *Who is Baldwin in the mid-century Black Atlantic moment?* This approach to reading Baldwin, an approach rooted in the epistemological and ontological crises arising in the moment of liberation from colonialism across the Black Atlantic, changes so many things about how his work resonates, how it stands in relation to broader questions of blackness and identity, as well as offering sharpened characterizations of his key ideas.

I have two aims in this book, then.

First, I want to offer a theoretical reading of Baldwin's nonfiction, a reading that is systematic and attentive to his shifts and turns across time and all the epistemic and affective registers of those shifts and turns. It is important to note that his nonfiction has not received any kind of sustained, rigorous philosophical treatment. In part, this is because Baldwin's own style is not particularly philosophical; the art of the essay, in his hands, is much more attentive to the intersection between personal narrative and witness to history being made in its moment.[4] To wit: At a number of points, when reflecting on his experience as an exiled writer, Baldwin will announce his return to the United States as driven by the desire or even need to be close to the history being made in the civil rights movement and other forms of liberation struggle in his home country. Or he offers close, critical commentary on a trending writer, film, or cultural movement as an intimation about the dramatics of his own life. When characterized and practiced this way, Baldwin's style entwines the intimacy of his own body and conscience with the same of the nation, which, in turn, underscores all the myriad ways in which political exigency is an existential question and demand. Baldwin's own life is so compelling, whether it is his childhood as a preacher-to-be, his wrestling with sexual identity and forms of masculinity, his relation to Black radicalism and varieties of white people, hope and shame, or witnessing the passing of literary and cultural giants. He ran in interesting circles. Those stories are enough for the nonfiction to be interesting. But none of that is particularly *natural* to philosophy and philosophical exposition. We do not find a plainly recognizable philosophical essay in Baldwin's nonfiction because he was not that sort of witness to place and moment.

That said, I have always said that it is a fatal mistake in understanding philosophical work to seek a sense of the philosophical inside the style of the text itself. Inside any given text, we *might* find philosophical tones and conventional formulations of questions, methods, approaches, and argumentation—the conventional expressive medium of the institution "philosophy." However, and I think this is always worth noting, the act of identifying such features is not itself philosophy or philosophical analysis, but instead a kind of literary criticism and classification that answers to questions of genre and categorization in an assessment of style. This is one of the funkier ironies of philosophy's chauvinism. More interesting to me and in opposition to the chauvinisms of philosophy is conceiving and practicing philosophy as a *method of reading*. A method of reading, that is, in which the reader pursues and critically seeks, in a given text, responses and responsiveness to questions of being, knowing, valuing, morality, culture, and politics. This puts *us* as critical interpreters in the position of creating philosophical readings no matter the stylistic features internal to the text—embracing our place in the transformative work of the hermeneutic event. If the text is responsive, and Baldwin's nonfiction is *always* capable of generating interesting insights into place, time, memory, identity, knowledge, and being, then the text *gives* us philosophy if we frame it as such. The personal essay becomes philosophical *in the act of reading philosophically*. And it is worth noting here and everywhere that this is absolutely essential if we, as scholars and readers, are to understand the profound and enduring philosophical insights produced by subaltern intellectual traditions—in this case, the African American intellectual tradition, which has since the beginning engaged all modes of expressive life in order to generate vocabulary for being and knowing under specific conditions of life and social death. Philosophy is not the antithesis of literature and the arts. Rather, philosophy is a way of reading literature and the arts, including the art of literary nonfiction and the personal essay.

Second, and perhaps more ambitiously, I want to reframe how we understand *what* was James Baldwin. We have a strong sense of *who* James Baldwin was, whether we draw from extensive biographical studies by David Leeming, Herb Boyd, and James Campbell or other detailed literary historical work linking Baldwin to his friends, critics, and interlocutors. But Baldwin was also an *event* and, like all events, he initiated a comprehensive reorientation of thinking about African American and interracial American life. This event, the event of his fiction and nonfiction and their afterlives, gathers force by simultaneously drawing the past into his words and in the labor of juxtaposition of his thinking into the innovations in thought that surrounded him in his moment. How do we reckon with this event? For the most part, if not near exclusively, Baldwin has been read in relation to his direct interlocutors in the United States. For example, if we peruse the essay collected in two outstanding Cambridge University Press volumes—*The Cambridge Companion to James Baldwin* and *James Baldwin in Context*—we see no serious comparative work that locates Baldwin's thinking outside the United States.[5] There are of course essay-length treatments of exile in Europe and Turkey, but all of those are of the literary historical or biographical variety whose purpose is to document the persistence of Americanness in Baldwin's reflections, even when far away from home. As well, across the number of years of publication, in the *James Baldwin Review*, a truly excellent journal, only a handful-plus essays put Baldwin in any kind of significant critical conversation with figures and ideas from outside the United States. This is all just so remarkable to note, given how explosive and vital the mid-century moment was for Black Atlantic thought. But, in noting the national focus of scholarship on Baldwin, I am not offering criticism of any collections, journals, and related scholarly media. In addition to explaining why the pages that follow are light in citation—a feature of doing imaginative critical work with little precedent—I am here underscoring how deeply connected our reading of Baldwin is to the context of the United States. This is no criticism precisely because the texts themselves ask for this characterization and approach to reading. Yet, and this animates the chapters that follow, Baldwin *also* belonged to a moment in history: the mid-century and all its drama around the transformation of Black life across the Atlantic world. Baldwin can *also* be read in that context, not only in a comparative voice—which is no small part of the reflections that follow—but also, and this is important to emphasize, in the critical work of reading for absences, reckoning with interpretative fabulation, and, in that alternative space of critical encounter, producing *another frame* for understanding his work. This framing otherwise is the widest ambition of this project. To read Baldwin differently. To read another Baldwin altogether. To see Baldwin's moment in the milieu of the Black Atlantic.

In a certain sense, we could describe this as reading Baldwin under erasure. Reading under erasure, an approach I of course draw from the early work of Jacques Derrida, is a critical method in which we discover elements of esoteric discourse without appealing to the author's intention(s). This approach forms a kind of intersection between deconstruction and critical fabulation. Why is this approach important? And what does it offer readers of such readings? Consider the fact that Baldwin takes no serious interest in Africa, African thinkers, the Caribbean and Black Latin America, or Caribbean and Afro-Latinx thinkers. This fact is striking. All of these regions irrupted into the mid-century's critical cultural and political moment with the profound, rigorous accounts of so many themes that we find in Baldwin's pages. But those pages barely name Black Atlantic thinkers, and when they do name them, it is largely in the form of roll calls or blank reportage rather than critical engagement. Given this *absence*, how do we proceed reading Baldwin in a Black Atlantic context? There are three possibilities. One is to let the text guide us and repeat that lack of interest as we attend to Baldwin's prerogative. This is a legitimate strategy and one that is largely practiced in Baldwin studies, whether that be philological attention or literary historical study. Baldwin was African American, never wanted to be otherwise, and never described himself otherwise. If we take that seriously, then we stay faithful to both the letter of the text (philologically motivated study) and the stated aspirations and status of the author and his immediate national-cultural world (literary historical study). A second option is to offer a critique from the outside, wondering and musing and critically rereading his work from the perspectives of those he found so uninteresting and unworthy of serious reading and engagement. This is a risky mode of critical reading. Reading what Baldwin *did not* say back into the texts as a critique forever flirts with what is, to me, an underproductive and largely uninteresting genre of critique that boils down to the declaration: *I would have written these essays differently.*

Sure, every essay could have been written differently. Criticism from the outside that leverages another tradition *against* Baldwin, while not being inside the Baldwin text itself, can show the limitations of Baldwin's worldview and readerly sensibilities. This can show us how Baldwin failed to fully understand his moment and how, with a better understanding of that moment, his work might have been taken in different directions with different conclusions and sensibilities. But such work really tells us less about Baldwin the thinker and more about the author writing such criticism. We all have our ideas and our libraries, after all. They make us the writers we are, even as commentators. Should we export our literacies and critical positions to another's work? This is an interesting methodological question that is also ethical and political. Scholarship has room for all sorts of prerogatives.

And still another option, the one I have chosen in writing this interpretation of Baldwin's nonfiction, is reading for absences. When we read for absences, the text is present to us, first, as an explicit discourse, and second, but coextensive with the first, also lodged in a historical moment that speaks *around* that text. The work of fabulation renarrates the origin and milieu of a given work or trajectory of thought, reading what it does *not* say as much as reading what it *does* say. This kind of reading is certainly paradoxical and always complex, but productively so. This is important when reckoning with Baldwin's nonfiction. He was a worldly person who traveled and lived abroad; we know a lot about him as a cosmopolitan personality. He also had his finger, however skeptically, on the pulse of the revolutionary world. Baldwin's primary focus was on the civil rights movement and the provocative, radical critics in the Black Panther and Black Power movements. Whatever his time writing in exile, Baldwin was a reader and listener to agitations and revolt in the United States. Why would we imagine that Baldwin would not know about the work of, say, Aimé Césaire or Frantz Fanon or Kwame Nkrumah, none of whom shows up in any significant way in his nonfiction meditations on race, nation, and identity? The Black Atlantic in revolt was loud, emphatic, and obsessively covered across the north Atlantic world of Baldwin at home and abroad. What would it mean to fabulate this relation as a relation of distancing and negation? What would it mean to do that reading for absence and under erasure alongside critical comparative work? If we engage both modes of reading, making his texts speak to this wider moment, then we do the important work of reinscribing Baldwin in his moment and therefore inscribing him more deeply than we would in an analysis limited to the context of the United States. It is a reinscription that reveals the reader as well as the absences in the text.

Let us always be revealed and reveal ourselves as readers. Hermeneutic confessions are never self-indulgent but instead honest presentations of the conditions for the possibility of critical assessment and theorization. Readers of readers are better for it. But any and all explicit characterizations of how and why we offer the readings we do are also about connecting a given reinterpretation to the deepest, widest interests and prerogatives of a thinker or texts under consideration. Rerouting and resiting a thinker is expansive and productive, opening new paths of understanding at and on unfamiliar margins. Reading for absences, reading Baldwin back into the mid-century Black Atlantic moment, is in that way an occasion for engaging and extending the path Baldwin sets us on. *In search of Black life.*

Introduction

✦

In Search of Black Life

"This world is white no longer," Baldwin writes in "Stranger in the Village," placing himself in history's interval. "And it will never be white again."[1] Baldwin is here indulging in a bit of fantasy, prompted by the surge *against* the meaning of the Atlantic world for centuries, a world composed of murderous and genocidal supremacy—in acts of insurrection, civil disobedience, armed revolution, and negotiated terms of independence. The mid-century was a radical moment that shifted how we understood the world until this moment of rupture. The old still held on, of course; Baldwin is never naive. But something different emerged in the mid-century moment and was owed his witness. Atlantic world history is unthinkable without the presence of "white"—whether white people, white culture, white supremacy, white imperialism, white gazes, white identity, or white violence. What could Baldwin possibly mean when he says that the world will *never* be white again? He surely does not mean the world is unstained by that memory. Centuries do their work. But he surely means something about whiteness as a fantasy, how a fantasy of purity and self-making has no future. It might not even have a past. Pure invention. Pure violence as its result. And so it is history.

James Baldwin's nonfiction is in many ways one long reckoning with this kind of history. A reckoning with history, yes, but also that memorial dimension that makes and shapes historical movement, abstraction, and forces into something intimate and existential. To be sure, Baldwin typically writes the self; his lived experience and movement through the world—Harlem, Switzerland, France, Atlanta—is always a focus. Part of his appeal as a writer lies in that intimacy—the personal essay, the writing of experience. He led an exceptional life, and that life is fascinating. But that lived experience is also, and first, animated by the bearing of history and memory on his body, language, and sense of both belonging and nonbelonging. This bearing creates the interracial world and sustains its work of pain, pleasure, exploitation, resistance, and refusal. The whole complexity of the world. He writes in the 1965 essay "White Man's Guilt" that history "is not merely something to be read. And it does not refer merely, or even principally, to the past. On the contrary, the great force of history comes from the fact that we carry it within us, are unconsciously controlled by it in many ways, and history is literally *present* in all that we do. It could scarcely be otherwise, since it is to history that we owe our frames of reference, our identities, and our aspirations."[2] What is this history? What is our framing of it and how does it frame us? This is a critical query because history itself has histories and geographies. How the history of history, how we think about where history begins *for us*, resonates and registers in our "frames of reference, our identities, and our aspirations" will already tell us much of the story.

For Baldwin, it is the history of the Americas. This history is the history of pain and new identities forged in and through that pain. The name "Americas" is itself synonymous with genocide and the trafficking of bodies. This is where we begin. This is where Baldwin begins.

A long note on this: What is the Americas?

In its first iteration of 1492, a decade before Vespucci would lend his name to the hemisphere, that traffic was the work of genocidal violence, moving from life to not just social death or individual death, but to collective mass murder. Killing, disease, abandonment. Arrival in the West Indies, however lost Columbus and his fellow *génocidaires* might have been, initiated a particularly intense form of violent conquest that has few if any precedents, antecedents, or parallels in global history. It was not enough to subjugate the indigenous peoples of the archipelago. Slavery, which was initially the fate of the indigenous of the continental Americas, was somehow not enough. Conquest in this *first* moment of contact, the arrival in Hispaniola, meant mass death and the obliteration of the indigenous peoples of the archipelago. This mass death buried memory in quotidian places that now appear as fragments, traces, bits and pieces reassembled in what remains: patois and creole, mixed identities, and, with those few who survived, their descendants. In a bit of historical irony or cruelty or enigma, those reassemblages became the task of another population. Reassemblages are what make the Black Americas, a sense of making worlds that is saturated with pain, but also saturated with making. Always. For the indigenous people of the Caribbean and massive swaths of the settled, colonized continent, the complexity of beauty and pain that now sits as a signature feature of the culture of the Americas was the work of another people altogether. This is where we begin, with genocidal conquest that becomes gruesome colonialism and imperial domination. A first founding wound.

And there is the other founding wound, one in the immediate wake or even in the midst of the first. In the wake of the bureaucratic crisis created by Bartolomé de Las Casas's liberation of the indigenous enslaved, an effort in what we now call Latin America, the depopulated islands of the Caribbean, cleared by genocidal conquest, were rapidly and massively repopulated by enslaved Africans. The bureaucratic crisis was of the worst imaginable sort but also adhered to the basic principle of empire: How can the resources of the New World be maximally extracted? An account of the origin of the transatlantic slave trade can be located here, setting in motion an unprecedented history that forms a persistent and insistent specter haunting the hemisphere. On Enrique Dussel's rendering, this is also the origin of European modernity: a bureaucratic crisis in search of modes of calculation and models of efficiency that could maximize extraction in the New World, no matter the cost in human lives.[3] What remained as a cultural or intellectual task for Europe—and the history of the concept of race shows this with particular clarity—was not simply proving that the cost was either *not* human or *not fully* human but also a deployment of the infra- or subhuman in the interest of greed, accumulation, and unrestrained domination; the *actual* humans with their legitimate needs and desires were first, but that firstness and the fact of atrocity needed justification. All of Europe's intellectual resources were rallied to make this case for racialized subordination. Philosophers, scientists, travelogue writers, literary figures, and theologians converged around these questions in order to justify the death and suffering of enslavement, but also, in the missionary iteration of colonial domination, their imagination created and expanded a vision of what colonial rule and enslavement does to a subjugated population. That subjugation was a total project. In no way was it the boutique concern of merchants and political elites. Rather, the whole of European culture was dedicated to transforming every element of human life under the control of white Europe. And yet, it was a vexed project at and in its very foundation. Whatever the effort to eliminate the personhood of persons, there is still the persistence of the human as such, something that perplexed enslavers and motivated missionary work in its strange and also vexed mix of condescending aspiration and absolute brutality. A new *people* becomes possible. Colonialism, conquest, enslavement—all of these wanted to render the infrahuman a kind of robot precursor, controlled and controllable in the service of unremunerated labor and endless accumulation of both material and psychological capital. Yet the human is obstinate. New senses of identity and culture emerge, for the subjugated for sure, but also for the perpetrators of empire. On what terms? And in what memorial horizon?

The response to indigenous genocide—the creation of the Caribbean plantation system, mimicked later in the Southern United States, and the entire intellectual apparatus attached to its justification and praxis—was a seismic event that reordered an entire world and entire peoples. The Middle Passage severed cultural, social, and psychological ties to Western Africa in the belly of the boat. The plantation reproduced this severed tie across generations through interdictions on African language and religious practices (the missionary element), the abjection of African life as cultural contagion (the shame element), deliberate production of imperial language domination (foundational alienation), and so on. A total project. Reckoning with the aftermath of all this, something that was undertaken underground in the midst of enslavement and then more emphatically across each generation postemancipation, is the process of world-building against all these kinds of hegemonies. Institutions might fall, be abolished, and end up relegated to history books, but forms of life and social death born from those institutions persist in social habits and in morphed and morphing institutional practices. This is history's refusal to comply with time. The past is never quite past enough. We owe so much to history, perhaps everything.

The story of how Atlantic world white supremacy and racism(s) transformed the lives of the conquered, enslaved, and subjugated is familiar enough. That is the story of abjection and oppression. And questions of racial justice, however controversial to conservative-minded folks, circle around the political presence and insistence of Black and brown peoples in the Americas. What does repair look like? How can we craft an ethical relation to the dead? How ought we reckon with the complexities of inheritance, which so often mixes pain and pleasure, the grotesque and the gorgeous? This is the memory work of the oppressed. But it is important to emphasize *also* and at the same time that the Middle Passage also fundamentally changed white Europe. Modernity's entwinement of reason, calculation, and imperial conquest, coupled with all the moral work to justify enslavement and colonial subjugation, sets thinking about infra- and subhumanity inside the foundations of culture and identity. This is something about Europe that has gotten much too little critical treatment. If all of Europe's intellectual resources were gathered to the site of subjugating enslaved Africans, and intellectual resources are the cornerstone of culture and identity, then we have to reckon with how Europe, not just its victims, was radically changed by its own violence. Anti- and decolonial work attaches itself to the European project too, even if that work has rarely if ever been part of Europe's postempire world, and is a part of the white Americas as well, of course, which is one of the key outposts of modernity's racial project. Colonialism and enslavement were machines of production. I am thinking here of Antonio Benítez-Rojo's description of the plantation as a "machine of machines" in *The Repeating Island* and how he writes Europe back into the machine of its own violence. He writes, and I quote in full because the embellishments are so crucial:

> We can speak, nevertheless, of a Caribbean machine as important or more so than the fleet machine. This machine, this extraordinary machine, exists today, that is, it repeats itself continuously . . .
>
> The singular feature of this machine is that it produced no fewer than ten million African slaves and thousands of coolies (from India, China, and Malaysia). All this, however, is not all: the plantation machines turned out mercantile capitalism, industrial capitalism (see Eric Williams, *Capitalism and Slavery*), African underdevelopment (see Walter Rodney, *How Europe Underdeveloped Africa*), Caribbean population (see Ramiro Guerra, *Sugar and Society in the Caribbean*); they produced imperialism, wars, colonial blocs, rebellions, repressions, sugar islands, runaway slave settlements, air and naval bases,

> revolutions of all sorts, and even a "free associated state" next to an unfree socialist state.[4]

We owe history for our frames of identity and experience, which are generated by this Atlantic world machine. There is so much here, but the key is Benítez-Rojo's articulation of the machine as a machine of both difference—complex notions of identity, dispersion, and reassemblage of languages—and hegemonic sameness. It is a machine of European creation, and the titles Benítez-Rojo puts in parentheses loop the creator back into its creation: Capitalism is intertwined with slavery, the underdevelopment is the initiative and constant labor of Europe, and sugar transformed European economies and cuisines. We could say the same about other commodities, noting in each example how the production of the commodity entails a brutalization of the enslaved or colonized laborer *and* the desire, world-visioning, and cultural production of the enslaver or colonizer. The machine produces sameness in the sense of making the colonizer and the colonized part of the same moral, cultural, and political logic and then produces the obvious differences between victim and perpetrator, the one who suffers and the one who lives well because of that suffering, an interracial world that, for Baldwin, will comprise the puzzle of thinking "the Negro" in the United States—a production that is formative of history, is the frame of a long history of identity and identification, and is local in the very same moment that it is hemispheric. This is a broad structural claim. But it is also an ontological and epistemological claim about regimes of being and knowing inside and outside the system produced by the machine: the logic of Black in an anti-Black world, the logic of white in an anti-Black world, and what it means to share that world while living in what Baldwin in his best novel's title just calls *another country*.

Benítez-Rojo helps us reckon with the long historical arc of this world and this logic. What ontologies and epistemologies are produced in this machine of difference? How destructive is the machine? And how fecund is the intersection of survival and resistance in the heart of this machine?

These questions dominated the Black Atlantic's mid-century moment, a moment that saw the Global South erupt in struggles for independence—some bloody, a few unsuccessful, so many putting direct colonial rule in the distance, nearly all struggling with neocolonial recurrence—and confront, even in the midst of revolutionary mobilization and action, problems of postcolonial culture- and statecraft. An old world collapsing. What sort of new or remade world is possible? What languages, institutions, values, affects, and senses of being and knowing are properly "post" in the postcolonial? The colonial machine destroyed knowledge and senses of being, belonging, and place. What is produced in the midst of, then after, that destruction? Or is destruction *actually* total, everything imperial power hoped it would be? Or does the work of resistance and refusal invert destruction with unexpected, even impossible, fecundities? The mid-century moment, in its Black

Atlantic iteration, was defined by the diverse reckonings with these questions, urgencies, and moral and political demands from a future we cannot know, drawing on a past and present that is unspeakably painful and full of revolutionary rage. Two events in this moment stand out for me. First, the publication of Aimé Césaire's epic confrontation with colonial abjection in his poem "Notebook of a Return to the Native Land"—first published in 1939, then revised in 1947 and again in the authoritative edition of 1956—which invoked and gave real texture and content to the concept of Négritude. Second, and building from that concept, there was the 1956 Congress of Negro Writers and Artists, which gathered together some of the most important writers and thinkers in the Black Atlantic world, including Césaire, Léopold Senghor, Alioune Diop, George Lamming, Frantz Fanon, and Richard Wright. Baldwin was dispatched to produce a report on the Congress for *Encounter*, which was published as the essay "Princes and Powers." Baldwin's report contains his one sustained engagement with this moment in the Black intellectual tradition. It is also his most sustained, and therefore most revealing and suggestive, intervention in emerging Caribbean and African thought. Something important about Baldwin's thinking and philosophical sensibilities emerges in "Princes and Powers"—we will return to it often in the pages that follow—but that *something* fades very quickly. In the moment of the transnational contact, Baldwin suggests and muses, then immediately retreats to his home nation context. The fact is, Baldwin was never much of a commentator on transnational blackness and questions of diasporic identity. What are we to make of this?

Baldwin's quick and suggestive remarks on his Black Atlantic moment are remarkable because the 1956 Congress and the ideas that dominated it evoke so much of what preoccupied Baldwin across his life's work: the beauty of blackness, the vicissitudes of antiblackness in the Black psyche, the possibilities for resistance and self-creation under (and perhaps after) white domination, and the place of the past in imagining liberation. The machine of terrible difference. Why was Baldwin so reluctant to or completely uninterested in taking on this powerful, emerging intellectual movement? Why wasn't Baldwin drawn to the diasporic conversation and instead drawn, at every turn, to the context of the United States? This last part is what is most revealing: The Black Atlantic's mid-century moment was less about transatlantic solidarity and shared insight and more about how the diasporic functions as a foil for a specifically US sense of racial formation. Baldwin puzzles over this notion of diaspora, knowing full well about its status as a kind of foil, but in the end the thinking in "Princes and Powers" is largely elliptical: no final word, no contestation or argument, no opening to new questions.

That intersection and Baldwin's departure from it form the core of the present project. Who was Baldwin to the Black Atlantic? And what or who was the Black Atlantic to Baldwin?

At the center of all this is the central issue of the meaning of the Black body—not as inert matter acted upon, but rather as a lived body in the condition of social death, as something de-formed and re-formed by the work of history. An incarnate historiography. History is written on our bodies; this is part of the movement of the word and how it bears on our subjectivity and intersubjectivity. We are embodied creatures, and our creatureliness is indebted in part, if not largely, to history and memory and the vicissitudes of inheritance. I am thinking here of Benítez-Rojo's appeal to the heteroclitic archive in *The Repeating Island*, an appeal that reinscribes embodiment—from speech to gesture to the rhythms of dancing and walking—into the accounting of Black life and its formation under unspeakable, yet always spoken of and from, conditions. For Benítez-Rojo, any thorough reckoning with the history of the colonial machine must take seriously how the body itself bears not just history and memory as the colonial prerogative but also the entire bearing of refusal of and resistance to that prerogative. The body carries memories that mourn and that are melancholic. But the body's saturation with history and memory signifies what it meant (and still means) to live, move, and breathe through death worlds. In that way, the body is an epistemological site: reflection, interval, deferral, mixture, reassemblage, feeling, process, production, and reproduction. Or, to anticipate the chapters that follow, dialectic, identity, affect, speech, home, and multiracial signification.

The Négritude movement and its peak moment at the 1956 Congress threaded all of these questions of embodiment through an elaborate and elaborated conception of blackness. Baldwin's witness to this moment was formative of his encounter with history's framing of our identity and identification. On the one hand, the iteration of Négritude expressed and defended at the 1956 Congress was plainly essentialist. Césaire's reference to Africa, written from the diaspora (he was Martinican, after all), is an appeal to a geography of reason, locating the *origins* of essential forms of knowing, being, and creating in a specifically racial space. Senghor, the Senegalese poet, offers an account of rhythm, emotion, and embodied relation that produces the same sort of claim from the continent of Africa. For both, Négritude is not a biological conception of race or some such thing, but instead a philosophy of life, spirit, and vital urge that animates cultural differences across the continent and its diaspora with a core *spirit* of civilization. Aesthetic, affective, and intellectual characteristics form Négritude's essentialist core. Critical suspicion around the Négritude movement is nonetheless warranted; the histories of Négritude and other sorts of essentialism have never been particularly kind. Essentialism is a risky endeavor. On the other hand, the Négritude movement and its relation to the mid-century moment is a deeply compelling, deeply engaged memory project and retrieval of a lost historical framing of identity, one that locates the meaning of race in the history and histories sedimented in the Black body. Affect and the aesthetic are incarnate sites of knowing and being. How does sedimentation in the body work?

History in the sedimented body is *discovered* by Négritude theorists in the diaspora as a thread of unity that binds the scattered seeds to the continent and Black histories, said now as a *plural* term, and denotes the specificity of Black life lived in *place*. History and stories thread tightly together in order to make identity possible, but they are also said in two different registers in order to make space for robust cultural difference. The intersection of the singular and the plural, identity and difference or differentiation, is therefore the intersection of two memories in the body, two histories lived as civilizational, cultural, and political temporality. The time of origin. The time of origins.

In many ways, the present project takes up Baldwin as an interrogation of precisely these two times and the question of both *how* and *whether* they intersect. In that intersection is verticality (first an origin, then its fallen states), horizontality (multiplicity without rank), and/or a chaotic mixture (rhizomatic and nomadic conceptions of life). So much of the second half of the twentieth and twenty-first centuries in Black Atlantic theory can be organized around such debates and characterizations, and Baldwin's relation to the Black Atlantic is a particularly interesting version of these disputes when we read him back into that context. At the heart of these disputes and Baldwin's interventions in them are questions of the meaning of history's pain, the origins of that pain, and the meaning (or nonmeaning) of survival as *life*. Survival as life—to survive, yes, but also to live in all of the complexity of being human. What is Black possibility? How does that possibility draw on the Black past? For Négritude and so many of its companion dissenting movements in the mid-century moment, the question of the past raises the question of Africa. What is Africa to the Black diasporic subject? Or, for someone like Senghor or Diop at the 1956 Congress, what is Africa to the African postcolonial?

For Baldwin, these questions have a quirky twist. As he puts it in *The Fire Next Time*—the name under which the short letter "My Dungeon Shook" and longer essay "Down at the Cross" are gathered—the question is not about the spread of diasporic meaning. Rather, he asks, "How can the American Negro past be used?"[5] This query emphasizes both the "American" (it is geographically specific, neither hemispheric nor the Atlantic world) and "Negro" (a specific racial formation with a specific past, however that past is configured), as well as that blank space between the words, never quite a hyphen, which becomes in his work its own kind of subjectivity and collectivity. Like any honest reckoning with blackness in the Atlantic world, Baldwin's formulation and the particularity of his discursive work draw on, in his words, "the Negro past of rope, fire, torture, castration, infanticide, rape" that produced "death and humiliation; fear by day and night, fear as deep as the marrow of the bone."[6] Coupled with his repudiation of the status "ward of America," a status that seals colonial and segregationist forms of domination and superiority, Baldwin claims instead that he is or is the descendent of "one of the first

Americans to arrive on these shores."[7] With that firstness and the paradoxical claim to Americanness, Baldwin begins to articulate a peculiar, singular, and compelling incarnate historiography. It is one whose inheritance is tied to the wake of the auction block rather than the slave ship and point of no return, drawing from histories of local vernacular cultural formation rather than nostalgia for and retrieval of lost civilization. This is a sense of blackness articulated at the mid-century moment in a tense, unraveling relation to Négritude and its political-epistemological imperatives.

The meaning of incarnation, history, memory, and identity after this shift, cast in light of Baldwin's thematization of "the American Negro," is nuanced and layered. The departure from Black Atlantic theorizations of similar racial, historical, and memorial dynamics helps us register a cluster of relevant things for interpreting Baldwin interpreting blackness in a transatlantic milieu. First, it sets Baldwin in a larger context within which his texts have limited contact. Yet this is a context that we as readers can render with hermeneutic clarity and precision; as readers, we both document relations in philological exposition *and* create relations through imaginative interpretation. This latter kind of work has not been undertaken with any seriousness in scholarly detail, save for a few essays here and there. For scholars of his work, Baldwin largely remains a creature of the United States and not of a wider Black Atlantic moment. Second, and more broadly, reading Baldwin in a Black Atlantic frame deessentializes blackness as a critical concept, which is something very much in keeping with his own sensibilities. Such deessentializing work is done by reiterating the complexities and differences of historical and memorial inheritance. Sites and siting in the south Atlantic world—geographic, national, linguistic, cultural, and political work—reveal different bearings of history and memory in the Black body to such an extent that the term "Black" itself must be retheorized. Indeed, we could say that this is the project of the 1956 Congress and of so much work in the mid-century moment that follows from it. In what direction do we theorize? Toward the proliferation of difference on the model of what Édouard Glissant called chaos? Or is critical theoretical work better put in service of ordering those differences and setting foundations of race, ancestry, and spirit on the model of strong notions of diaspora? Baldwin is set inside this debate, and much is to be gained by reading him *there*. Third, Baldwin's specificity focuses on the problematics that arise from a sense of blackness in the mode of *becoming* and *social reproduction* inside a multiracial social and political space, as well as inside the life of the imaginary that animates sociality and politics. The dynamics of an interracial milieu of blackness-becoming, with their intricate apparatuses dedicated to reproduction of certain racial forms, is part of the uniqueness of the African American situation generated by *this* machine of difference. To be sure, the continent has its interracial states defined by white rule and brutalization—Zimbabwe and South Africa, in particular—but in terms of the dynamics of social production and reproduction those states are organized around the political form of the settler colony. The United States is a settler colony, to be sure, but the dynamics of that form to not attach to African Americans in relation to white people but rather to indigenous peoples of the nation and beyond its borders. Baldwin sees this unprecedented and singular dynamic for what it is and reckons with ideas of race, identity, and the like inside this social form.

And so, as a fourth note, we can see the limits—but also enhanced possibilities, which always emerge from marking limits—of the colonial model for theorizing blackness in the Americas. The United States very well might demand its own, nongeneralizable model for thinking about Black life and its incarnate historiography. This approach by Baldwin and other writers, as well as the scholars writing on them, is often cast as an objectionable type of "American exceptionalism." I never like that phrase being applied to Baldwin, in part because it collapses his prophetic and witnessing work into imperial foreign policy (the origins of the phrase), which is plain distasteful and sophistic. But, aside from the sloppy and frankly weird rhetoric, it misses the point: Baldwin's nonfiction offers a long, sustained, detailed, and conceptually and phenomenologically rigorous account of and argument for what I call "the African American difference." Difference is not synonymous with hegemonic exceptionalism but is instead just this: difference documented as uniqueness of social, cultural, and political economy. African Americans have been at the bottom of the well since the mythic 1619, but few if any aspects of American cultural production are possible without African American artistry. If we take art seriously as not just aesthetic but also epistemic and ontological work, then this needs accounting. Baldwin gives us an important accounting of all of that. Lastly, if we read Baldwin in a Black Atlantic context, we see how profoundly he calls into question the meaning of diaspora as a critical and identity-naming concept. Baldwin is not a diasporic thinker, and he borders on being, and may be outright be, an *anti*diasporic thinker whose work nonetheless reflects the deepest love of blackness and African American life. This raises origin story questions, questions of the relationship he and his work have to the machine of machines. What kind of body and trauma initiates the inheritance of blackness? Is it the sea as a figure of dislocation, pain, and loss? So much of Black diasporic thinking turns on a notion of a People of the Sea, a kind of African iteration of the Judaic notion of a People of the Book. Or is the auction block the originary moment of pain and identity founded *after that form of loss*? The mid-century moment in the Black Atlantic turns to the sea and its history. Baldwin, however, withdraws from this, turning his eye toward the auction block, its violence, what is inherited from it and what is lived in its aftermath and its afterlife, marking the body and memory with so unimaginable a price. This is Baldwin *after* the Black Atlantic, but also *of* the Black Atlantic, *in some sense*. How does this *after* and *of* make a form of thinking and a trajectory of thought?

This is the puzzle across the chapters that follow.

✦

Baldwin's nonfiction tells a complex story across four decades of writing. I am always struck by the strange temporality of Baldwin's essays, the way he sometimes moves in a single sentence between mourning the past and raging against the present racial order and its violence, while imaging all along alternative futures and dimensional aspects of the past and present that are infused with hope, democratic actualization, and a reordering of all things. The complexity of the time of his writing and its infusion with all the surging moments of the Black Americas is what make Baldwin's essay work so philosophically intriguing. But in his telling the story of blackness—the "American Negro" and its vicissitudes—Baldwin's complexity becomes particularly compelling. This moment tells a complex story because of Baldwin's commitment to a fundamental principle that persists across his many shifts in temperament, interest, and theme. This principle is articulated in one of his very first essays "Everybody's Protest Novel," in which Baldwin intervenes in the (largely) Manichean conflict that animates what he calls Harriet Beecher Stowe's "very bad novel" *Uncle Tom's Cabin*, full of "the ostentatious parading of excessive and spurious emotion," and Richard Wright's character Bigger Thomas in *Native Son*, whose "bitterness bubbling up like blood" marks nothing if not distance from sentimentality.[8] In this conflict, Baldwin offers an important gloss on race politics and affective life in the United States, setting into place the very terms of thinking the substance of race and identity. Stowe and Wright write from different subject positions, of course, and the two write with very different relations to sentimentality and moral lessons. Stowe the abolitionist; Wright the nihilist. There is excessive emotion. There is bitterness and blood. Yet, provocative as it seems (and certainly unimaginable in terms of the affects and politics of each), Baldwin argues that there is an important unexpected and uneasy proximity of *Uncle Tom's Cabin* to *Native Son*. Both novels are locked into a leveling of humanity, rendering their protagonists and centerpieces of moral-political lessons one-dimensional: the slave reduced to his suffering of injustice and the Black man reduced to his rage. The subjectivity that emerges out of the two reductions is a subject in protest: the abolitionist shaming of enslavement from the position of the vulnerability and meekness of the enslaved and the man fleeing murderous antiblackness who journeys through acts of violence, evasion, and frustration, expressing them as acts of resistance. Two different affects of protest, but, nevertheless, two novels of protest. In both cases, protest *makes* Black subjectivity. That is, in both *Uncle Tom's Cabin* and *Native Son*, that subjectivity arises in reactive formation. Responses to antiblackness, whether vulnerability or redemptive violence, *create* subjectivity.

This generates a question of enormous significance for thinking ontology in an antiblack world, a question that Baldwin puts to Wright and one that could be put to the entire Black intellectual tradition. What does it mean to anchor *protest* against racism in that dimensionality of Black life that is made *by* white people? Reactive formation roots ontology in the world, but is that the *entirety* of the world? In terms of *Uncle Tom's Cabin* and *Native Son*, how does the white gaze underpin and sustain both novels, despite—or perhaps because of and energized by—the differences in affective character? The violence of the white gaze can be rendered sentimental or enraged in the sensibility of protest. But how does that sit with the truth of life or what Baldwin calls "devotion to the human being"? This is his pursuit, always: in search of Black life in its truth, not its fabrication in the gaze or the reactive formations that populate the world made by that gaze. That truth, that devotion to the human, is our glimpse into Baldwin's funky version of existentialism. The search for the human in the infrahuman, the humanity of "the Negro" under the racist gaze and social institutions of white people, is a project of reading the *histoire*—stories, history, History—of Black people for irruptions of freedom as well as the text of freedom written under erasure. Baldwin writes in "Everybody's Protest Novel," "But that battered word, truth, having made its appearance here, confronts one immediately with a series of riddles and has, moreover, since so many gospels are preached, the unfortunate tendency to make one belligerent. Let us say, then, that truth, as used here, is meant to imply a devotion to the human being, his freedom and fulfillment; freedom which cannot be legislated, fulfillment which cannot be charted."[9] This last remark, that a certain resonance (or nonresonance) of freedom cannot be legislated or charted, is particularly suggestive. And Baldwin leaves it that way: suggestive. In some ways, we can say that this passage is a signal of what is to come in his nonfiction and of what compels him as a writer to explore the absence of Black freedom in texts of unfreedom. Bigger might spend half of *Native Son* in flight, but that flight is no freedom. It is only the same rage that Uncle Tom sublimated as sentimentality, lived more viscerally and wholly unmediated.

It is important to note here, too, that Baldwin reading blackness and Black freedom under erasure is not purely the act of imagination. Quite the opposite, in fact. What it means for Baldwin is that we are called to a creative, critical fabulation that is also wholly familiar, reasonable, and visible. The novelist, committed to the complexity of life, documents this freedom by reading Black life under erasure rather than as a sociological phenomenon. Baldwin puts it this way: "In overlooking, denying, evading his complexity—which is nothing more than the disquieting complexity of ourselves—we are diminished and we perish; only within this web of ambiguity, paradox, this hunger, danger, darkness, can we find at once ourselves and the power that will free us from ourselves. It is this power of revelation which is the business of the novelist, this journey toward a more vast reality which must take precedence over all other claims."[10] This is in many ways Baldwin's calling card as a thinker and no small part of why he remains such an enigmatic thinker. "Precedence" is another compelling term, set here in the context of an exhortation to eschew the sociological novel—*Uncle Tom's Cabin* and *Native Son* are two sides of the same sociological coin, as it were—and instead engage literary gifts and possibilities with a view toward an urgent end: Black life as a vast reality. That vast reality means a sense of life that exceeds, or at least *possibly* exceeds, what the sociological makes of Black existence; Baldwin is sensitive to how the sociological has its truth, but he refuses to concede to its one-dimensionality. To give precedence to complexity is to emphasize and embellish the vastness, the ambiguity, and the deep, wandering paradoxical character of African American history, memory, and cultural formation. In history, memory, and cultural formation is the making of identity, world, and a people. Stowe and Wright want the right kinds of things. Whether through sentimental appeal or fearsome rage, each wants to subvert the social that makes Black abjection. Baldwin affirms this. But that desire in Stowe and Wright extracts an unnecessary price, a price paid by both the social circulation of the meaning of blackness *and* the meaning of Black literature: "The Negro" is barely more than abjection, and the moral call to dissolve that abjection, a kind of apocalyptic moral thinking, comes from a sense of what Black people could *be* without that being having any content whatsoever. What if we start instead from the extant complexity of Black life, if we write in search of that and make such searching our first priority? This is Baldwin's first and final question as a writer.

If we begin with Baldwin, then, we begin with a peculiar sense of the object of writing. What is it that appears in literature and the critical essay? Refusal, resistance, pleasure, and joy, but also the vastness of suffering and the spiritual and soulful abyss that vastness has created and continues to create. The latter documents the work of white racism; the former documents the life and humanity of Black people living under a violent cultural and political regime. But for Baldwin all of that must be done without retreating into the fantastical storytelling of mid-century diaspora theory. In this way, the 1956 Congress organizes so much of Baldwin's thinking even if only one of his essays treats it. The questions raised by "Princes and Powers" and more broadly by the Congress turn us toward the most urgent and most fraught issue: *Where* and *to what* does "the Negro" belong? History and memory, from colonialism and enslavement to independence and postemancipation, tell a story about nonbelonging. Africa is the nostalgia that motivates so much of the 1956 Congress and so much of the mid-century moment of the Black Atlantic. How can a place be imagined, retrieved, then (re-)made, where Black people belong? How is a world to be made in which belonging is constitutive of the foundations, rather than, as with modifications to colonial or related rule, a random and fleeting addition to a burning house? The chapters that follow provide an answer to these questions, questions that orbit around the general problem of home: that deep sense of belonging that blends questions of place with identity. To theorize home and homelessness, and even to ask, in the case of the African American experience, whether there is any real distinction between location and dislocation, is to ask about everything that matters in human life both individually and collectively. Indeed, as we will see, the meaning of affect, language, and identity formation draws on the meaning (or absence of meaning) of home for the Black Americas broadly, and for African Americans specifically, across Baldwin's work.

In many ways, we can simply say all of this in the straightforward observation that Baldwin takes Black humanity *seriously*. Not that he recognizes or appeals to Black humanity; that is in many ways the terms set by the protest novel, whether that is the humanity revealed in the sentimental tale or the humanity revealed in the capacity for violence. Humanity irrupts into an antiblack world in these kinds of moments, and for that reason the protest novel, no matter its limits, does important cultural and political work. But to take Black humanity *seriously*, to give that humanity work and to let it do its work, is to reckon with Black humanity as a critical concept. Like all critical concepts, taking Black humanity seriously helps Baldwin see aspects and features of Black life in their bold and vivid appearance in the cracks of a terrifying world. It is helpful here to turn to Baldwin's note in "Princes and Powers" on what binds the 1956 Congress together. That bond is not the racial heritage of a metaphysical order, but instead a sense of resolute desire. A desire to be a human in the world and therefore not one who forever risks one's humanity simply by stepping into the world and declaring a place in the sun. Baldwin writes:

> And yet, it became clear as the debate wore on, that there *was* something which all black men held in common, something which cut across opposing points of view, and placed in the same context their widely dissimilar experience. What they held in common was their precarious, their unutterably painful relation to the white world. What they held in common was the necessity to remake the world in their own image, to impose this image on the world, and no longer be controlled by the vision of the world, and of themselves, held by other people. What, in sum, black men held in common was their ache to come into the world as men. And this ache united people who might otherwise have been divided as to what a man should be.[11]

Their unutterably painful relation to the white world. Baldwin here defines the Black Atlantic in much the way George Lamming did at the very same conference in his essay "The Negro Writer and His World": The violence of Europe creates a people. This creation is that common thread that Césaire described as a kind of *horizontal solidarity*. "Horizontal solidarity," Césaire writes in his contribution to the Paris Congress, is a sense of solidarity "created by the colonial or semicolonial or paracolonial situation that has been imposed on us from without."[12] While Césaire goes further and subordinates horizontal solidarity to vertical solidarity (the unity of a people through shared civilizational origins), this moment in Baldwin's reflections sets out a shared agenda across the Black Atlantic. But it is a shared agenda that leans so heavily on cultural difference that it risks the point of blending culture with ontology. In that blend, the very notion of race itself is upended.

This notion of race, as we see across the chapters that follow, draws on the historically violent and memorially constitutive relations between white and Black people. It is a dialectic of sorts: Whiteness as an identity and hegemony turns on the abjection of blackness, and the white gaze, with all of its hegemonic work at the level of body and psyche, traps blackness in a circle of troubled affects. Black Atlantic critical theory, in its anti- and decolonial registers, has always engaged with the impact of colonial rule on the entirety of subjectivity; thinking, feeling, knowing, and being are all structured from the inside by the work of colonial abjection. This is not Césaire's vision, but it is a logical extension of the economy he names with the phrase "horizontal solidarity." Césaire wanted to gather the diaspora around the spiritual work of African civilization. He also wanted to gather that same diaspora around the rage shared across colonial subjects; the white gaze makes solidarity possible. Although Césaire doubles the discourse of solidarity—vertical and horizontal, both constituted by white violence and foundational as a cornerstone of a philosophy of life—the end of his discourse is always the unity of diasporic identity. And while Baldwin's remarks in "Princes and Powers" underscore the purchase of this description across the Black Atlantic, leaning into the horizontal solidarity of shared abjection, he always returns the scholarly gaze to the United States. Herein lies the limits to Baldwin's transatlantic dossier: engaged with the elements of Black solidarity, but hesitant to write that solidarity as ontology in any sort of epic or mythic form. So herein also lies Baldwin's caution and careful reflection on history and memory. How are history and memory linked to place? And if linked intimately to place, how does specificity form and re-form how we think about being and knowing? The mid-century's ambition is what makes the theoretical moment so exciting and productive. It is also why that moment can be excessive and hyperbolic. Baldwin enters the mid-century moment with a sense of restraint and caution that derives not from racial conservatism or anxiety about transatlantic contact but from an attention to the details of refusal, resistance, and cultural production.

The chapters that follow tell this story, and it is a story both coherent and actually quite straightforward. For all of Baldwin's time in exile, for all his articulation of themes central to the work of Black Atlantic thought in the mid-century, he is not in any significant way a diasporic thinker. That is, Baldwin himself has no interest in the idea of diaspora beyond empirical histories and heritage. Against so much of his moment, Baldwin comes back, again and again, to the claim that African Americans are entirely their own *people*. That sense of *people* needs detail. So far as terminology goes, it is important to note how this notion of "a people" pushes cultural and memorial meaning to a different level than that of its traveling companion terms "identity" and "ethnicity." Baldwin is absolutely staking claim to "African American" as an ethnicity. This is beyond dispute. One could pair that with the idea of race to express what race thinking thinks best: identity and difference at the same time. This kind of project, revolving around the unity of a group (race) that can also account for important and often profound differences in cultural practice (ethnicity), is the foundation of diaspora theory—a bare and low-content foundation, but an important foundation nonetheless.

A foundation is only a foundation. Something is put atop a foundation. What do we make of its embellishments? Are those embellishments only decorative or flourishes of meaning, or do they recur in ways that revise, perhaps even entirely rewrite, any and every sense of foundation? One of the signature features of Baldwin's work is his desire to articulate, sustain, and indulge joy in a sense of cultural production *specific to place* in ways that exceed the merely decorative, the merely different, and the mere manifestation of a deeper unity. Diaspora talk *needs* that sense of a deeper unity and also a sense that cultural production is secondary or tertiary work in relation to more primary racial questions; the scattering of fertile and capable seeds, after all, is only possible if the tree is healthy, fully rooted, and productive. But for Baldwin that sense of a shared, single root is displaced and replaced by a genuinely robust and developed notion of *tradition*, which, in turn, is critical for what we conceive as a sense of *a people*. To think Baldwin's nonfiction as a story about history and memory and thus generative of traditions is to think Baldwin in the midst of these utterly compelling and profoundly important debates around Black identity, heritage, and the meaning of Black life in the past, pivoted to the future. What was and is blackness? What will blackness be, in the wake of history's cruelty and also in the wake of independence, emancipation, and all the next steps in liberation struggle? History has exacted an unimaginable price. Who and what is Black life *in* and *after* that price? Who and what is Black life that struggles with or against the unimaginable but is also abundantly full of the imaginable?

✦

We have rearrived in place. The United States. What does it mean for Baldwin to claim such a strong sense of Americanness in the mid-century moment? This was a moment awash in reinventions of all sorts: names, stories, practices, authenticity claims, race and racial identity, origin, Africa, oceans and seas, machines, machines of machines, and so many aftermaths.

My insistence here is simple: We have to read Baldwin in a Black Atlantic context in order to understand, in the most expansive sense, the ultimate significance of his claims *against* Atlantic world diaspora storytelling. Baldwin never worked from an uncritical habit or sense of specialness about him and his place or origin. He was, instead, working in an intellectual milieu that revolutionized ideas of blackness, racial identity, diaspora, and all the moral, cultural, and political imperatives that come with it. What does that revolutionary work mean?

In order to grasp the extent of this context and how it bears on *understanding* Baldwin, on coming to terms with his thinking, I stage a series of readings below that draw out the details of that thinking in relation to emergent themes in his moment and also after. This is not, properly speaking, comparative work. Comparative work draws thinkers and/or traditions closer and then draws finer distinctions between those thinkers-traditions that mark difference(s) in some significant way. Setting Baldwin in a mid-century and after Black Atlantic context works from both distance and deep intimacy. The distance is geography and intellectual sensibility, but the intimacy has a different and more provocative place on the world stage—or at least on the south Atlantic stage. Whatever the differences, Baldwin's place in the mid-century moment and after is threaded tightly around the matter of racial identity, its enigma, and the sense that that identity is still to be articulated on the terms of Black people, Black life, and Black memories, histories, and experiences. Blackness, after all, was itself an invention of imperial power and the colonial gaze. Yet, it is also a term that attaches to profound literary, cultural, and political traditions, nearly all of which exceed anything made by the imperial, colonial gaze. How does blackness show up when it emerges as both a lived experience and a cultural-historical concept between Black people and Black traditions of thought? A different machine, a different difference. This is also different than placing, say, the question of race and diaspora between Africa and South Asia, a comparative context with a lot of richness but also very different historical experiences.[13] This is different than reading race as a genealogical project and production, which centers Europe and the work of whiteness over centuries of enslavement and colonial domination. Horizontal solidarity, while not a final note on diasporic identity formation, is how Baldwin asks questions that make the Black Atlantic world a world: full of pathos, reckoning, diversity, and transformative cultural production. So, Baldwin's question is the question asked across the Atlantic: Who and what are we without the white gaze? How is who and what we are structured by that gaze? How do we think outside the knot of antiblack racism, especially when it shows up as a psychic structure *inside* the oppressed? What emerges when we are freed from that knot?

In order to get at these questions and read Baldwin's work within this frame, the following chapters take up a cluster of critical concepts and motifs: the sense of origin, the production of racial identity, affects and their bearing on conscience and consciousness, language as world making and world sustaining, the concept of home, and the place of pessimism in an interracial world animated by necropolitical violence and its institutional structures. In the opening chapter, I put Baldwin's work in critical relation to that of Édouard Glissant and his obsessive return to the Middle Passage as a womb-abyss, a reckoning with catastrophic loss that births a people. That natal trauma of the Black Americas for Glissant is not the assignation of melancholy to the afterlives of slavery, but instead a sense of beginning that births the myriad and expansive possibilities of composite culture. Working from W. E. B. Du Bois's and Alain Locke's theorization of the Spirituals, I demonstrate how Baldwin's turn to the auction block rather than the Middle Passage in his account of African American origins positions the auction block as a critical concept that organizes African American identity and life in ways that are both melancholic and fecund. This is not unlike Glissant's reckoning with the Middle Passage, although, and this is crucial, Baldwin works with importantly different characterizations and senses of tradition. Origin stories matter, however much they may eschew grounding and single root arguments. In those stories, we catch sight of formative experiences-become-concepts that underpin traditions and identities of peoples.

That identity, what Baldwin will call with some ambivalence "the Negro," is produced in the origin story of the auction block's long, diverse resonance of the motherless child, which is then reproduced in the fraught interracial space of fantasy, brutal reality, and the complex internalization of both. The second chapter takes up this formation and reproductive work in three parts: the image of three Africans in Baldwin's work, the complexity of two white Americans, and the intertwining and dissimulation of the African fantasy and the white gaze in the first iteration of "the Negro." This takes us into Baldwin's nostalgic reflections on Haile Selassie, his strange failure to even mention Kwame Nkrumah and Ghana, the white imaginations of William Faulkner and Norman Mailer, and then to his greatest interlocutor, foil, and precedent in African American thought, Richard Wright. Out of this collage of images, absences, and visceral conflict emerges a sense of African Americanness that forms a sort of infrastructure to Baldwin's nonfiction. The third chapter takes up the question of the ghostly presence of the white gaze, a specter in the infrastructure of thinking, in comparative context, exploring the affective life of antiblackness in Frantz Fanon's work and Baldwin's reflections on the painful African American past from enslavement to the ghetto. A comparative context helps us see the proximity of Baldwin's thinking to central motifs in mid-century Caribbean thought. In particular, it helps us understand how vernacular cultural production represents and embodies profound senses of refusal that operate at the level of ontology and epistemology—how one is and how one knows—rather than, as it is for Fanon, simply the function of metacathexis for the energies of antiblackness.

The dynamics of racial formation and the affective life it produces and reproduces frame each of the chapters that follow. Chapters 4 and 5 examine Baldwin's conception of language and of home, two critical meditations for understanding the specificity of his account of race, nation, and identity. In what are for me some of his most important essays, Baldwin describes the origin and practice of what he calls "black English," a conception of English that sits in interesting relation to how theorists of creole and creolizing languages—Glissant in particular, although also Kamau Brathwaite, Patrick Chamoiseau, and others—understand the formation of expressive culture in the Black Americas. For both traditions, vernacular language practice is a matter of world making, world sustaining, and world reproduction. To speak a language, as Fanon puts it in *Black Skin, White Masks*, is to inhabit a world and culture. As well, language practices are inextricably intertwined with origin stories; Baldwin himself ties Black English to the auction block and its wake while, at the very same moment, theorists from the Caribbean tie creole and creolizing languages to the Middle Passage and its afterlife. Fanon is right: Language and culture, language and world, are inextricable. One *needs* language for world and world for language. If language and world are so intimately entwined, then how does this sense of language and world impact the conception of *home*?

The fifth chapter takes up Baldwin's paradoxical conception of home, a conception that sits with a sense of both being at home and nonbelonging at one and the same time. Home is won through the payment of an unimaginable price. For me, this is where Baldwin's work ultimately leads us: to an aporetic conceptual space crossing ethical and moral sensibilities in strange and estranging ways, and also the most complicated existential space in his nonfiction. It is one thing to articulate outrage, bear witness to atrocity, and document what has *not* been done. Baldwin was never a political revolutionary in terms of vision. It is quite another thing to set outrage and atrocity at the center of your work and *then* witness to senses of home forged in the interstices of the nation's putatively closed system of white supremacy and antiblack violence. The nuance and subtlety of Baldwin's thinking is in this moment, and chapter 5 tries very hard to make best sense of it.

The final chapter moves Baldwin's work from its mid-century Black Atlantic moment and its immediate aftermath to the contemporary with a consideration of Afropessimist ontology and its prospects. In a bit of comparative work, I demonstrate how Baldwin's intervention in the question of pessimism—something he already knew by way of Richard Wright's Black subjectivity-making work in *Native Son*—is not an affective claim against the dispiriting meditations of the pessimist tradition but instead a series of epistemological claims that bear on self- and collective knowledge. For me, this is a crucial intervention in the debates around Afropessimism and shows the ongoing relevance of Baldwin for contemporary thought. Most critical responses to Afropessimism object to the affective dimensions, positing the significance and presence of joy against pessimist sensibilities or appeal to the richness and complexity of African American cultural production by naming it as a site of resistance. What we can learn from Baldwin, especially when set in the frame of his dispute with Wright's conception of Black subjectivity, is how joy and cultural production are *symptomatic* of a deeper alternative to Afropessimism, one that argues with pessimism on pessimism's own terms:

the being of the world and the sociogenic principle of subjectivity. This in no way overturns Afropessimist claims, claims with which Baldwin has so many points of agreement, but instead clears conceptual space for a philosophical argument about the place of pessimism and optimism in theorizing Black bodies, Black life, and Black (or ~~black~~) being. Perhaps Being—what transcends and structures the life of a being and beings—is not antiblackness but instead a fractured space marked with interstitial formations. These are the formations that Baldwin, with all paradoxes in place, simply calls *home*.

Where do we begin this account of home? What is its origin story?

Chapter 1

Black Atlantic Origin Stories

Whence our identity?

Everything has an origin story. So does everyone and every *people*. The story of a people? These are always stories, of course, and never scientific studies. Stories are neither mere embellishments nor ephemera nor thin fictions. Stories of a people tell a history saturated with and inside of memory, drawing upon the imagination in order to reckon with what might be beyond our grasp, outside our reason, and unimaginable to even the most creative and empowered parts of us. Indeed, in the context of the United States and perhaps the Americas as a whole, the unimaginable lies at the heart of who and what we are. That is the price we pay to exist, to be, and to know. The Black Atlantic origin story, for Baldwin, is a story of unimaginable pain and its price. "Our dehumanization of the Negro," Baldwin writes in "Many Thousands Gone," a key early essay, "is indivisible from our dehumanization of ourselves: the loss of our own identity is the price we pay for our annulment of his."[1] This is a remarkable observation, one that marks out the space of Baldwin's conception of an identity forged in what he describes as "a fruitless tension between the traditional master and slave. Impossible and fruitless because, literal and visible as this tension has become, it has nothing to do with reality."[2] A fabrication with material consequences. The birth of racial nihilism. The beginnings of Afropessimism. With real conciseness, Baldwin has already here articulated the difficult and impossible condition of interracial life in the United States: identities built on illusory foundations, identities lived as lives of violence, pain, and terrible inheritance. The illusory foundations are lived as pain because there is also the matter of *reality*. That is, there is both the illusory foundation of racial meaning, how that meaning makes lives in interracial space possible and necessary and how that meaning is reproduced across time. But there is also the possibility of another kind of relation to identity and meaning. How can we think identity *between* illusory foundation and reality? This is the crossroads of racial origin stories. Whence our identity? The illusory or the real? And how does that sense of the illusory and the real hinge on the meaning of history and its infusion of memory? How do we become who we are across time? For Baldwin and the Black

Atlantic, it is a straightforward problematic: How we remember slavery—its origins, its cruel practices—means everything for our inheritance(s) of history.

Let me pause for a moment and reorient this discussion in order to set a context. Baldwin's remembering of slavery is an origin story in the deepest sense. All of African American identity moves from that origin point, but as an origin point it is already a shift in the Black Atlantic's storytelling. How does beginning make the aftermath of origin work, create, and know? So much of Black Atlantic intellectual history is in this question, and that history shapes Baldwin's specificity as a thinker. Let me return to Baldwin after a critical excursus into the Black Atlantic question of origin, story, illusion, and reality.

In a series of provocative books published since his paradigm shifting *The Black Atlantic* (1993), Paul Gilroy has set out an ambitious and often controversial agenda of theorizing the meaning of race and racism without raciology. *The Black Atlantic* argued with measured success that what we might think of as the African American intellectual tradition has a less steady anchor in the nation and its historical experience than we might expect. The *roots* of the tradition are replaced, in Gilroy's careful study of cornerstone figures, by *routes*. (It is also noteworthy that Baldwin's work does not show up in significant ways in *The Black Atlantic*.) Gilroy's work after *The Black Atlantic* is concerned with that same kind of conceptual complexity, dislodging common anchors in our language of race while also understanding the persistent significance of them, accounting for what remains after critical assessment, and attending to how new critical vocabularies emerge as necessary. We see this project of complicating our notion of race first appear in the collection of essays gathered under the British title *Between Camps* (2000), a collection that begins an earnest and sustained inquiry into this problematic of race after raciology. The American retitling and issue of the book *Against Race* in 2001 only serves to underscore both the ambition (how is thinking possible without racial categories?) and the controversy (how is it possible to understand without race?). The motivations for Gilroy's multibook project are clear. Any biological claims to something like "race" have long been debunked, so any use of the concept of race that appeals, explicitly or implicitly, to scientific foundations ought to be disputed and rejected. At the same time, as we all know, the phenomenon of race is not just a feature of our world but, especially when paired with its old companion racism, an organizing principle of it. How do we think these two things at the same time? What is race without raciology? And what is racism without scientific foundations?

Of course, Gilroy is neither the first nor the last person to undertake such an enormous project. What I find so interesting about Gilroy's work on race, however, is how he takes our postraciology world seriously without retreating to a smug, nonworldly posture of being "beyond" race. Race still matters, and what makes his project all the more complex and urgent is the incorporation of—and deep commitment to—an insistent racial justice program. That is, even without the concept of race, we have moral and political imperatives ranging from reparations to preferential treatment to revisions to models for rights that sit at the center of our conscience. Concrete demands issue from history and memory and how both are written in the body of encounter. We need words for these demands. These are demands, after all, that strike at the heart of our social and political organization in the Atlantic world. Without raciology, how can one ground a sense of racially specific sensitivity and justice? What notion of race can be simultaneously stable enough to do justice work and unstable enough to not repeat the speculative sins of the past? How to tell the truth, to witness, without falsehoods? No small questions. Biggest stakes.

Gilroy's bold intervention on these questions is not without controversy and visceral debate. Matters of race and identity are fraught as well as deeply important for thinking about culture and politics, so putting the concept of race under real scrutiny—not unlike putting the national character of an intellectual tradition under the same, it should be noted—raises so many critical questions and initiates so many critical debates. Many objections to Gilroy's project miss this latter commitment to racial repair and address, however, and therein bypass what is most compelling about his postraciology work. For all his movement away from conventional, rooted ideas of race, and for all of his insistence on the roots and routes being theorized in the plural, Gilroy remains committed to some kind of blackness: blackness as a social and cultural formation that bears with it urgent questions, as well as important denotations of cultural production, collective understanding, and senses of belonging. Across his nonfiction, too, Baldwin's commitment to the same set of principles—that there is no science of race and that racial obligations, outrages, and justice are fundamental moral and political imperatives—pushes against the bolder, mythic conceptions of race in Black Atlantic theory in the postwar period. That period saw a revival of essentialist notions of race, whatever the nuances and embellishments to those notions, as terms of liberation and not just terms of oppression; reversals of conceptual fortune animate a lot of Black Atlantic mid-century thinking, especially in the Négritude movement. Baldwin rejects essentialism. He rejects it not for ideological reasons (although that would be plenty) but for reasons deeply rooted in an ontology and epistemology of African American life and subjectivity. It is possible to be and know blackness without raciology. Between Gilroy and Baldwin, there is this crossed path.

It is always important to note that the rejection of essentialism is not a rejection of a robust, enduring, and politically and culturally motivating conception of racial identity. Quite the opposite, in fact. That rejection is fundamentally a *revitalization* of racial hope, pride, accumulation, embellishment, retrieval, appreciation, and politicocultural activation. Baldwin's adoration of Black life in its interstices, in the margins of American life, as well as his rage against the brutality of interracial life, is the central aim of his fiction and nonfiction both. Whatever the racial complexities of *Another Country*, for example, the message remains that being Black is a mortal risk precisely because of the presence of white people in a shared world. But *Another Country* is also about the brilliance and exuberance not just of Black people but of blackness as an earthy and atmospheric presence in a terrifying, violent world. That terror has no basis beyond the cruelty of whites; Baldwin has no compulsion, *pace* the Négritude movement, to rethink an essentialist root to race and revalue its values. Which is just to say, Baldwin's love of blackness eschews strong senses of root precisely because he wants that sense of blackness to have the cultural, memorial, and historical dynamism borne by it over centuries of suffering and world making. He begins with the difficulty of essentialism's long shadow, writing in "Many Thousands Gone," "Today, to be sure, we know that the Negro is not biologically or mentally inferior; there is no truth in those rumors of his body odor or his incorrigible sexuality; or no more truth than can be easily explained or even defended by the social sciences. Yet, in our most recent war, his blood was segregated, as was, for the most part, his person." This passage raises the obvious question, one that threads together so many themes from Baldwin's work: If race is not a natural, transgeographic identity, then what do we mean by "race"? And if raciology is fundamentally *wrong* and *without grounds*, then should we think, act, and be without racial categories? How does segregated blood become the marrow of justice claims, with all its painful history, yet also the heart of sublime cultural production? This is the enigma of beginning without root, of thinking without fixed, essential categories, yet also loving what blackness has been, is, and will be. This is Baldwin's complicated task.

Baldwin, not unlike Gilroy, refuses to affirm this second question—thinking, acting, and being without racial categories cannot make sense in the world as we know it. That is, it is not a question of thinking and acting without race as a structuring and guiding question. Not at all. In fact, and this is the nuance, delinking the question of racial identity and blackness from all essentialisms is *precisely* how the fecundity of racial identification is possible—how beautiful blackness, love for it and cultivation of it, comes to ground all of Baldwin's work and his intimate, yet distant, relation to mid-century Black Atlantic theory.[3] In many ways, the present chapter and the chapters that follow revolve around just this question and how this imperative guides Baldwin's fiction and nonfiction meditations. But as we begin here, it is first a question of beginning: How do we tell the *origin story* of Black and blackness? If race is not a fixed biological or metaphysical fact of the world, then how does race arise as an identity? Where does that identity begin, and how does beginning animate the history/histories that follow? And, to the Black Atlantic question, how are origin stories linked to the particularities of the geography of reason, to how thinking is linked to place, its historical experience, and the folding of specificities of memory into time's existential expanse? This is Baldwin conceived and read in the Black Atlantic context, that space of diverse and divergent origin stories that frame wide, expansive forms of thinking.

Geography as a critical concept—roots and routes that make a place—is crucial here as both a common site of inquiry (the Atlantic world) and the uncommon formation of identity (place specificity). For all of Baldwin's travel and time writing in exile, his gaze always returns to the nation and the origin story of blackness within it. How, then, is Baldwin's commitment to the specificity of the United States—what he calls "Americanness"—formative of his vision of both the nation and the meaning of race inside the nation? And how does that vision distinguish his thinking from broader thinking in the Americas and set itself up in productive relation to key ideas in the African American intellectual tradition?

Sorrow and Memory

In the closing chapter to *The Souls of Black Folk*, Du Bois makes a compelling case that the Spirituals, far from an ephemeral expression of suffering, sit at the very foundation of the African American intellectual tradition. Musical pieces introduce each chapter of *Souls of Black Folk*, which, as a matter of rhetorical structure and style, asserts how expressive life in sound is crucial for understanding the argument of the text as a whole and what is inside each essay in particular. In the closing chapter, "The Sorrow Songs," Du Bois explicitly argues for this through an invocation of sound as the medium of memory, something hearkening back to Frederick Douglass's aside in *Narrative of the Life of Frederick Douglass* that the sound of enslaved people singing in a plantation field haunted him throughout his life, placing the memory of pain *in sound* at the heart of his own work toward emancipation.[4] If *Narrative* was a foundational piece in thinking emancipation as a critical moral concept, we can say that *The Souls of Black Folk* is the same sort of piece for epistemology in an antiblack world: how African Americans know themselves and their origins and what memorial knowing bequeaths to the present and then future. Both Douglass and Du Bois root their reflections in sound and presume the genius of expressive life: philosophical, aesthetic, political. "And so before each thought that I have written in this book," Du Bois writes, "I have set a phrase, a haunting echo of these weird old songs in which the soul of the black slave spoke to men."[5] This last turn of phrase, "spoke to men," is crucial. Du Bois deploys this characterization in order to ensure that we as readers, then as listeners, understand the epistemic and ontological significance of the Spirituals; the knowing and being specific to Black life is in the Spirituals (thus, worthy of being spoken "to men"), which tells an important story about culture, politics, and subjectivities both individual and collective. Indeed, composed just a few years prior, Du Bois's essay "The Conservation of Races" argued for a commitment to cultural production in order to put "the Negro" on the world stage alongside other racial and national groups. The Spirituals "spoke to men" in precisely this manner and manifest something essential about race and nation. Du Bois writes in *Souls of Black Folk*, "By fateful chance the Negro folk-song—the rhythmic cry of the slave—stands today not simply as the sole American music, but as the most beautiful expression of human experience born this side of the seas. It has been neglected, it has been, and is, half despised, and above all it has been persistently mistaken and misunderstood; but notwithstanding, it still remains as the singular spiritual heritage of the nation and the greatest gift of the Negro people."[6] *The Souls of Black Folk* reaches its climax as a dramatic text here, having documented the beleaguerment and pain of Black folk across chapters on subjectivity, intellectual work, education, economics, and all other ranges of inquiry. Du Bois ends by writing the Spirituals into the Americas and elevating or transforming the abject—the sounds of the enslaved—into the sublime, which then defines both a people and a nation. That last move, shifting discourse from African Americans specifically to the nation as such, is Du Bois's characteristic rhetorical flourish and political critique. He is right, after all. Expressive culture in the United States has *always* been rooted in African American traditions. Cooptation and appropriation work with something, after all. At the same time, the Spirituals are a particular inheritance for African Americans: animation of the present with memory of so unimaginable a price. But whether we follow his characterization to the level of the nation or reckon more narrowly in terms of African Americans as a *people*, Du Bois's account of the aesthetic as ontological work is critical for understanding the Black American origin story as the movement between unfathomable pain and sublime expression, and thus the origin story Baldwin wants to tell us.

Expressive life is nothing like an escape from the burdens of the world, an opium of the masses, or mere entertainment. Rather, expressive life is critical theory in sound. When it has philosophical aspiration, the genius of expression inheres in the ability to theorize the existential conditions of Black life in the aural and in that theorization reflect and create, produce and reproduce, senses of shared life, community, and belonging. We can think here of how Ralph Ellison describes Bessie Smith as a "priestess, a celebrant who affirmed the values of the group and man's ability to deal with chaos."[7] Smith's ecstasy, her ability to bend and blend time, is the condition of the blues *because* it inherits the craft and capacity of the Spirituals—God's blues, or a god's blues. She affirms and makes a world, no matter what the world denies about her and no matter how it assigns her outside its interracial meaning. The Spirituals and the blues are in that way *insurgent* discourses. They intervene in life and intervene in place—places both geographic and spiritual. Some years later, Alain Locke puts this sentiment plainly: "The Spirituals are really the most characteristic product of the race genius as yet in America. But the very elements which make them uniquely expressive of the Negro make them at the same time deeply representative of the soil that produced them. Thus, as unique spiritual products of American life, they become nationally as well as racially characteristic."[8] The invocation of "spiritual products" is interesting because it anticipates the kind of language we see in the Négritude movement around the question of *esprit*—a critical term taken and reshaped from European vitalist thought.[9] But whereas the Négritude thinkers had a broad, continental vision of that sense of spirit—the civilizational force of Africa across the continent and also the Atlantic world—Locke's sense of spirit is generated from the specific sense of place of *this country, another country*. In this way, Locke completes Du Bois's provisional thinking at the close of *Souls of Black Folk* by drawing on the Spirituals as a living resource for cultural production and racial development *in this place*. To this end, Locke links this expressive life to identity, yes, but also to soil. "The soil that produced them" describes a sense of nomadic rootedness that is saturated with life, death, mourning, ecstasy, pleasure, suffering, and melancholia. Sound is born from that milieu, from that earthy and embodied sense of relation to the world. What does it mean to think that mixed saturation as not a sense of the tragic but as a sense of life, meaning, and world making? It means to think paradox and the necessity of the impossible, a reckoning that resonates more with the development of poststructuralist thought a half century later than it does with the high modernism of Négritude and its companion movements. What is this spirit-sonic deconstructive space, and what does it tell us about origin stories?

This moment in Du Bois's work and Locke's embellishment and extension of it, as well as how both gather together so much about the African American intellectual tradition, open up an important and interesting comparative moment between that tradition and the post-Fanon trajectory of Caribbean thought, in particular Édouard Glissant and the creolists. Both traditions or trajectories speak to a troubled and troubling sense of beginning, an origin point that mixes the unrepresentable, death world pain of the past with the persistent insistence on *life* both in the midst and in the wake of too much violence, which then bequeaths to the present and imaginable future too much impossibility. It is first a question of production and then reproduction, a massive yet discrete and specific story of origins—a story Glissant and Antonio Benítez-Rojo tell as a maternal story, a story of the womb, and which Derek Walcott renders as a matter of the surname, identity, and paternity in "The Muse of History."[10] For others, we see the same problem of death, melancholia, pleasure, and life in broader terms and ontological puzzles: How can one *be* in a world that produces natal alienation and social death? First: yes, alienation and death. Also: yes, life and beginning again. There is birth at the shore of the unimaginable place, in the wake of unimaginable loss, but this is a peculiar birth that Glissant calls the womb-abyss, a birth space that, upon arrival of the born, becomes immediately and irretrievably absent. In the wake of enslavement and on this shore, Du Bois hears the sound of slavery and finds himself in that sound as its descendant. Yet the birth origin retreats at the very moment of hearing it. The sound is *weird*, by which Du Bois means uncanny, from another world, and yet intimate to his own. In this sense, the Spirituals function as a trace that leaves no trail. In each iteration of this birth from radical absence, we hear the echo of another Spiritual, the refrain that has to be sung and heard to know: Sometimes I feel like a motherless child. Sometimes. Motherless. A child. *I*—the subject, being, knowing, doing, feeling, making. We will return to this refrain as a comparative frame.

The figure of the maternal, blended with loss and melancholy, tells a particular origin story and sites its iteration in sound. That sound is for Glissant both in the place of orality in the formation of Caribbean culture and in the echoes of broken-off fragments of language and expression in creole languages across each island. This repetition with difference is what Benítez-Rojo calls the repeating island. The sound of language—oral traditions, creole, patois, pidgin—carries the origin into the present and puts it in a fecund, not meaning-evacuating, relation to the future. This is the enigma of Glissant's thought and of so much post-Fanon Caribbean theory. To put it plainly, Glissant's origin story positions the Middle Passage as the rootless root. Baldwin does the same with the Auction Block (here capitalized in order to designate its status as event and critical concept). In both cases, it is a matter of positioning the unpositionable. In both cases, the sometimes, the feeling, the motherlessness, and the child—with all the temporalities and ontologies carried by those senses of the abyssal, the orphan, and the nomadic—function, in the formation of the "I" of subjectivity, as origin stories that are not origins, yet are the birth of community, identity, expressive life, and all of the resonances and significations of cultural production. The life of social death and life lived *against* social death: This is the paradox of Black life in the Americas. It is no coincidence that Baldwin, Glissant, and others tell an origin story that begins and also arrives at this same aporetic position. Origin stories are at once epic tellings of a particular sort and the initiation of an interpretation of or reckoning with historical experience as sedimented into the marrow of everyday life. Telling an origin story of the Black Americas, and telling it in the terms of the historical and memorial experience sedimented in Black life, tells as origin precisely what history's hegemonic actors wanted to deny and forbid. The origin story is an assertion of life as the *after* of unrepresentable violence, a certain kind of denial of social death's scope and power. And so we ought to think of the Middle Passage and the auction block as critical concepts and emphatically *not* as historical or personal events. That is, the Middle Passage and auction block both function to organize being and knowing across time. Seeing that function work in the cultural and political subconscious allows us, like with all theoretical interventions or claims, to see and hear something that might otherwise lie hidden. The feeling of the motherless child, an historically sedimented affect, becomes a knowing of a very particular kind—nomadic, rhizomatic, nimble, and ecstatic—and it places a sense of being between pain, survival, and *poiesis*, the capacity to make worlds despite the massive, centuries-long effort to deny such possibility.

What, then, is an origin story? And how does it transform violence into an after*life*?

Memory Sounds

The opening chapters of Glissant's *Poetics of Relation* (1990) tell a complicated story. His opening conceptual moves draw our attention to a new constellation of thinking, moving quickly from a threefold notion of *abyss* to nuanced appropriations of Félix Guattari and Gilles Deleuze's formulations of nomad and rhizome to hesitations around conventional modes of storytelling to the generation of the critical conception of plantation. Glissant takes us quickly and with incredible nuance from the Middle Passage to the contemporary shoreline, haunted at every turn by and welcoming of the ghosts of the Caribbean landscape. That welcome is a way of *honoring* and also the first bit of foundational work for a radical sense of difference or diversity. Everything is gathered to this moment: Crossroads of the world, unthinkable disaster, centuries. The abyss is the belly of the boat, the loss of root(s) in the continent of Africa, a first encounter with the unfathomable. Then the abyss is the sea, with its depths that inspired nothing like fear or awe, but only reminded, if not invited, the mass death at the heart of forced migration. And then the arrival at the Caribbean shore, the unknown and unfathomable of a terrifying future, a third abyss that begins again. What remains of what was lies "in the blue savannas of memory or imagination."[11] This is Glissant's iteration of the motherless child.

The continent, the mother-who-would-be, is left behind; arrival is the work of islands on consciousness, conscience, and world making. It is always worth returning to a detail or two of Glissant's account of the archipelago and its origins in the opening of *Poetics of Relation*. That account of how we begin thinking about beginning is set forth concisely in the "Errantry, Exile" section of the text. "Roots make the commonality of errantry and exile," Glissant writes, "for in both instances roots are lacking. We must begin with that."[12] Glissant asks us to begin with the sea, a shift in the language of locality and diaspora away from mythic and epic stories of continental roots and toward the abyss as a world-birthing space of catastrophe, loss, and beginning. Like Baldwin, Glissant is no thinker of strong notions of diaspora. Memory that begins at the shoreline is paramount. He writes, "For us, and without exception. And no matter how much distance we may keep, the abyss is also a projection of and a perspective into the unknown. Beyond its chasm we gamble on the unknown. We take sides in this game of the world. We hail a renewed Indies; we are for it. And for this Relation made of storms and profound moments of peace in which we may honor our boats."[13] For me, there is no more important passage in Glissant's work, and in many ways this comment of his, bursting with possibility, tells the entirety of the origin story and its recurrence in the present. No origin story is absent the present. The story reminds us. This is its moral force. It reminds us to honor the boats. The boat is origin. The boat is past. The boat is present. The boat is also the pleasure of the water. Enjoyment. Skill. Sociality. Abjection in memory. Trauma. Storm and peace. All paradoxes that not only defy resolution but, in their refusal of resolution, give life in the fullest, most complex vitality: composite culture, creole identity, all in motion, all drawing from multiple roots.

To what and where does this moment of honoring the boats, standing simultaneously in storm and peace, lead us? What does the origin story tell Glissant about *how* to be, about the *I* who feels in the Spiritual? This account motivates what Glissant calls a *poetics of diversity.* And here the poetics of diversity is neither simply a metaphysical or ontological claim, nor is it reducible to the epistemology of displaced and scattered subaltern groups. Rather, the poetics of diversity affects the very terms of composition. Indeed, when asked by an interviewer about the nature and character of his 1993 work *Tout Monde*, Glissant replies that "it's a novel that engages with the *substance* of the world, that is as expansive as the substance of the world, and I don't have a problem with that. It is also a work that risks going beyond established literary genres."[14] This is a compelling framing by Glissant for a number of reasons. First, it helps us read a work like *Tout Monde* in a very particular way; while I am in no way bound by authorial intent as a reader (such is the nature of reading), this does describe and justify the quirky sense of what the book is seeking to argue, as well as how and why it is composed of such varying voices and registers to the point of chaos. Intentionally so, it turns out, *Tout Monde* is a literary engagement with the very meaning of its title. Second, Glissant blends together "substance" and "expansive," a key creolization of terms that in the white Western tradition have stood in opposition. Substance is typically the limit of expansion, the obstinate character of *res extensa*, but here Glissant parallels his critique of Being by reforming substance *as* expansiveness. If paradox is built into the very notion of beginning, then a certain abuse of language and concept is in order. Third, and to the comparative argument with Baldwin, this remark by Glissant clarifies the force of origin stories—as narratives of history, but also as nascent regulative ideals for a poetics of the present and future—for thinking the possible, necessary, and ethically commanded *respectful, adventurous* life of the globalization of cultural forms. Risk, which is here a matter of taking the unknown and the abyssal as a guide for knowing and being, is constitutive of life *after* the origin story. Not as a moral imperative or political challenge but instead just as a direct description of the terms of relationality.

In that context, I also think Glissant's sense of origin story, set alongside his critique of myth and epic in *Poetics of Relation*, orients a reading of two early works that *seem* to traffic in the languages of mythic and epic origins: the poetry of *The Indies* (1956) and the novel *The Fourth Century* (1964). To be sure, these are very different works. *The Indies* is a sweeping, quasi-epic story of conquest, the Middle Passage, the plantation, and how the swirl of all creates what Glissant will later call the rhizomatic character of the archipelago and plantation worlds. *The Fourth Century* is an intimate novel, telling a family and community story that places us in the dramatic unfolding of generational memory of slavery, its traumas, and the capacity to make world(s) in the midst of, then after, catastrophic violence. But even *The Fourth Century* is told with a certain grandeur; the notion of *four* centuries is already an epic narrative, telling the story of the beginning of the Black Americas in the archipelago. The sweeping narrative of *The Indies* is supplemented by, and not juxtaposed to, *The Fourth Century* in the sense that both tell origin stories in different registers, sweeping or discrete. But there is no argument for a rooted experience in either one. Rather, each tells an unrooted and unrooting story, stories that set adrift, make nomadic, and understand the struggle to link memory and history—the life, not social death, of motherless children. In both works, the positivism of history, the compulsion to tell the master narrative and make an intervention in myth and epic (there is an interesting element here about the relationship between positivist values and the work of root making), is overwhelmed by the work of memory. How else to make sense of the utterly strange Columbus that emerges in *The Indies* or *The Fourth Century*'s staging of Martinique's birth in terms of the enslaved, the maroon, and the fraught conciliation of families? But memory is no personal matter. Memory functions here as a way of *saying* origins in the origin story. It is a way of saying the unsayable and letting that unsayable resonate and produce an atmospheric effect that shapes the contours of affect in each work.

Honoring the boats.

The distinction, then, between the mythic/epic story and origin stories is clarified in this interpretative frame. The effect of the abyssal beginning of the archipelago—the loss of root in Africa, the loss of life and meaning in the belly of the ship, and the loss of language and connection at the shoreline—is akin to the loss of the possibility of history as a metanarrative History. Walcott was right in his 1992 Nobel Prize lecture "The Antilles: Fragments of Epic Memory": The sigh of History is a sigh over ruins that give life, not ruins that signify the loss of life and abject suffering. Losing the possibility of History is not *also* a loss of a sense of place. Place and its world-making labors *is* the work of memory. Memory tells origin stories in very specific ways. Memory tells origin stories in the grammar and timbre of the ghost. Learning how to understand ghostly language—the echo of the abyss in composite culture, the uncanny pain in the Spirituals—and to see and hear the temporality in it requires us to attend to the work of memory in sound. This is why the notion of orality is so critical in Glissant's thinking, and indeed in any thinking that takes creole language and, like Baldwin, vernacular cultural formation seriously. The *sound* of the past and the resonance of origin stories in the everyday is elemental to the present and future—elemental, here, in the sense of the building blocks of a particular human reality and also in the sense in which water is a fish's element, that in which it moves, breathes, and lives.

To hear memory in sound is to hear the origin story, a trace with a bit of a trail; every trace does point *somewhere*. This pointing, this very peculiar indicator, directs us toward the maternal as trope, the womb-abyss, who cannot show herself or itself. Yet, here are the children. That moment of the origin story never gathers the abyss to presence. Creole cultural forms, vernacular expressiveness, and the Spirituals are languages of the plantation world. The motherless child, motherless, yes, but yet a child. Children make worlds out of what lies before them.

Auction Block Sounds

In turning to Baldwin, we see a different yet critically related movement into origin stories. Glissant's account of the womb-abyss, his reckoning with how the Middle Passage tells an origin story of creolization and relation, takes as one of its *leitfäden* the composition of creole language, seeing in that composition the work of memory through sound and errant syntax. Baldwin is surely better known for broad reflections on race and American life, but his attention to language and sound in often lesser-known pieces tells an important origin story. As always with Baldwin, this is an African American story. And it is one that helps us understand the resonance of epistemology and ontology in the motif of motherless children. This is important given *both* the sense in which slavery is for Baldwin the origin story of African American life and speech *and* the sense in which he spends so much of his writing, from the earliest reflections on Harlem to the late book on the Atlanta child murders, reflecting on the meaning (or even searching for the existence) of Black childhood.[15] What is Baldwin's womb-abyss? What is made in that abyss and what does it give to the world?

The child, on Baldwin's reckoning, is the site of both the playful ecstasy and the reproduction of Black life. Angularity, as Zora Neale Hurston characterized it, is in children's speech and gait and play, but also in their sense of inheritance. Speaking is knowing. Speaking is being. Rhythm, song, asymmetry of posture and tone, all of that. Language lies at the center of our reckoning with inheritance. Black English, as Baldwin calls it, is an entire language, one that makes identity out of the African American experience while affirming a version of the proverbial nation within a nation. But the history of enslavement, the demands abjection puts on the making of subjectivity, means that the African American relation to language is forever one of intervention, transformation, and expressive life in what Ellison calls at the close of *Invisible Man* "the lower frequencies." Just as language was a first site of the exercise of exploitative power, language is the first site of remaking the world after or in the midst of catastrophe. Language is play and world making. It is also—as a blend of play and work making—the act of creation itself. For each Black writer in the Americas, Baldwin claims, the work of remaking is a fresh, demanding imperative. "Writers are obliged, at some point," Baldwin writes, "to realize that they are involved in a language which they must change. And for a black writer in this country to be born into the English language is to realize that the assumptions on which the language operates are his enemy."[16]

The enemy here is not merely the power of the white gaze in the colonizer's judgment around diction and the like; Baldwin is not the Fanon of the early pages of *Black Skin, White Masks*, who characterized colonial language as a space of nonbeing, alienation, and fate to failure. Rather, what concerns Baldwin about the racial politics of language is the moment of self-knowing and collective self-knowledge that comes with Black English. This is knowing that connects the self to community in shared vernacular. We can think of this as an African American iteration of Patrick Chamoiseau's description of writing and the proper name in the opening of *School Days*, in which the main character chalks out his name with frantic energy "in order to proliferate and avoid genocide."[17] Everything is at stake in terms of self-knowledge. To embrace the world-making power of Black English is for Baldwin to embrace what it means to know who one is in relation to the world of other African Americans *from the beginning* because of a shared origin story. And here we have to say "African American" precisely because Baldwin, like Glissant and the creolists, insists on the specificity of historical experience and on the embeddedness of memory in the sound of speech. Origin stories matter. To know *that* world, its origin and the afterlife of it all, is to know a form of authenticity in motion. Origin stories set in motion and that motion comprises a dynamic of identity and difference: sharing the form of motherless children, evolving and modifying in moment, eras, places, and the demands of time. We are never the same across time, so this is never fixed speech. It is speech in the mode of becoming, a collective and intersubjective improvisation and meaning making in the cracks and on the margins that is both resistance and refusal. It speaks against the hegemony of white power and the gaze, but it also declines participation in both the rules and the rule to participate in the rules.

A sense of origin story is at stake as well. Like Du Bois's reckoning of the Spirituals as the foundation of the African American intellectual tradition, Baldwin turns to the origin story of slavery resonant in the Sorrow Songs, in particular to the *event* of the Auction Block. The Auction Block is a critical concept, working in a certain parallel relation to the Middle Passage in Glissant, but also very different in important ways. The Middle Passage is abyssal, animated by the absolute silence of loss and memory drown at the bottom of the sea. The Auction Block is animated by the cry of loss, an echo of rage and grief in language that begins at the moment of commodification, separation, and sale, and all the layered brutality. That brutality is transformative of the world; African Americans know and live in its afterlife because the brutality of it all upends the entirety of thinking. It is an event in the sense that Martin Heidegger gives to *Ereignis*: an appropriation of thought and being by a moment in history, an interval, that is then iterated across time, giving shape to place, people, and community. The *life* of a lifeworld, even if that life lives in relation to social death and its ghosts. The Auction Block is a moment of iterated trauma, unspeakable in its pain but heard in the sound—melancholic, beautiful, sublime, mournful—of music and speech. Baldwin writes in the essay "Of the Sorrow Songs":

> It is out of this, and much more than this, that black American music springs. This music begins on the auction block.
>
> Now, whoever is unable to face this—the auction block; whoever cannot see that that auction block is the demolition, by Europe, of all human standards: a demolition accomplished, furthermore, at that hour of the world's history, in the name of "civilization"; whoever pretends that the slave mother does not weep, until this hour, for her slaughtered son, that the son does not weep for his slaughtered father; or whoever pretends that the white father did not, literally, and knowing what he was doing, hand, and burn, and castrate, his black son—whoever cannot face this can never pay the price for the "beat" which is key to music, and the key to life.
>
> Music is our witness, and our ally. The "beat" is the confession which recognizes, changes, and conquers time.
>
> Then, history becomes a garment we can wear, and share, and not a cloak in which to hide; and time becomes a friend.[18]

There is so much in this passage, much of which I will revisit in a reflection on vernacular language below in chapter 4. Here, however, let me underscore a few elements. The beat, an incarnate historiography through and through, has its *price*. An unimaginable price that is nevertheless concrete, embodied, and aural. Baldwin will come back to the motif of price in a number of essays, but here it is a note struck in the most painful moment of African American history and memory: the separation of beloveds and the sale of human bodies. The auction block is the site of the commodification of human bodies, of human life, and the site of separation, physical brutality, and death. We know that much about the practice of slavery. But Baldwin shifts that witness moment of historical vision to the memorial presence of such pain in sound, embodiment, and existential movement; the auction block makes music, and in making music, it makes life.[19] Again, the paradox of origins: to die of unspeakable pain while living a certain kind of world-building beauty. The fractured, ambivalent sublime.

Baldwin's capacity to see life emerge in the memory of the most abject space is then further transformed in his short reflection on time—an ecstatic stretch of the African American origin story. The violence of slavery was *intended* to halt time, to suspend the enslaved in the present without connection to the past or hope for a future, and so to deepen subjection beyond physical domination to the subjugation of the element of human temporality to white cruelty. But Baldwin is claiming here that the beat contains confession (the sheerness of the truth of the past, abject and cruel), witness (hearing and recognizing both pain and the insistence on persistence), and the ability to conquer time *as constructed by the white gaze and its lash*. In that sense, the beat, the musicality of speech and expressive tradition, is first a moment of resistance that then becomes the cultural habit of the lower frequencies: refusal to see oneself in relation to the white gaze and its now, postemancipation, sublimated sense of lash. The auction block becomes the Auction Block precisely when its history becomes a garment, something to adorn and *honor* the past in the present, then future. Honor the boats, honor the block. This is the ultimate purchase of origin stories: identifying sites of mourning, honor, and birth. The Auction Block, like Glissant's Middle Passage, becomes a critical concept precisely when time becomes (or can become) a *friend*, an intimate companion with whom one has peace, conversation, respect, exploration, openness, vicissitudes, and the sort of kindness that does not eschew pain but is also capable of understanding pain as part of the fecundity of resistance and refusal.[20]

That is to say, Baldwin makes the Auction Block an origin story with obligations, inheritances, honors, beauty, terror, and world. Ontology and epistemology. An origin story of loss, yes, but also a loss *inside* the Black Americas. It is important to note that we do not find Baldwin musing on the Middle Passage, thinking through its wake and legacy and resonance. In that moment of temporal choice, he marks a distinction between his thinking and the Caribbean tradition beginning with Aimé Césaire's critical reflections on abject life in "Notebook of a Return to the Native Land" and especially post-Fanon Caribbean theory around questions of creole, patois, and composite culture. Instead, with Baldwin we find this moment of separation and the spectacle of Black suffering placed at the beginning of another beginning. It is the mother's weeping for the brutalization of her son, the child's melancholia after loss of the father and the mother. Literally, in this case, an origin story of the motherless child. The Spiritual's refrain is the *feeling*, that affective life that forms subjectivity in the beat, of being motherless, and we might hear in the companion verse "far, far away from home / a long long ways from home" a story about Africa. There is no reason to render the Spiritual's resonance and location one-dimensional; they are polyphonic and polysignifying.[21] But for Baldwin, the resonance is back to this founding wound of separation, death, wandering, and loss that *begins* African American historical experience, not in the belly of the boat, but in this other womb-abyss we call the Auction Block.

✦

In a certain sense, we can identify a kind of deconstructive practice at the heart of these origin stories, a practice that refuses to identify the persistence of death across time—the melancholia of Black Atlantic memory—with the negation of life. Deconstruction works with supplements to systems in order to demonstrate both the opening of closure and the impossibility of systematicity to be what it wants to be. The trick with deconstruction, of course, lies in the *affirmation* rather than refutation of what it wants to complicate and critique. So, in theorizing the possibility of life, deconstructive practice begins with the terms of death worlds and their claim to closure—the claim that nothing escapes the proscriptions and hegemonic work of killing, death, and dying. This is particularly important when we think about the white gaze and its violent racial hegemony. Rather than contest the gaze with resistance, deconstructive approaches like Baldwin's and others telling a Black Atlantic origin story embed thinking inside hegemony's terrible work in order to mark its limits and the opening of/at those limits. Glissant's and Baldwin's origin stories, although they split in important ways around the question of sites of loss and what they bequeath, enact this deconstructive practice. This is an important element of the Black Atlantic intellectual tradition. I have in mind here Du Bois's iteration of the origin story, in which he begins "The Sorrow Songs" chapter in *Souls of Black Folk* with an epigraph from the Spiritual "Lay This Body Down":

> I walk through the churchyard
> To lay this body down;
> I know moon-rise, I know star-rise;
> I walk in the moonlight, I walk in the starlight;
> I'll lie in the grave and stretch out my arms,
> I'll go to judgement in the evening of the day,
> And my soul and thy soul shall meet that day,
> When I lay this body down.

The thematic of this Spiritual is the labor—impossible yet imperative—to die a certain kind of death that the plantation makes impossible. This is a death suffered on one's own terms in the presence of the sacred. *I walk through the churchyard.* The sacred is here in the moment of passing, a death in slavery that is an escape from worldly suffering, for sure, but it is also a death that sees in hope (if hope is the right word) the possibility of life *after* slavery's generations. It bequeaths the possibility of living *otherwise*, remembering the auction block as Auction Block, but also living in a world not wholly dedicated to abjection. A lifeworld inside the death world, which might someday become a lifeworld lived on its own terms. And so, to this, Du Bois comments that out of the Spirituals "rose for me morning, noon, and night, bursts of wonderful melody, full of the voices of my brothers and sisters, full of the voices of the past" and also that the melodies and voices "came out of the South unknown to me, one by one, and yet at once I knew them as of me and of mine."[22]

There is a peculiar and important temporality in this. It is *ecstatic* in every way, in the sense that Du Bois describes a sense of seating Black subjectivity in the Americas in a stretch of time rather than as or between discrete instants. The past folds into the present, not just as a ghost, but as a kind of connection that is a nonauthoritarian, nontotalitarian sense of filiation, making connection and relation without ordering hierarchy and power. Connection and origin typically denote relations of hierarchy and power, but here Du Bois is describing relation without the specter of violence that white racial filiation has always brought to thinking. In this way, however much Du Bois was a thinker of the nation within a nation, he was never a nationalist. Nor was Baldwin. We here catch sight of a sense of productive comparative relation to Glissant's ethical imperatives against filiation, myth, and epic as conditions of exclusion and domination. This is important because it characterizes inheritance as fecundity and open possibility rather than subjection to memory and the unbearable, death-bringing weight of pain. There is plenty of pain. The Middle Passage and the Auction Block are critical concepts, but they are also names for the unimaginable. Baldwin's nuance, which is also that of Glissant and Du Bois, is to think the unimaginable as a price paid to be and know *as* Black people in the Americas. To be and know in relation to the unimaginable, but never merely melancholic.

Similarly, Du Bois's introduction of the Spirituals into *Souls of Black Folk* embeds temporality in sound, which among other things embeds inheritance in the everyday and in cultural production. Time does not work as an abstract container, however flexible that container might be, but is instead entwined with the body, conscience, consciousness, and therefore subjectivity and identity in their most concrete sites of production and reproduction. Du Bois links the Spirituals to the dramatics of African American existence—"sorrow, despair, and hope"[23]—but the temporal dimension of this deepens both his appreciation of the meaning of those dramatics and how they link the present and future to an origin story. The past is at stake here, but a very particular resonance of that which has passed. It is not *only* the voice of the enslaved that persists across time in sound, but the origins of that birth, the origins of the sound's origin. An *oblique* or *elliptical* indicator, a sign that points not to the memorial and what can be remembered but to the immemorial and the absent that nevertheless *gives* life to the reproduction of death worlds, the reproducible abyss of loss, and the ever-renewed struggle to make and maintain worlds in our now centuries-long necropolitical event.

Part of what Du Bois helps us see, I think, is the resonance of the motherless child in the Black Americas as not abjection but as the melancholia built into the very being of place. Baldwin repeats this gesture in linking sound and voice to the Auction Block. We are historical creatures, after all, and the memorial register of historical experience and its capacity to *create* us, to set us in Being and Becoming (that relation remains always complicated, if not impossible to reckon), has to be understood on its own terms. Not on universal terms. Always on the terms of the memorial register. It requires origin stories attuned to memory and history, which, in the case of the Black Americas, means coming to terms with the complexity of orphan narratives generated out of abject spaces become worlds of vernacular expressive life, its sounds, and how community is *made* of subjects and *makes* subjects in acts of social-cultural reproduction. Historical experience makes *communal* or even *national* identity through kinds of origin stories. This is the historical function of epic and of myth but also of the antiepic told in the aftermath of violence. An after*life.* We can see here an interesting twist on Walter Benjamin's reading in "Theses on Philosophy of History" of Paul Klee's painting *Angelus Novus*. Blown into the future by the pain of the past, by the melancholic energy of the ever-increasing pile of corpses, the angel looks at the catastrophe of history but also at the movement of progress, the time of what is to come *after*. This is futurity after catastrophe. For Benjamin, writing in 1940s Germany, this is wholly melancholic. The Black Atlantic iteration of this motif, however, is not merely a melancholic story. It is also or even first a story of the persistence and inventiveness of Black life itself. The capacity to face and be faced by the past in word and sound, to hear melancholia but also the pleasure and world making of language and its play. To be is to remember and be in sound. To not be is to forget.

If we can recast Benjamin with Toni Morrison, then, as a last word: sixty million angels of history or none at all.

Chapter 2

The Negative Dialectics of Race

If Baldwin's Black Atlantic origin story begins with the auction block, after the Middle Passage yet haunted by its ghosts, then we have already told a significant part of his intellectual story. He is a descendant of motherless children. But the Black Americas have that other narrative about the mother, about the mother-land, about the motherland. Aimé Césaire and the iteration of Négritude he represents turned this narrative into a metaphysics of race and identity. With Africa, there is the memorial mother, abundant rather than abyssal. Baldwin bears an ambivalent relation to this story of origins before the origin story. I am thinking of this remark from a review essay, "*A Lonely Rage*, by Bobby Seale," in which Baldwin writes about the wild contradictions at the heart of Africa's presence in the American imagination, in his imagination, and how that presence buoyed a desire for another world while also threatening this world with a regretful, sad death. Baldwin writes, "The time of my youth was far less hopeful. I speak of this savage irony because the political and spiritual currents of my very early youth involved a return to Africa, or a rejection of it; either choice would lead to suicide, or madness, for, in fact, neither choice was possible."[1] This passage bears within it so much of Baldwin's intellectual infrastructure: ambivalence, ambiguity, commitment to complexity, refusal of binaries of remembering and forgetting, refusal of nostalgia, refusal to dispense with nostalgia's gifts. The keystone of this ambivalence and ambiguity and their myriad refusals is the fact of the mixed racial space of the United States. That mixed space means everything for Baldwin, from terror to promise.

Indeed, one of the more compelling aspects of Baldwin's fiction and nonfiction is his commitment to thinking through the complexity and contradiction of interracial space and place. This is one of the more peculiar moves by Baldwin, but also something that shows real fidelity to the specificity of his nation of birth, a kind of intellectual challenge as burden and birthright. We are, after all, an interracial nation marked by a certain inexorable whiteness while also always something otherwise. The otherwise is always possible, necessary, and most importantly *actual*. All of that is navigated in relation to whiteness even when the imperative is to think the outside of whiteness and its world.

Baldwin not only activates the complex workings of racial formation in the United States but entwines, in that account of formation and adjacent phenomena, the pain of origins with the pleasures of Black life.

We see this in his accounting for the relation between race and memory. The memory of the auction block is formative of the African Americanness of African American identity—what Baldwin simply calls "the Negro," which is, helpfully and productively, a simultaneous racial and ethnic term. Linking race to memory creates a deeply fraught sense of origin. As we have seen, Baldwin, and also mid-century and after Caribbean origin stories, must reckon with senses of the abyss. Founding wounds and loss are catastrophic. It *might* seem like this sense of origin, the origin story Baldwin tells of being American and Black at the same time, wraps "the Negro" in melancholy, loss, and at some ontological level a dependency on white people, white violence, and whiteness in all of its varying manifestations. In a certain sense, this is true. Inexorable whiteness in an interracial world places terrible demands on us. It exacts an unimaginable price. When Baldwin evokes blood bled into the land as the cornerstone of a claim to place in "Princes and Powers," writing that "nothing, in any case, could take away our title to the land which we, too, had purchased with our blood,"[2] we have to understand that he is evoking generations and generations of suffering. *That* is what grants title to the land, title to being in this place as not just a formal citizen but as an existential being whose home is made here and only here.

This connection to place and commitment to the complexities of such a connection is the thread across each of the following chapters, but for the purposes of the present chapter we can sharpen focus on the relation between racial antagonism, racial fantasy, and racial formation. I am interested in a dialectic of sorts in Baldwin's work, one that counts down from (3) the fantasy of Africa and African identity to (2) the strange and estranging beleaguerment by whites to (1) the reconciliation of fantasy and estrangement in the formation of Richard Wright's conception of Black identity. This is an important movement for a number of reasons. In terms of a fantasy life that motivates so many questions of identity—the imaginary dynamics of becoming subject is always a part of who and what we are—the place of Africa in the African American imagination has deep and abiding roots. What is Africa to African Americans? We can think of how Countee Cullen's question "What is Africa to me?" organized so much thinking and making in the Harlem Renaissance and after. How does Baldwin intervene in that question and also, in his intervention, produce a nonexilic, nondiasporic vision of blackness? Alongside and always in tension with the question of Africa and blackness, there is the troubled role of the imagination. How is that imagination of Africa-to-me a projection or desire and in what measure is it a reckoning with legacy, heritage, and inheritance? This is the mid-century question for and from the Black Atlantic par excellence. But if Baldwin conceives of African American identity in terms of the interracial space of the

United States, then the question of whiteness and white beleaguerment has to be raised, addressed, and in some manner resolved. What does a resolution look like for Baldwin? It means entering the space of refusal, but also of resistance. Out of refusal and resistance both, another kind of relation to the white gaze and its identity-making aspirations becomes possible. What comes of this encounter with the gaze outside the specter of Africa? And what does it mean to move from Africa to the white gaze and back to the question of *what is the African American*? This is the moment of fraught resolution: Wright's conception of the Negro, an identity at once fully produced by the white gaze and fully standing in possession of its resistance and rage. Wright plays such a special role in Baldwin's thinking here.[3] At once the African and the African American, Wright's conception of blackness is for Baldwin the sublation of the negative dialectical movement between Black fantasy and white violence. This is a sublation that does not surpass but is instead dragged without cessation into the morass of making a new beginning.

Out of that fraught and terrifying beginning, Baldwin catches sight of another kind of blackness. But it is only out of and in relation to a fraught and terrifying beginning that Baldwin is able to gain this clarity. And so we begin with him before his beginning.

What is Africa to James Baldwin?

3: Baldwin's Three Africans

Among the many paths into Baldwin's work, very few scholarly works have examined his engagement with the post–World War II francophone tradition. I have in mind here how Baldwin emerges as a serious writer at the very same moment that the francophone tradition, having set out from origins in the early Négritude and surrealist movements in Martinique, emerges as a revolutionary intervention in theorizing the meaning of blackness, liberation, and revolutionary culture. All of which, of course, proceeded from a sense of solidarity—horizontal and vertical, in Aimé Césaire's formulation, between Black people across the cultural geography of the diaspora. The francophone-inspired proposal for such solidarity was metaphysical and unrestrained, taking the ultimate chance on blackness by putting identity in old roots, the singular ancient root: the geographic and spiritual wellspring of Africa. This root tells a now familiar story. Between genealogy and what is spiritually *real*, *effective*, and *affective*, Africa functions as the animating force for so many postwar diasporic thinkers: a source of pride and unity and as the final appeal of diasporic thinking's alpha and omega—what makes us a people?

In the francophone tradition, forged by demoralized and revolutionary students in Parisian cafés, the postwar moment was nothing if not a moment of excess and exuberance. Aimé Césaire's blend of René Ménil's Afrosurrealism with a cultural and civilizational commitment to Africa as a metaphysical force set the itinerary for a quarter century of work dedicated to the imagination of an unbroken and unbreakable blackness. The promise of Négritude was that such unbrokenness, reborn in the imagination and borne by the poetic word, could become culturally actual, effective, affective, real, and, in the crucial word of the movement, *vital*. However, this vision of Africa is hardly set out from a place of desperation or despair. Rather, and this is part of the force of Césaire's work as an essayist and poet, this vision of Africa describes an intensity of life and creative explosion that seeks to account for how and why life and creativity is still possible amidst the ruins and ruination of colonial violence. Africa, in this moment, is not strictly speaking a savior or saving force precisely because the poetic word and its life vitality do not need saving. Precarity under colonialism is not equivalent to being lost. There is no need for words of salvation. Something, perhaps *everything*, survives. Like the *morne* of the Martinican landscape, the survival of Africanness sat quiet and suppressed. Or, after independence, perhaps *repressed*. For Césaire and a particular constellation of Black Atlantic thinkers, poetry makes the explosive madness of the word happen. In the madness of the word, white colonial space is revealed to have never fully occupied the Black body. The life of that body has always been African through and through. Négritude is not famous for its modesty.

As we track this discovery of the intractable, suppressed, then released *élan vital* of blackness and Africa in the mid-century francophone world that witnesses the grandeur of its liberatory claims, we find no better contrast to it than the early fiction and nonfiction of Baldwin. I am thinking here of "Princes and Powers," the key work for what follows below. In that essay, Baldwin carefully examines the existential, metaphysical, and affective attachments of the mid-century moment, in particular its fixation on Africa and how that fixation, for him, says too much about the meaning of blackness. And yet we can find compelling thinking on Africa and the African across Baldwin's work, albeit written under erasure, irrupting in moments of memorial flourish and also as a foil for his larger aims.[4] What can be said about that presence? What is Africa to Baldwin? Who is the African to him, and how does that meaning speak to how Black identity and the meaning of history function in Baldwin's imagination of African American life?

I want to draw out three impressions of Africa and Africans in Baldwin's work here. These impressions tell us a bit of the story of Baldwin's relation to Black Atlantic theory in the post–World War II era. This era was saturated with figurative Africans across the Négritude movement, in anticolonial struggle and independence victories in the Global South and as part of the pan-African shift in the Black Power movement in the United States. Baldwin's place in all of this is very much like his impressions of Africa and Africans: ambivalent and always a bit, if not entirely, viewed from the outside. *Exilic*, in a word. And yet there is the constant intimacy with, even necessity of, his three Africans, both as a site of imagining the self beyond antiblack racism and as a note of contrast that brings the Americanness of African American identity into better focus. Baldwin will never have a moment of ancient rivers growing his soul deep. Baldwin's Africans instruct otherwise.

This "instruction otherwise" is in part derived from Baldwin's treatment of memory and history and how Africa figures with such ambivalence in his theorizing of blackness and identity.[5] I have in mind here a bit from "The Price of the Ticket" where he writes, "Later, in the midnight hour, the missing identity aches. One can neither assess nor overcome the storm of the middle passage. One is mysteriously shipwrecked forever, in the Great New World."[6] This is a stunning remark. Baldwin has never been a writer of the Middle Passage, preferring instead the intersection of past folkways with the fraught present and an often messianic sense of the future. Now, to be sure, Baldwin will evoke the echo of the auction block in essays dedicated to the Spirituals, Black English, and related issues, and yet the Middle Passage itself is rarely taken up with any real seriousness. But here, in "The Price of the Ticket," Baldwin suggests something important about his thinking—namely, that the Middle Passage changes everything, suggesting that the register of all things concerning blackness and identity emerge from a shipwreck. His three Africans, too, come from that shipwreck. A wreckage within which "we must first crack the American image and find out and deal with what it hides."[7]

First, then, the question of the virtual African.

What is Africa to the Americas? And how does the spectacle of Haile Selassie figure in Baldwin's work on race, memory, and identity?

For Baldwin, this is a relation largely constituted in the imaginary. By "imaginary," I here mean both Jacques Lacan's and Édouard Glissant's deployment of the term.[8] From Lacan and Glissant, we see the power of the imagination in the formation of identity in relation to the spectacular/specular image that allows one to see one's self through another (Lacan), as well as the transformative capacity to imagine the poetic word and the world otherwise (Glissant). The psychoanalytic context is important here, especially if we recall the treatment of imagination and identity Frantz Fanon gives in *Black Skin, White Masks*. Lacan's imaginary becomes in Fanon's hands a racialized story about sociogeny: how the self is made into a self through identification with the image, how the other of the self makes the self into what it is, and how the self gathers, through the image the capacity to say *this is me, I am this*. This is perhaps another language for what Du Bois called double consciousness. Inside sociogeny lies the deepest violence of colonial domination, but also the possibility of liberation through the image. Glissant's imaginary tells a slightly different story. Rather than the specular image of identification, which is made all the more important for theorizing blackness (and Africa) in Fanon's sociological rewrite of Lacan, Glissant conceives the imaginary first as alienation (the colonial occupation of language and possibility), then as a decolonized imagination reinvested in the radical openness of the future and the chaos of creole language and cultural production. For Glissant, this is the power of the poet to create a vision of another world. This twofold sense of the imaginary and its relation to Africa defines so much of the Black diasporic moment in the postwar period. Africa in this moment and period is a myth-making and epic-inspiring force, functioning as a specular counterimage that liberates Black subjectivity from centuries of alienation. Or at least begins that process as *a*, if not *the*, centerpiece of anticolonial struggle.

In this horizon, we find Baldwin's first African: Haile Selassie or "the first black emperor I ever saw."[9] A first image, the virtual emperor, and thus the counterimage of Black specularity, settles the importance of Selassie inside the young Baldwin's Harlem imaginary. The appearance of the emperor on Baldwin's childhood television screen interrupts the sociogeny of African American life as death and abjection. It does not cure, but it does interrupt. On the screen, something about a narrative of Black possibility that inevitably turns into Black actuality and fate is put into question. The image, functioning as the specular in Lacan's sense, opens Baldwin to another imaginary and how its future becomes possible, as it is made virtually visible, for the first time. Let us pause for a moment here and consider how Selassie is able to garner such interruptive force in the first place. How does blackness first emerge in Baldwin's work of memory and the image?

I am thinking here of two screens, two visual media.

First, a word on the screen we know best: Baldwin's rescreening of Harlem in his early fiction and nonfiction. This screen—often reported as if literal observations from behind a window, some floors up from the abjection, yet still immersed in the crashing sensory waves of despair—is simultaneously a screen that re-presents and re-produces the African American lifeworld. Baldwin's early work re-presents the African American lifeworld as a kind of memory work, traversing the personal and collective memory of suffering in the screens of his fiction and nonfiction, thereby reproducing the affects of that world. Baldwin's memory work identifies the abjection of Black life. Harlem is no place for hope outside of the messianic force of love, something that is fully articulated in *The Fire Next Time*. This visual medium, the writer's gaze from the child's window or walk through the neighborhood—no *flâneur* to be sure, only a witness to the repetition of historical trauma—is like any re-presentation: a re-production. That is, the screen of Harlem streets and their abject life hosts both testimony *to* and sites and sights *of* remaking the same abjection across generations. We could say that Baldwin's version of an Afropessimism, such as it is, takes root right here, in and on this screening of Harlem. The reproduction of abjection is what provokes his sadness and rage, sighting and citing here the origin of Baldwin's well-known remark in "Many Thousands Gone" that "no American Negro exists who does not have his private Bigger Thomas living in the skull."[10]

And there is a second screen.

This second screen repeats a familiar intervention of a sense of hope or shift in imagination that comes from abroad, from an elsewhere. This is not yet exile. That will come later and with very real disappointments. This first moment of hope, this second screen, hosts an optimism about another possible future for Black identity that comes from a familiar source in diasporic thinking: Africa. On the second screen, Selassie's televisual appearance recalls for Baldwin the child's racial imaginary. This location is utterly crucial, for Baldwin always places Black children in a peculiar, decisive space between innocence and initiation into abjection. Selassie and Africa intervene in this between space. In "East River, Downtown," a retitled essay originally published in *The New York Times* as "A Negro Assays the Negro Mood," Baldwin writes Black hope back into the landscape of despair:

> My first hero was Joe Louis. I was ashamed of Father Divine. Haile Selassie was the first black emperor I ever saw—in a newsreel; he was pleading vainly with the West to prevent the rape of his country. And the extraordinary complex of tensions thus set up in the breast, between hatred of whites and contempt for blacks, is very hard to describe. Some of the most energetic people of my generation were destroyed by this interior warfare.[11]

Interestingly, seventeen years later, in a short piece on Bobby Seale's memoir *A Lonely Rage*, Baldwin remarks again on the "visible heroes" of his youth and mentions Father Divine and Joe Louis again, but drops Selassie—the virtual African, the newsreel of Selassie registering objection, outrage, and a righteous plea. In 1961, this stands alongside the visible hero Joe Louis as an intervention from elsewhere, a reminder or suggestion of another vision of self and world.

Selassie triggers another imaginary. In triggering another imaginary, the emperor and perhaps Ethiopia itself as an *idea* and *fantasy*, Selassie *might* function as a paternal figure for another phase, moment, and future of blackness. Selassie repairs and replaces the kind of affects and ontology we find in the eschewal of paternity in Derek Walcott's "The Muse of History." Selassie *might* play the role of father, insofar as he *might* restore the virility and reproductive power—an imagined figure never fully damaged by colonialism and subjugation—to diasporic identity. Perhaps Selassie revives and revitalizes the bodies stricken with torpor in Césaire's "Notebook of a Return to the Native Land." And yet the Rastafarian movement, the New World inheritors of this paternity, never quite make it into Baldwin's nonfiction and therefore never carry this particular imaginary of Africa into Baldwin's depiction of the African American lifeworld. This is partly because the movement does not transform racial life in the United States, but also because of the particularities of the moment: Ethiopia is a signal of *crisis* and reactivity, not emancipation. The visible hero is heroic because of how he shifts of dynamics *inside* the white-Black racial struggle of the United States, while also standing outside the locality of conflict, so Baldwin also evokes Selassie in order to mark a generational shift and change. In "They Can't Turn Back," Baldwin writes of groups of Black students that they "were born at the very moment at which Europe's domination of Africa was ending. I remember, for example, the invasion of Ethiopia and Haile Selassie's vain appeal to the League of Nations, but they remember the Bandung Conference and the establishment of the Republic of Ghana."[12]

Bandung and Ghana, as we shall see, function very differently in Baldwin's imagination of Africa. But Selassie here plays a double role, altering the imagination of blackness in relation to empire—the appeal to the League of Nations is no small piece—while also embodying the "interior warfare" that destroyed so much of Baldwin's neighborhood, community, and colleagues. Selassie is intimate enough to be specular but different enough to promise a spectacular something else. A paradoxical situatedness in space and time.

This shift from Harlem to Ethiopia, we could say, enacts a shift from materiality to imagination, and in so doing it enacts a shift in the structure of memory. Harlem's memory is memory in the present; Baldwin's gaze writes the history of that present, which then becomes a terror that comes from a paradoxical memory of the future. We all know what will happen because we know what has happened. The fate of Harlem will be the fate of Black children. In "The Harlem Ghetto," Baldwin links this memory to the significance of the Hebrew Bible in African American religious culture. "This same identification," Baldwin writes in the 1948 essay, "which Negroes, since slavery, have accepted with their mother's milk, serves, in contemporary actuality, to implement an involved and specific bitterness."[13] From milk to the screen, then, two figures or images of the reproduction of abjection. The memory of Selassie's appearance on the newsreel screen, however, is that moment of memory that comes from the future. A memory to come, yes, but also a memory that has already been. Selassie is already the past when he appears in Baldwin's essay, a screen that preserves the past in and for Baldwin's memory. And yet this visual medium, the counternarrative to what he hears from Father Divine and from the screening of the Harlem landscape, rescreens the future, promising a memory that has not yet arrived. Even if Selassie does not quite have an invincible imaginary of the Brown Bomber (prior to the catastrophic loss to Rocky Marciano, that is), the virtual African's specularity shifts the field of imagination. The screen of Harlem does not end the imagination of Black life. But it frames that imagination with abject memory.

Second, then, the question of the para-African.

Baldwin's report from the 1956 Congress of Black Writers and Artists in Paris, "Princes and Powers," offers his most sustained reflections on Africa, Africans, and the question of identity. Difference and geography are written across that question. "But it was clear that our relation to the mysterious continent of Africa," he writes, "would not be clarified until we had found some means of saying, to ourselves and to the world, more about the mysterious American continent than had ever been said before."[14] Africa as mystery. America as mystery. It begins there and locates the question of African between those geographies. Indeed, what is so compelling about "Princes and Powers" is the appearance of Richard Wright as the central figure of the African. A para-African in Léopold Senghor's metanarrative of diasporic fiction at the 1956 Congress, the case of Wright's writerly identity opens a space in which Baldwin can articulate, then disarticulate, Africa and the Black American imaginary.

The 1956 Congress was a remarkable event for many reasons. A companion to the Bandung Conference held one year prior, the Paris Congress marked a twofold shift in thinking about the Global South. Bandung was about anticolonial struggle, marking and re-marking the colonies and newly independent countries as unified by the colonial experience. The rage and outrage in the heart of that unity, Bandung seemed to say, was plenty full of revolutionary potential. But the shift to Paris and Césaire's and Senghor's lead role transforms the discussion from anticolonial political struggle to the question of blackness and its diasporic cultural politics. Coloniality gets racialized in very specific ways: It is a Congress of *Black* writers and artists. This is exactly Baldwin's game. From the very beginning, Baldwin's fiction and nonfiction pursue the cultural politics of survival, resistance, and all that might be said to exceed what white people have said about and done to Black people. The function of Africa at the Congress, however, raises no small conundrum. Can Baldwin pursue such cultural politics without Africa? Or can a figurative African in "Princes and Powers" reconcile the Africa imperative with Baldwin's commitment to the screens of race in his United States?

"Princes and Powers" places Alioune Diop, Césaire, and Senghor at the center of the conversation. This was no speculation or invention by Baldwin. In that moment, Diop was the editor of *Presence Africaine*, the journal in which the Congress's proceedings were published, and of course Césaire and Senghor were intellectual innovators of diaspora theory in both the continental and archipelagic iterations of Négritude, which was then at its peak. For all three, Africa is the force that unifies the diaspora. For all three, the cultural difference found in nations and territories, the diaspora's identity, lies in the civilizational *force* and *vitality* of Africa. We ought to hear this in a metaphysical and cultural register. The ultimate reality, and therefore existential authenticity, of Black life is rooted in Africanness, which means, in turn, that diasporic cultural production ought to be (or even just is) measured by its proximity to that force and vitality. Césaire's contribution to the Congress, "Culture and Colonization," lays out this crucial distinction between culture and civilization and, from that, carves out space for difference in the diaspora that does not threaten a deep and rooted sense of identity. It is then up to Senghor to draw out one of the most dramatic consequences of this claim: Richard Wright is to be counted among the great African novelists.

In the programmatic moment of this claim, Senghor writes in "The Spirit of Civilization" that "the spirit of African Negro civilisation consciously or not, animates the best Negro artists and writers of to-day, whether they come from Africa or America. So far as they are conscious of African Negro culture and are inspired by it they are elevated in the international scale; so far as they turn their backs on Africa the mother they degenerate and become feeble."[15] Senghor's intertwining of "African" and "Negro" means everything here, mixing the geography of identity with the language of race and therefore noting or promising the transmission of racial meaning across geographic location and dislocation. Without that transmission of meaning, writing becomes and remains degenerate and feeble. These are bold words, But, again, Négritude was never know for modesty in claims.

Senghor makes this bold claim and Baldwin finds it odd, even audacious. The audacity provokes a strange turn in tone and rhetoric. We see Baldwin speak very differently about Wright, dropping his typical polemics and critique in order to simply register his confusion. Who could be more American than Richard Wright? Mississippi, Chicago, New York City, then exile. It is the standard script of the mid-century African American writer, Wright's original script through and through. And yet here is Senghor, claiming Wright for Africa. Baldwin summarizes this claim: "[Senghor] went on, somewhat later, to make the point that the heritage of the American Negro was an African heritage. He used, as proof of this, a poem of Richard Wright's, which was, he said, involved with African tensions and symbols, even though Wright himself had not been aware of this. He suggested that the study of African sources might prove extremely illuminating for American Negroes."[16] *Even though Wright himself had not been aware of this.* We do not need to be wedded to old-fashioned notions of authorial intention to find this to be a bold and excessive claim by Senghor. Part of Baldwin's objection to Senghor here is simple and straightforward. Wright has no knowledge of such tensions and symbols, and Senghor himself displays no appreciation of the particularities of American life, the history of race in the United States, and all the formative experience in that life and history. In other words, Senghor cannot fathom the racial imaginary of a Black American writer—the Negro who is not the African Negro. Therein lies the second part of Baldwin's objection. "In so handsomely presenting Wright with his African heritage," Baldwin writes, "Senghor rather seemed to be taking away his identity."[17] The assignment of African identity to Wright, rendering him a para-African, is not just an aesthetic judgment with metaphysical implications but also a total claim about Richard Wright the person: who he was, who he is, and how he should be understood. It is just too much for Baldwin.

This strange moment of assignation and withdrawal, of Senghor's massive reach and Baldwin's claiming his fellow countryman back, hearkens back to an earlier passage in "Princes and Powers" that describes the racial ambivalence of the Congress. As the Congress gets underway, Wright calls Baldwin over to the American delegation. All in the delegation are African American, and yet Baldwin is struck by how peculiar it is to have been gathered together "in this courtyard by our relation to the African continent." John Davis, who served as the delegation leader, was, according to Baldwin, asked repeatedly if he was "a Negro." The answer is of course *yes*, but that answer is itself a question. What makes him "a Negro" when his skin color suggests, to the Africans gathered in Paris for the Congress, that he is white? "He is a Negro," Baldwin writes of Davis in "Princes and Powers," "a Negro by choice and by depth of involvement—by experience, in fact."[18] Choice, involvement, depth, experience—all of these mark the identity of the delegation, and so too of Wright, with the production of a complex process of racial formation through law, practice, and, yes, *lived experience*. The "para" of the para-African cannot survive this moment of insight. What puzzles the Africans makes perfect sense to the Americans. Racial identity, and so then all of the terms of Wright's fiction, is an experience undergone *outside* the shadow of Africa and *inside* the fraught and frightening shadow of American history. Wright is no African, to be sure, but Senghor's speculative claim is important. In that claim's exuberance, Senghor underscores and illuminates the very thing it wants to exceed: that there is no place like home for Wright, even as he is no African. He is at most a *screen* on which the supplement, the "para" of the para-African, can be projected. That is plenty meaningful for Baldwin's racial imaginary: Blackness incorporates Africa at the very moment Africanness is rendered a projection, a screen memory of sorts, blocking, per Sigmund Freud's formulation, the destructive force of trauma while also maintaining the fecundity of denial in the construction of another kind of self.

Yet, like the virtual African, the para-African is not yet Africa or African.

Third, then, the question of the actual African.

The actual African presents us with an immediate puzzle: Baldwin's lack of direct, sustained engagement with Africa in his nonfiction. Baldwin himself is clear on this, as he notes in a talk from 1961, delivered at a forum on liberation struggle in Africa: "I'm not an African; I've never been to Africa," he writes. "I'm talking only from my experience in this country and my experience of the West."[19] How does Africa beyond the screen and the para-representation appear in his thinking?

Baldwin counters the memory of Harlem with the screen memory of Haile Selassie, the virtual African whose literal screen life provokes critical and crucial resistance to shame, to white hegemony, and to certain forms of cultish religiosity. Resistance plays the double role of a fantasy of the unconquered and the reality of resistance in the cultural formations of everyday life. Abjection is never the final story in Baldwin's work, of course, and yet the terror of living under antiblack racism is always a centerpiece—even in moments of hope, messianic love, or everyday traditions of resistance and refusal. In that sense, we can say that Baldwin's work is never melancholic, depressed, or immobilized without cure or curative compulsion. It is, rather, the work of witnessing that is full of outrage, but never just rage. Bigger Thomas might be inside of his and every Black person's skull. There is also outrage at the heart of race. Outrage marks a sort of moral rectitude or righteousness of *not being the violence*. We can think here of when Baldwin in *The Fire Next Time* rejects any notion of wanting to be white or even just like white people: "Do I really *want* to be integrated into a burning house?"[20]

Whatever Senghor's fantasies of diasporic identity, Wright, the author of every Black person's conscience, is intractably that American who, whatever his own refusal of the burning house of integration, complicates any supplement of blackness with Africanness. The para-African Wright remains for Baldwin a sign of Négritude's excesses, akin, in some ways, to Selassie leaping out of the screen in Harlem and transforming the landscape with a wave of a metaphysical wand: a vision of redemption, yes, but one too discontinuous with *having already been* shipwrecked in the Great New World.

Baldwin's adult and writerly life had another such figure at its center: Kwame Nkrumah. Selassie was the screen of Baldwin's youth, a newsreel moment accompanying Joe Louis in the formation of the Black hero and Black alternative to the materiality of Harlem life. What kind of center could Nkrumah have occupied? Why note this name, figure, and revolutionary place when Baldwin's nonfiction offers no engagement with the Ghanian leader? Indeed, Nkrumah's name does not appear in either *The Price of the Ticket* or *The Cross of Redemption*. This is peculiar and for that reason exceptionally instructive.

Nkrumah's place in the mid-century Black Atlantic imagination is rightly mythic. If the diaspora was a question following the 1956 Paris Congress, wondering how culture and politics could possibly make sense of over four and a half centuries of scattering seeds, then Nkrumah's victorious moment in Ghana's independent struggle is the answer—however provisional, however wrought and fraught with projections of anxiety and desire that answer might be. We can recall here James Campbell's account in *Middle Passages* of postindependence Ghana and the meaning of Nkrumah for the African American imaginary.[21] Older American radicals were drawn to the moment, including most prominently W. E. B. Du Bois and Paul Robeson, but also younger cultural and political figures from Baldwin's own generation, including Maya Angelou, Malcolm X, and of course Wright, who wrote extensively about Ghana in *Black Power*.[22] Even his beloved friend Lorraine Hansberry evokes historical Ghana in *Raisin in the Sun* with dialogue about the Ashanti empire. And yet we get no sustained words from Baldwin about Nkrumah or Ghanaian independence and the impact that figure and moment have on the Black imaginary.

Perhaps, then, if we read under erasure, if we read for absences and how they structure explicit and intentional discourse(s), we could say that Nkrumah is Baldwin's most important African. The virtual African, Selassie, supplements Joe Louis in order to instill or at least propose a screen for unconquered and unconquerable blackness. Wright is supplemented by Africa, described as a great African novelist, and while Baldwin concedes something to the *possibility* of the racial unconscious, his foil from Mississippi remains just that: his foil from Mississippi. The para-African is linked to the racial imaginary by Senghor in a grand gesture of Négritude poetics but is then taken back by Baldwin in "Princes and Powers" to the travails of painful American history. The actual African, Nkrumah, appears neither on a screen nor as a motif for a poetics of diasporic consciousness. Instead, the actual African appears in Baldwin's social circle, at the edges of his political sensibilities, and on every sense of the cultural screen of thinking and rethinking blackness. Yet, we have no words on Nkrumah, which is remarkable if we consider this: Nkrumah's time as the first prime minister of Ghana, 1957–60, then as president from 1960 to 1966, coincides with arguably the most productive, ambitious, and provocative period of Baldwin's nonfiction writing.

Nkrumah tells a bigger story in his *absence* in Baldwin's nonfiction. Ghana's independence transformed a generation's racial imaginary, moving from whatever kind of screen a figure like Selassie creates to a living imagination of thinking identity otherwise. For this imaginary, which is less specular and more spectacular, Nkrumah transforms dislocation into the possibility of relocation, which inverts history and accelerates its transforming meaning. That is at least the *promise* of Ghana in 1957. Whatever the inevitable discontent with Nkrumah later—heroes always get complicated—the independence moment is a real moment, and one cannot help but wonder why Baldwin does not discuss Ghana and the diasporic imagination at any length, or even offer a few analytical words. Is it merely a difference of generational imaginaries? It is true that in his second evocation of Selassie in "They Can't Turn Back," Baldwin marks both the Bandung Conference and Ghanaian independence as generation gaps; Ethiopia's appeal to the League of Nations is the first screen for Baldwin, whereas the college kids he describes in that 1960 essay come of age during Nkrumah's leadership. "But they," Baldwin notes, "remember the Bandung Conference and the establishment of the Republic of Ghana."[23] So, is it really just a matter of generation gaps or ideological preferences?

We have to read Baldwin's note of "they remember" with a bit of skepticism. Or at least read the absence of Nkrumah as a real articulation of identity and cultural politics, not just a generational split. After all, Angelou and Malcolm X are exactly Baldwin's generation, caught, for a short bit at least, in the new spectacular imaginary. I would suggest here that Nkrumah the actual African is Baldwin's most profound challenge, having mobilized so many fellow African American intellectuals around the diasporic racial imaginary renewed by independence. Nkrumah's and Ghana's absence says everything about Baldwin's ontology of the African American subject. Dis-location, that shipwreck in the Great New World, *is the origin story*, even if it is only the first chapter of a story that becomes the critical work of the Auction Block.

The other origin story, the origin of Black culture in the United States, is Baldwin's primary and most complex preoccupation. In that preoccupation, he will repeatedly turn to what "Many Thousands Gone" calls "the relationship that Negroes bear to one another,"[24] a relationship of Black people who have a very specific shared geography. Not transatlantic geographies or diasporic connections. *Local.* And so, when Baldwin puzzles in "Alas, Poor Richard" that the Black American and African cannot know what to make of their encounter when set face-to-face, the meaning of the absent actual African, Nkrumah, comes into a strange and estranging focus. The puzzlement is a statement about the imagination: The screen means something. The actualization of the virtual, the promise of homecoming, is not just a mirage, but, for Baldwin, an epistemological gap that cuts to the very heart of thinking the being of blackness. Baldwin does not deny the historical *fact* of historical root in Africa or how that dis-location sets in motion alienated, even abject life in the Americas. Of course not. Instead, the actual African and his absence prompts a new insistence, perhaps Baldwin's most fundamental insistence, that dis-location and arrival do not demand the imagination of re-location. The obstinacy of the African American imagination, rather, has made primary, rooted, and *at home* location *after* dis-location. We can call that *after* by its proper name here: tradition. The African American tradition.

Nkrumah's absence is necessary for this notion of tradition. A supplement that makes the systematicity of "the Negro," the African American, *work* in Baldwin's conceptual system. The virtual African reminds Baldwin that resistance is possible or even already accomplished in the fact of being unvanquished. The para-African reminds Baldwin that theorizing diaspora puts American identity in a precarious place. The actual African, however, puts the question of land and language at the heart of resistance and diaspora, offering re-location as the curative agent against the painful memory of dis-location. In his absence from Baldwin's text, Nkrumah underscores the fecundity of pain *after the shipwreck*. Plymouth Rock may have landed on Black people, as Malcolm X famously quipped, but Baldwin is here to remind us that an entire people were forged under that rock. And so there is no compulsion to speak of the actual African. Plenty of tradition is already here, on this land, made out of dis-location. Tradition as the reterritorialization of Black identity. Baldwin's conceptual work after the actual African, then, becomes an epistemological project of reckoning with what is known about the self, about community, and about the specificity of "the Negro's" history and memory. "We were not transformed when we crossed the ocean," he writes. "Something else happened. Something more serious. We no longer had any way of finding out, of knowing who we were."[25]

Baldwin's wandering encounters with his three Africans tell us less a story about Africa than a story about Harlem, ancestry, and the recurrence of home even from points of alienation, rage, and exile. The perplexity in a piece like "Princes and Powers" about the reach of the idea of Africa and the African, peaking in Senghor's designation of Wright as a great African novelist, tells a certain kind of exile story—exile story as origin story. For Baldwin, this means existential exile and mass displacement, not merely geographic relocation and imagination; the latter is the story of Paris, Istanbul, and the mountains of Switzerland. Baldwin's three Africans instead put the African American in question, which prompts a reframing of territory and existential-cultural meaning, resettling it on the grounds of the Americas and in the United States in particular.

It is interesting to note here that in "Alas, Poor Richard," Baldwin's final good-bye to his great foil Richard Wright, the stories turn again and again to the question of Africa and Africans. Africa, Baldwin notes, failed Wright, just as did Europe and the United States. All failed Wright because he sought a curative moment on each continent and in particular in the faces of Africans. "Time brought Richard, as it has brought the American Negro, to an extraordinarily baffling and dangerous place," Baldwin writes. "An American Negro, however deep his sympathies, or however bright his rage, ceases to be simply a black man when he faces a black man from Africa."[26] In this sharp remark, he articulates, with sympathy for once, Wright's sense of alienation. Baldwin writes with some sympathy because he shares this same experience with his foil: exile and exilic fantasies crash so quickly. In that crash, Baldwin catches sight of the limits in thinking through Africa and Africans in relation to Black identity. This identity, disentangled from virtual, para, and actual Africans and the fantastical imaginary they engender, has to be thought from a deeper sense of exile. Glissant says just this in *Poetics of Relation* when he reflects on the Middle Passage as an origin story of irreversible exile and simply remarks: "We must begin with that."[27] For me, this is precisely what Baldwin means when he evokes the shipwreck in the "Great New World." Exiled space is made into home, not through a sense of greater belonging but through the obstinacy of work, survival, and cultural formation on the margins of an antiblack world. "The land of our forefathers' exile," Baldwin writes in "Princes and Powers," "had been made, by that travail, our home."[28]

In this travail, Baldwin's three Africans are rendered echoes and absences. An imaginary that slowly lets it all go and returns to a home that had already been made.

2: Baldwin's Two Whites

Africa is a site of fantasy. White people? White people is a site of reality.

What is the reality of white people? Baldwin's broad take on white people is neither particularly shocking nor particularly boundary pushing in the African American intellectual tradition. At the same time, white people play an essential role in his conception of racial formation and identity, a role that binds both white and Black people together in the very idea of the United

States. Baldwin's nonfiction and fiction both are full of interracial ambivalence. White people are perpetrators of the greatest crime: the transatlantic slave trade, the auction block, the architecture of segregation, police terror, the production and reproduction of the ghetto, and the cruelty of everyday life. White people are also an intimate part of what it means for African Americans to live and breathe in the United States and Baldwin, for all of his visceral criticism and deep spirals into nihilism, never quite takes the step of absolute rejection of the "inter" in interracial, for reasons both ethical and ontological. We can think here of how his criticism of the Nation of Islam in *The Fire Next Time* revolves around the possibility of a different kind of white person or how the first half of *Another Country* explores exactly these moments of not quite redemption of *a white person* (forever in the singular, never in the general), but something approximating it. What and who are Baldwin's whites? And what and who are Baldwin's white *people*?

Two particularly important whites occupy Baldwin's imagination of the racial nation: William Faulkner and Norman Mailer. The aloof white and the visceral white. Both are attached to the time of relation, to two importantly different times of relation that mark one and the same American specificity of the white gaze. That gaze is neither colonial nor merely anthropological. It is political and embodied. For Baldwin, the incarnate character of interracial proximity marks the particularity and unicity of the United States, and, in terms of the time of that relation, it anchors the time of the nation. "Any real change implies the breakup of the world as one has always known it," Baldwin writes, "the loss of all that gave one an identity, the end of safety."[29] White racial safety and Black racial safety are of course very different things altogether, and yet the fact of existence, of being-in-memory and being-in-history, means that inheritance—politically racial, violently antiblack—is how we make sense of the world. Inheritance secures places in place. The negative work of blackness in relation to whiteness, of whiteness in relation to blackness, generates Black and white as identity categories. This is the dialectical move Baldwin charts across his work. And of course these are not just categories but rather existential realities, investments, and senses of possibility. The dialectical formation of racial identity *requires* memory and history; the dialectic is not atomistic in resolving conflict as Black abjection and white supremacy but instead is the bearing of *what has been* on *what is* and *what is imaginable*. From racial necessity to possibility. This is complicated by the fact that the nation's history is written on our bodies and forms the stage of interracial encounter. The terms of those memories and histories—always plural, always filtered through both race and nation, Black/white, and Americanness—are vulnerable to our interventions, transformations, and revolutions if not also refusals. This last bit opens the system of white supremacy. But, first, we have to understand its profound work to shape who and what *we* are. The first person plural is important here, of course. At stake in the dialectic of racial formation is not just the abjection of blackness and Black life but also and just as much the sense of what it means to be white. *We* become in this dialectic.

The generality of Baldwin's argument gains specificity in his early essay "Faulkner and Desegregation." Written in 1956, just two years after *Brown v. Board of Education*, the essay is at first glance nothing other than a scorching critique of Faulkner's famous urge around desegregation in the United States: "Go slowly." The demand to shift pace in racial justice movements is both to be expected and, in 1956, widespread to the point of being almost common sense. Baldwin rejects this bit from Faulkner with a simple yet devastating, query: "And it is, I suppose, impertinent to ask just what Negroes are supposed to do while the South works out what in Faulkner's rhetoric becomes something very closely resembling a high and noble tragedy."[30] This is a searing assessment, bluntly put, and wholly without ambiguity. Faulkner's desire to render Black liberation and white concession as a kind of tragedy already tells a lot of the story, in particular the story of white innocence and vulnerability. Dialectical relations, especially the side of dialectic that discovers itself to be dependent upon negation for its own being, will always be structurally vulnerable to what negates. In a theoretical field, this is the meaning of Baldwin's oft-repeated claim that Black people understand white people better than white people understand themselves: The one who subjects is subjected to a relation of dependency that is both epistemological and ontological. But this gets us a few steps ahead of ourselves.

Baldwin's commentary on Faulkner drips with contempt and sarcasm. The sarcasm comes from the simple fact that on Baldwin's reckoning Faulkner has never taken the needs, desires, and demands of Black Southerners seriously. Or seriously enough. Thus, the contempt. Everything is at stake for African Americans in this moment in terms of both strategy and senses of self and community to come.[31] Desegregation pushes the logic of the Civil War to its post–Civil War conclusions: no more racial caste system, no more hoarding of institutions. In addition, if Reconstruction was about enforcing the inclusion of Black Southerners in civil society (and beyond), then desegregation rejoins that struggle through institutions of education and the franchise. These are the stakes: citizenship uncompromised. But this is also a question of memory. For the white Southerner, the purity of negative dialectical racial formation comes into focus. Desegregation requires, at the very least, a massive renegotiation of identity and meaning, ranging from the term "white" to relations of place, family, history, and memory. *Go slowly, for these are huge stakes*. For the Black Southerner, the contingency and remainder of racial formation comes into focus in the form of delays and deferrals, living in the deconstructive space composed of racial violence, segregation, and the promises of humanism, rights, democracy, and personhood under a certain legal and moral regime. Desegregation moves the promise of freedom, suspended in the "to" of the well-worn trope *from slavery to freedom*, into a moment of possible and near-actual fulfillment, which is its own kind of renegotiation;

life was made in the "to," in the transition, in the sublation of the experiences of enslavement into cultural forms of survival, creation, and thriving. Reinvention is promised in this reordering after the promise. A doubling of deconstructive space, for sure, but also an exit of the system in the sense of departing from its logic, possibly making a new logic, and certainly remaking an already remade world.

Both of these movements initiate a crisis and draw out the peculiar temporality of white Southerner racial formation, identity, and its reproduction. Baldwin writes of Faulkner that in his work and political commentary "so compelling is the image of ruin, gallantry, and death thus evoked that it demands a positive effort of the imagination to remember that slaveholding southerners were not the only people who perished in that war."[32] Faulkner's literary memory is of course by ontological design, not simply political and cultural conservatism. To be sure, Faulkner's work, if Baldwin is correct, effectively minimizes or even erases the humanity of Black Southerners, but the emphasis on ruins and death speaks to a deeper question about white identity. Ruins preserve memory, and, although produced through destruction and death, ruins function as simultaneously the denial of death and the conservation of life in their wake. This conserved life is critical for the maintenance of white identity after dialectical relations of negation shift and make identity precarious; Black liberation threatens the conservation of white life in the ruins. Thus Baldwin writes, "And the segregation which Faulkner sanctifies by references to Shiloh, Chickamauga, and Gettysburg does not extend back that far, is in fact scarcely as old as the century. The 'racial condition' which Faulkner will not have changed 'by mere force of law or economic threat' was imposed by precisely these means. . . . The North, in winning the war, left the South only one means of asserting its identity and that means was the Negro."[33] The potential loss of Black abjection and subjection is for Faulkner an entirely existential event. Faulkner is not wrong, and in fact Baldwin's account of racial formation articulates precisely this logic for him. If whites have always needed Black people to be at the bottom of the well, and if *measure* and *comparison* is the logic of racial formation—a thought that draws Baldwin into proximity with Frantz Fanon's account of identity in *Black Skin, White Masks*—then emancipation and liberation are akin to or perhaps exactly an abyssal crisis for whiteness. There is no white identity without abjection of blackness and Black people. The *sanctification* of Southern white history, which is practiced in the production of ruins and their link to gallantry, is a move *against* that crisis and an attempt to forestall the abyss. Sanctification of ruins functions as a kind of epic or mythic refounding, in this case a refounding of identity linked to place and ruin. The battlefield that made emancipation possible, like the South's battle flag that flew above those fields, fundamentally changes the temporality of racial formation for white people. Thus, sanctification becomes not so much a ritual of honoring sacrifice and debates over the moral worthiness of those sacrifices, but instead an intervention in the time of subjectivity and calcification of identity in frozen time(s).

So, the precarious *time* of Faulkner's whiteness is key and what is most deeply at stake in Baldwin's reading of him underneath the at times bitter and searing polemic. We can think here of Faulkner's famous line from *Requiem for a Nun* that "the past is never dead. It isn't even past."[34] In the context of *Requiem for a Nun*, it signifies Faulkner's concern that acts of the present might be absolved, or at least mitigated, by meanings from or in the past, but writ larger it is also a story about how we cannot extricate our moral and political feelings and judgments from relations—just, unjust, and ambivalent—in the past. This is a kind of ecstatic time, but also a time of ontological dependency that shows up when Faulkner confronts the process of desegregation. This is not far from Baldwin's own claims about history. Indeed, as he put it in a 1980 address at Wayne State University, under the title "Black English: A Dishonest Argument," "I want to suggest that history is not the past. It is the present. We carry our history with us. We *are* our history. If we pretend otherwise, to put it very brutally, we literally are criminals."[35] A quarter century after his critique of Faulkner's reckoning with desegregation, Baldwin repeats the famous sentiment from *Requiem for a Nun*, but with a twist and a different moral emphasis. The moral emphasis here is in the characterization of flight from history as *criminal*. To think or place ourselves outside history—certainly a common gesture of white American innocence after desegregation—is to transgress the very law of our being in the world.

But the outside of history, as Baldwin smartly notes, is not simply to be outside time itself. The meaning of the *now* as an atomistic, isolated temporal kernel separated from the ecstatic stretch of time is its own kind of neutralization of history—perhaps one of a most potent, dangerous sort. The strange twist in the dialectical formation of racial identity is that in neutralizing history the white Southerner *ought* to be *also* neutralizing the possibility of himself. But that only reiterates the importance of ruins. With ruins in place and functioning as reification and reproduction, history can be neutralized with identity intact and the time of identity's genuine social, political, and temporal transformation can be deferred without a closure date. At the end of "Faulkner and Desegregation," Baldwin writes, "But the time Faulkner asks for does not exist—and he is not the only southerner who knows it. There is never time in the future in which we will work out our salvation. The challenge is in the moment, the time is always now."[36] It is important to see how Baldwin, in this short passage, mixes senses of the *now*. Faulkner's sense of the now is an isolated moment that pauses, for racially specific reasons, a reckoning with the past and creation of an unprecedented future in the interest of sitting in an isolated now. That now preserves the present as if white Southernness were already a highly valued fossil, itself a ruin that freezes time in the present and postpones unprecedented futures. "The time he pleads for," Baldwin writes of Faulkner, "is the time in which the southerner will come to terms with himself."[37] *Waiting* for that time means disrupting how revolt, protest and its demands, animates existential and political temporality with the desire for justice and for reckoning with the painful past. Why wait for white people? While it is true that "there isn't any Negro problem, there is only a white problem," as Richard Wright famously put it in an interview,[38] time itself is not a white prerogative. This fact is already a refusal of racial logic. Baldwin's push against Faulkner means exactly this: a struggle over the meaning of political time itself, which, for white Southerners and African Americans, is always already existential time.[39] Justice time is the heart rhythm of both.

If Faulkner appears in Baldwin's writing as an impossible patience and struggle over the politics of racial time, then Mailer's presence in Baldwin's thinking is more visceral and therefore, in certain ways, more intimate. In part, this is the case because Mailer was part of Baldwin's writerly world in New York City, but also because the former was so obsessed with blackness and its consumption. Faulkner wanted to gain some moral distance from the past of interracial life while also seeing its immediate presence in every aspect of resistance and refusal. Faulkner's slowdown of time in thinking about the political meaning of segregation and desegregation reflects a certain kind of white conservatism—something in no small supply in that moment—and it also reflects a desire to pause time and resist a sense of break, rupture, and fissure that might mark a new beginning. The time of Mailer's "The White Negro," which is a centerpiece of Baldwin's commentary and critique in "The Black Boy Looks at the White Boy," is very different. Urgent, violent, and consumptive, Mailer's (in)famous essay "The White Negro" (1957) *wants* blackness, partly for a sense of objectionable exoticism (to put it lightly), but also for a sense of the intensity of the political and cultural moment, which was for Mailer defined by sexual libertinism (or the dream of it) and unrestrained expressive life, both of which he imagines to be endemic to African American life. For Mailer, desire and its manifestation is enough to constitute a break with the past. A strange kind of erotic recast of apocalyptic thinking.

Mailer's erotic apocalypse is the projection of two kinds of fantasy. First, it is a fantasy that both embraces and reproduces a sense of exoticism in the white gaze, looking at African American life as an idealized form of what white life is *not*. This is the part where Mailer eschews whiteness without taking into account the hegemony of his own gaze: the power to construct an exotic other. Second, this is a fantasy that links sexual desire (in the broadest sense) to time and, in alternative renderings of carnal want, the possibility of breaking with time's dictation of racial inheritance. The desire for blackness, for the Negro in the White Negro, is the desire to eat the other and draw a more authentic life from consumed, digested flesh. So, for Mailer, if white people are not bound in any significant way by their relation to antiblack history (an odd but also coherent white existentialist notion of freedom), then consumption of the racial other, the assimilation of it into the white body, and digestion of this strange kind of violent mixture *might* promise another kind of being, another kind of world, and so another kind of Being. Mailer the ontologist and existential revolutionary. Thus, after a series of descriptions of alienated white life, full of caricature and epochal rhetoric linked to war and nuclear arms, "The White Negro" names its redemption. The redemption is here formulated in terms of racial type, and it reveals, the hyperbole of Mailer's prose notwithstanding, the presence of fantasy and the fantastical in the white imagination. The abject other becomes the exotic and ecstatic other. Mailer writes:

> Knowing in the cells of his existence that life was war, nothing but war, the Negro (all exceptions admitted) could rarely afford the sophisticated inhibitions of civilization, and so he kept for his survival the art of the primitive, he lived in the enormous present, he subsisted for his Saturday night kicks, relinquishing the pleasures of the mind for the more obligatory pleasures of the body, and in his music he gave voice to the character and quality of his existence, to his rage and the infinite variations of joy, lust, languor, growl, cramp, pinch, scream and despair of his orgasm.[40]

Mailer goes on to claim (or evoke, a difference that might matter) that jazz bears all of this inside itself and serves as the crucial, vital interval for the white person and their emerging hipster identity desires. For Mailer, this is a moment of transformation that upends the racial order. In a certain sense, he is right, at least at the level of fantasy and the white gaze. We really do learn a lot about how the white gaze imagines itself transformed by itself—what deep narcissism, which is consistent with white hegemony and innocence—in "The While Negro."[41] Mailer's cultural-political sentiment reflects a peculiarity of the mid-century moment that persists into the contemporary: Black people produce our popular culture as a nation; white people consume it, and that consumption eats the abject-now-exotic Other and so carries with it anxieties about contamination of the purity of race as a cultural phenomenon. All we have to remember here is how even a white artist like Elvis Presley set off white fears of a Black contagion, purely from the swivel of a hip and grip of a microphone. Phallic and erotic, ontologically transformative—or so goes the fantasy.[42] Mailer simply revalues the values and casts the contagious abjection and exoticism as salvation.

In a strange turn, one that I think draws Baldwin's curiosity about Mailer and tempers his critique, Mailer takes this notion of the Hip and the hipster, with its identification with Black culture and life, as an *epistemic* site. It is an epistemic site because, for the white person, it is a site to (be)come and for the Black person it is a condition of being. "Since the Negro knows more about the ugliness and danger of life than the White," Mailer writes, "it is probable that if the Negro can win his equality, he will possess a potential superiority, a superiority so feared that the fear itself has become the underground drama of domestic politics."[43] Baldwin's own rhetoric about how white people do not understand themselves or their cultural-political milieu runs parallel to Mailer's sentiment here. If white people are ignorant of their own humanity, an ignorance lived as repression of desire and contraction of the body, then the *other* of whites, the juxtaposed abject, offers a nondialectical alternative mode of being and new possibilities for life. In the fantasy world of the white imagination, that is. Mailer's notion of the Hip and hipster takes root in this self-alienated white space and the exoticizing vision of Black alternative humanity in sound, movement, and sexual presence that appears as redemption, salvation, and reinvention of the self.

But that always remakes Black people in versions of the white gaze, eclipsing any sense of complex and vital humanity. What would it mean to reverse that gaze, to look at Mailer and his exoticizing gaze rather than looking *through* that gaze?

Baldwin's title "The Black Boy Looks at the White Boy" suddenly comes into sharp focus here. What drags down Faulkner's attempt (halfhearted as it might be) to understand the concerns of Black people and move them forward is his inability to understand that Black people look at themselves—introspectively, collectively—and also that Black people look at white people. In the case of Faulkner, we see this in his assumption of the place of white need(s); Baldwin is right that Faulkner's time, the time of a deferred future in white interest, is an existential fabrication. Black time, the time of justice demanded, surmounts white time and subordinates it to liberation praxis. If one organizes the time of collectivity around the white gaze, the result is invariably Faulkner's sentiment and plea. But the time of Black self-knowing and praxis confounds the white gaze. Necessarily. This notion of time and Black self-regard is also what makes Mailer's strange and estranging vision of the hipster, the white Negro, so fundamentally fucked up. It is not a matter of principle, either in the sense of an interdiction on learning from the other or in the sense of embracing the broadly (non–racially specific) ecstatic and sexual in response to a mechanistic, bureaucratic world. Both of those things are possible and, in many ways, probably still very urgent imperatives. What is so objectionable about Mailer's vision is that, per Baldwin's title, he does not understand that the Black boy looks *at* the white boy, and how in that gaze we might find distance, a mixture of contempt and ridicule at such bizarre attempts, and therefore a robust reckoning with the event of appropriation. I am thinking here of how in "The Black Boy Looks at the White Boy," using Jack Kerouac as a proxy for Mailer, Baldwin quotes a passage from Mailer that leers at Black bodies with sensual and objectifying desire, then adding, "I would hate to be in Kerouac's shoes if he should ever be mad enough to read this aloud from the stage of Harlem's Apollo Theater."[44] The Apollo stands in for the Black gaze directed at white nonsense about exotica, liberation, and orgasmic fixation on style and embodiment. For all of Baldwin's slow, plodding interest and allure for Mailer's schtick—his gaze at Mailer is complicated by all sorts of desires, political and cultural, as well as a fascination with the productiveness of the writer—his essay draws us back, time and again, to the quiet prison designed by hipster fantasies for the hipster himself. The twist, as it were, lies in the reversal of gaze. Pray for Kerouac if he ever read his leering exotifying gaze to the Apollo Theater crowd, but there is no correlating need to pray for those in the audience. They know themselves. They also know the white boy on stage. None of that is a surprise—none of those words, none of the hipster's fascination with Black bodies, life, and culture. What is surprising is that in imagining white liberation through becoming Black or becoming like Black, Mailer's hipster designs his own shameful prison.

The gaze reversed is whiteness estranged from its possibilities. That dialectic falls apart when the abject is taken away, when Black life is made present in the encounter. The Black boy looks at the white boy? The end of identification. The emergence of new possibility.

1: Baldwin's American Negro

Between Faulkner's innocence and ambivalence and Mailer's fascination and aggression, we catch sight of the limits of escaping the system of white violence, its gaze, and the delimitation of the racial imagination for Black Americans; the foil, the enemy, is made clear in both essays. But blackness as a counterideology or counternarrative is no quick fix. The African is a flight of fancy for Baldwin, an attempt to flee and deny the realities of American life. What Baldwin wants to sit with are those realities *inside* and *in the interstices* of that life and therein negotiate thinking and being otherwise. But, always, this is a movement toward an otherwise lodged inside the particularity and peculiarity of the work of history and memory on place. How can the hegemony of both flight from the world and the white gaze be destabilized?

Destabilization takes many forms, of course. The most prominent and familiar of them are rebellion and revolution. The apocalyptic tone of so much mid-century Black Atlantic thought—Césaire and Fanon stand out as pointed and important cases—is revolutionary in its desire to destroy the world as we know it and after that destruction imagine new possibilities for being, to think the unprecedented at the end of the world. Baldwin shares their nihilism in many ways, but it is never total. For Baldwin, the possibility of rebellion and revolution, whatever it might mean, must be rooted in a sense of place and how history and memory bear on it. In his work, this means working from the ontology of race and racism in the United States; Black people are not outside history but instead intimate to and even at the center of its meaning. This is critical for understanding the terms of the interracial composition of the world and racial identity. Baldwin characterizes this as an *advantage*—a funky characterization, but a rhetorical flourish that puts real demands on his thinking and on us as readers. He writes, "We in this country now—and it really is one minute to twelve—can really turn the tide because we have an advantage that Europe does not have, and we have an advantage that Africa does not have, if we could face it. Black and white people have lived together here for generations, and now for centuries. Now, on whether or not we face these facts everything depends."[45] Facing the facts of interraciality has multiple significations. For my purposes here, it is worth noting that Baldwin is insisting on the most difficult insight: Whiteness and blackness are both generated by the interracial composition of the lifeworld.

This composition is a dialectical movement, but one that does not follow any rule or principle of reconciliation. It is, rather, a *negative* dialectic in the sense Theodor Adorno that gives the term when he writes that he wants to "free dialectics" from "affirmative traits without reducing its determinacy."[46] The racial dialectic of the United States does not produce affirmative notions of race. It produces the violent innocence of whites and their hegemonic gaze and the abject category in which Black people are forced to live, existentially and institutionally. All split, no reconciliation. We see something very much like this in Baldwin's 1964 essay "The White Problem," dating from the period of the publication of *The Fire Next Time*. In this essay, Baldwin sets out what he calls "two levels of experience." These two levels operate as the dialectical tension within which whiteness as an American identity emerges. "In this country, for a dangerously long time," Baldwin writes,

> there have been two levels of experience. One—to put it cruelly, but, I think, quite truthfully—can be summed up in the images of Doris Day and Gary Cooper: two of the most grotesque appeals to innocence the world has ever seen. And the other, subterranean, indispensable, and denied, can be summed up, let us say, in the tone and in the face of Ray Charles. And there has never been in this country any genuine confrontation between these two levels of experience.[47]

What would it mean to imagine this confrontation? Baldwin is here imagining a confrontation of images, but they are of course the images that, in many ways, entwine to create the imaginary landscape of American culture and politics. What it means to *be* emerges from these images. To be sure, this is a very different confrontation for white and Black Americans; racial difference is lived as the founding and ever cruel antagonism of Black lives by whiteness. But racial identity as a *lived reality*, as an existential condition, emerges in both cases from this tension, these "levels of experience," between Doris Day or Gary Cooper and Ray Charles. If the tension is dialectical, then it is important to see how the meaning of these images is itself broken apart by the racialization of that meaning and the affective life of images across the poles of racialization.

For white people, the dialectic is anchored in the abjection of blackness. The white experience of racism—and it is important to underscore that whites experience racism as the efficient cause and existential outcome of or a category of existence produced from antiblack racism—establishes a sense of measure against and through which identity is constructed. Baldwin poses this identity construction as a displacement of "paying dues," a sense of how the racial other, for white people, carries the burden not just of the social cost of abjection but also of making the meaning of collective identity *for the very people who produce conditions of abjection*. The strangest kind of autoaffection. Baldwin writes, "In this country, the entire nation has always assumed that I would pay their dues for them. What it means to be a Negro in this country is that you represent, you are the receptacle of and the vehicle of, all the pain, disaster, sorrow which white Americans think they can escape. This is what is really meant by keeping the Negro in his place."[48] Whiteness is therefore not reducible to privilege or benefit. While it is true, of course, that white people benefit enormously from every manifestation of antiblack racism, Baldwin is proposing a deeper, more searching claim. Whiteness, he argues here, only makes sense as an existential category, as an identity in and across time, in relation to the abjection of blackness. The meaning of being white is inseparable from the experience and construction of privilege as an infrastructure of the lifeworld, along with the entire range of affects and psychological pathologies that come to those living from the abjection of the racial, social other.

Baldwin, in a move that is typical of so much of his nonfiction work, reverses the gaze. The desire to keep Black people at the bottom of the well is also the desire to *not see*. White people need Black abjection but also want that abjection to be hidden from view. What is hidden is the condition for the possibility of white life. The ghetto as critical theory. And this means everything for Baldwin in terms of formulating the terms of African American response. That response for Baldwin takes a form of knowing that *knows more* precisely because it is positioned *outside*. Baldwin writes:

> No one has pointed out yet with any force that if I am not a man here, you are not a man here. You cannot lynch me and keep me in ghettos without becoming something monstrous yourselves. And furthermore, you give me a terrifying advantage.
>
> You give me this advantage: that whereas you have never had to look at me, because you've sealed me away along with sin and hell and death and all the other things you didn't want to look at, including love, my life was in your hands, and I had to look at you. I know more about you, therefore, than you know about me. I've had to

> spend my life, after all—and all the other Negroes in the country have had to spend their lives—outwitting and watching white people. I had to know what you were doing before you did it. People talk about the new Negro, but he's been coming for three hundred years.[49]

Baldwin's evocation of the new Negro points back to Alain Locke's work and the famous anthology from 1925, but the appeal to the new is also crucial for understanding his interruption of racial dialectics. The new of African American life is not the outcome of resolution or sublation—some sort of integration and transformation of the world—but instead the turn to what is already there, to what is already here and, in that sense of being already, already transformative of (or against) how white people understand the dynamics of race and racism. This moment in racial dialectic recalls a key moment in "Princes and Powers" in which Baldwin argues that it was "the popular impulse to keep us at the bottom of the perpetually shifting and bewildered populace." Such an impulse is not simply cruelty but also, and first of all for Baldwin, because African Americans are, for whites, "almost personally indispensable to each of them, simply because, without us, they could never have been certain, in such a confusion, where the bottom was."[50] This dialectical *need* makes whites monstrous. It explains the monstrosity of Faulkner's delay of racial justice time. It explains the monstrosity of Mailer's exoticizing gaze and carnal desire. What becomes of blackness in this dialectic, in terms of both possibility and necessity?

The truth of African American existence is for Baldwin the truth of place and of those dynamics that not only comprise the terrors of interracial life but also make for the layered realities of Black existence in an ontologically antiblack world. The world is ontologically antiblack in the sense that Being itself is antiblack; this is Baldwin's flirtation with what we now call "Afropessimism." If Being is antiblack, then the kinds of beings we *are* is saturated with the same antiblackness. Antiblackness is a stain, a contaminant, and a forestructuring of relations to self and others both Black and white. It stains white identity with the compulsive need for the abjection of blackness. But what is blackness, Black identity, or "the Negro" in this same negative dialectical movement?

Wright's early fiction documents precisely this forestructuring. For Baldwin, Wright's *Native Son*, the one work of Wright's that occupies Baldwin's critical imagination, tells a story that is simultaneously truth telling about Black existence in an antiblack world and reification of a sense of nihilism that truncates our sense of the complexity of Black life. Through Wright's fiction, Baldwin sits with the nonaffirmative traits of dialectical racial formation. In thinking through Wright, Baldwin navigates a compelling path through the negative dialectics of race in search of both senses of "the Negro": a reactive subject consumed by abjection and at the same time a joyful subject living in the interstices of social and political life in the United States.

There is no more important foil in Baldwin's writerly and critical career than Wright. His critiques of Wright, which are varied in many respects but also circulate around a common claim, reflect Baldwin's deep suspicion about the *scope* of nihilism. The truth value or appropriateness of nihilism never concerns Baldwin. Rather, it is the *scope* of nihilistic claims that concern Baldwin and which for Wright are total and all-consuming. I will return to the Wright–Baldwin relationship repeatedly in the chapters that follow because of how profoundly it informs the substance of Baldwin's thinking, but for now, in the context of racial dialectics, what is most compelling and important is the relationship between violence and the white gaze. Bigger Thomas embodies this dialectical outcome and production. And so how Wright conceives and writes his characters is Baldwin's most pressing concern. Baldwin's concern is rooted in the text: This nihilism, this abject production of a negative dialectics, is on the page of most of Wright's significant fiction. One should not be at all shocked that Wright would write violence so viscerally into his novels and short stories. Antiblack violence, after all, is a national tradition, and Wright's own biography—Mississippi born and raised, time in Chicago and Harlem, then exile in Paris—is tantamount to a biography of the pain and rage of African American struggle, survival, and flight. But his fiction is rarely about survival and flight. Instead, it repeatedly returns to the experience of being the object, then subject, of violence. That interval is crucial: moving from object to subject, from reactive and enraged. Baldwin observes, "The violence, as in so much of Wright's work, is gratuitous and compulsive. It is one of the severest criticisms that can be leveled against his work. The violence is gratuitous and compulsive because the root of the violence is never examined."[51] What are we to make of this appeal to the root of the violence? The root is white hatred of Black people and how that hatred is expressed in the dehumanization of Black life and the rendering of the Black body as fatally vulnerable. The gratuitousness and compulsive character of Wright's violence comes from this vulnerability: a voice from the bottom of the well, unconcerned with how the well was built, but instead concerned with how it feels to inherit the memories of generation after generation living there, in the bottom, without hope.

For Baldwin, Wright's fiction, perhaps ironically, comes up short of its own aspiration—or the aspiration it *should* have. Any effort to describe the African American condition as the outcome of a negative dialectics of race is undercut by a consuming rage and the digestion of its own abject state. That is, by documenting the rage that comes with suffering centuries of the worst kinds of terror, terror lived in the abject conditions described in a social realist register and mode of political outrage, Wright's work *wants* to tell an entire story. *Native Son* opens with a bleak account of a decrepit home, a rat, and the hopelessness of existence. What is the cause of this? And what are the paths, if not *out of*, at least *against* this bleakness? Perhaps this is what Wright *wants* to tell us. But he instead *actually* tells a very limited story, one about the *internalization* of the story of antiblackness without all of the other politically critical elements of the construction of a violent, antiblack racist society. Baldwin puts this in the starkest terms in "Alas, Poor Richard" when he writes, "Thus, when in Wright's pages a Negro male is found hacking a white woman to death, the very gusto with which this is done, and the great attention paid to the details of physical destruction reveal a terrible attempt to break out of the cage in which the American imagination has imprisoned him for so long."[52] Wright's fiction is at once an expression of rage and an expression of revenge. That rage is satisfying because it documents what Baldwin describes, in a moment of despair, as the fact that "no American Negro exists who does not have his private Bigger Thomas living in the skull,"[53] even if that rage and sense of revenge is never in a (fully) liberatory register. Indeed, this is what seals Wright's nihilism as complete. Even acts of violent resistance turn out to be without meaning. Bigger Thomas is sentenced to death at the close of *Native Son*. Fred Daniels is killed by the police at the close of "The Man Who Lived Underground." Cross Damon is murdered at the close of *The Outsider*. Dave Saunders wanders off to places unknown and unanticipated in "The Man Who Was Almost a Man." And so on. Whatever the resistance, whatever the violence against violence, there is, in the end, only Black death. Wright's closing scenes for the dramatics of interracial life is, for Black people, only death. That truth lives inside the skull. But what is the *scope* of this truth, and what does it say about the possibilities and actualities of Black life?

I am always struck by how unforgiving Baldwin is in his reading of Wright. Baldwin renders all of these encounters with violence and reactive action as a reiteration with only the slightest difference in affect of white abjection of Black life. Bigger lives inside the skull. That is the truth. But there is also a failure in Wright's fiction to think Black life otherwise—not an otherwise *to come*, but an otherwise that is *life*, not social death, in the interstices of an antiblack world. First there is the indisputable, if despairing, truth of Wright:

> And there is, I should think, no Negro living in America who has not felt, briefly or for long periods, with anguish sharp or dull, in varying degrees and to varying effect, simple, naked, and unanswerable hatred; who has not wanted to smash any white face he may encounter in a day, to violate, out of motives of the cruelest vengeance, their women, to break the bodies of all white people and bring them low, as low as that dust into which he himself has been and is being trampled.[54]

This is Baldwin's moment of empathy and shared consciousness that links the negative dialectic of racial formation with history and memory. Wright does not write from nowhere. He writes from inside this history and memory, from the position of the one produced *by* the negative dialectics of racial formation. Baldwin knows this. But he also knows otherwise and writes in search of openings in the closed system of nihilism. Is the white gaze complete? Does it close the entirety of being and world? The affects of this gaze—hatred, disgust, dehumanization—live in the gaze itself but also inside the affective life of African Americans. And so Baldwin also adds the decisive twist: "no Negro, finally, who has not had to make his own precarious adjustment to the 'nigger' who surrounds him and to the 'nigger' in himself."[55] This remark is one of the most demoralizing observations in all of Baldwin's nonfiction. It brings him inside Bigger Thomas in an importantly new way. The rage of Bigger lives inside the skull. But so too lives what precedes that rage, the abject blackness carried *to* Black subjectivity by the white gaze that then has an entire life *inside* the skull, a life degraded that is also felt as if it were one's own, the feeling of the bottom of the well without the impulse to refuse the legitimacy of that feeling.

The negative dialectics of race produce this feeling, this subjectivity. It is lived without fantasies of Africa or the slow-moving, exotifying words of certain whites. What is the affective life of this internalized antiblackness, the blackness of "the Negro," and how might the vicissitudes of Black affect mark the limits of that despairing life? This is our next question.

Chapter 3

Affect and the Afterlife of Memory

In a famous interview with René Depestre, appended to the 2001 translation of his *Discourse on Colonialism* (1955), Aimé Césaire remarks on the affective life of Black people under antiblack racist regimes. Such affective life is produced by the racial dialectic of supremacy and abjection, which stalls and reifies the terms of exaltation and shame. Shame emerges for Césaire in gestures that avoid identification with being Black. He recalls, "Our struggle was a struggle against alienation. That struggle gave birth to Negritude. Because Antilleans were ashamed of being Negroes, they searched for all sorts of euphemisms for Negro: they would say a man of color, a dark-complexioned man, and other idiocies like that."[1] Frantz Fanon had expressed this very same sentiment just a few years prior in *Black Skin, White Masks* (1952) as part of his long exploration of the inferiority complex and its link to colonial abjection. Césaire's poetry, Fanon notes time and again, gave Black Antilleans a sense of pride and self-worth that proved indispensable to liberation struggle. That sense of pride and self-worth was of course never enough. There always needs to be more, a need for a deeper transformation of the psyche and language as well as of the material and cultural conditions of Black life. But shame is a critical moment in liberation struggle. It lives in a sense of self and also in those projections that might serve as counternarratives and counterattachments across the Black Americas. I am thinking of how Baldwin describes Father Divine and the continent of Africa as sites of shame in "East River, Downtown," which is less about those particular examples as exceptionally shameful and more about the structure of what Césaire characterizes as "a struggle against alienation" and Fanon names as the inferiority complex. This is the life of whiteness inside the Black psyche, which is perhaps the deepest damage and violence of antiblack racism. Shame is as atmospheric as it is site specific.

What would it mean to read Fanon and Baldwin alongside one another?

Fanon and Baldwin are two of the most important and certainly most provocative mid-century writers on questions of race, history, and the future of subjectivity for oppressed peoples. Fanon's eschewing of history in the name of a radically open future, with its companion notion of a new humanism, sits at the foundation of so much postcolonial thinking. Baldwin's account of the complexities of African American life under regimes of antiblack racism continues to be crucial for our understanding of cultural formation in the cracks and margins of the lives of the oppressed. And they share the mid-century moment in the Black Atlantic, a moment infused with the deepest rage against centuries of colonial domination as well as a decisive surge in liberation movements committed to the creation of new worlds. The two writers are also very different. Fanon writes from the Caribbean, then Algeria, in the midst of and immersed in colonial revolt. Baldwin writes sometimes from the United States, often from exile in France, Switzerland, or Turkey, in the midst of revolt but always holds that revolt at a certain distance.[2] Fanon is the insurgent. Baldwin is the witness. This is a difference that makes a difference.

Why would that matter? What does that difference mean for how we think about the place of antiblackness in the psychic and cultural constitution of Black life? The shared commitment between Fanon and Baldwin to thinking subjectivity, politics, and cultural production in relation to history and memory, embedding all in the expressive media of Black life, is compelling enough.[3] But the relation between Fanon and Baldwin on questions of affective life takes on a special kind of urgency when we see the enormous stakes of that relation. Between Fanon and Baldwin, we find the pathological effects of the white gaze internalized but also the various radical interventions *against* those internalizations. Fanon and Baldwin speak to questions of revolution and refusal in worlds composed by antiblackness and so too the relation between the past that bears on the present and how present appropriation of that bearing shifts and alters the meaning of the future. Affect is always embedded in time, in the time of oppression, and also in the time of revolution and refusal. Theorizing and documenting the vicissitudes of affect under regimes of antiblackness draws us into the dramatic afterlife of memory. Atrocity sits in memory. This is inheritance in an antiblack world. How does atrocity live after and in its memory?

My task in this set of reflections is really quite simple and straightforward: to examine how questions of affective life underpin the psychological, cultural, and ontological dimensions of both Fanon's and Baldwin's thought, as well as how affective life structures the present and future of Black subjectivity. The shared concern with interracial contact draws Fanon and Baldwin into a certain convergence, but their assessment of subjectivity *after* whiteness—and the comparative impact of cultural production—generates important counterclaims that speak to the geographical resonance of affect. It might make a difference that Fanon writes from the colony and Baldwin writes from the ghetto. The terms of racial proximity matter and vary across geographical difference. The convergences and counterclaims that concern me here center on the affect of shame, which is a common site of affective life under antiblack racist regimes in Fanon and Baldwin. For both Fanon and Baldwin, one of the crucial legacies of antiblack racism lies in its production of shame as an atmospheric affect—an affect that is not one among others but rather a mood within which all other affects, values, and aspirations are staged and framed. In that sense, shame is a mood that forms, and is therefore a constitutive component of, most affects in Black subjectivity. And so for Fanon and Baldwin shame is a critical site of analysis as both diagnosis (we must understand the affective life produced by antiblack racism and how deeply it is written into the psyche) and transformative resistance (the confrontation with shame is a moment of transforming subjectivity and the future, as well as, for Baldwin, a moment of retrieval of forgotten elements of Black history[4]). Differences between Fanon and Baldwin emerge here, and one thread that guides the following reflections is an interpretation of Fanon's Sartreanism—the break with history, the purity of the future, the abjection of memory—that identifies important limits in his legacy. Whatever his ecstatic visions of the future, Fanon insists throughout his work that the past is abject and only a future that says yes to another world by simultaneously saying no to history is a future worthy of revolution. Black subjectivity retains its freedom for Fanon even when that freedom cannot be drawn from cultural forms—an important claim given his characterization of so many Black cultural forms as colonized or too tainted by history's pain; Fanon's dismissal of blues, jazz, and creole languages is important here.

It is precisely around that question of the status of cultural forms under antiblack racist regimes that Baldwin breaks with Fanon. Whereas jazz and blues remain largely expressions of abjection for Fanon in *Black Skin, White Masks* and his groundbreaking essay "Racism and Culture," Baldwin sees in the same expressions not just elements but entire manifestations of cultural resistance, uniqueness, refusal, world making, meaning, and, in a word, *life*. This simple split regarding the status of cultural production is returned to history and memory as a difference between Fanon and Baldwin—and therefore a difference in mid-century Black Atlantic thought. It is a difference surrounding the crucial question of what the past offers to the revolutionary Black subject. Baldwin's distance from Fanon is the kind of distance that so many post-Fanon Caribbean thinkers also seek to establish, which in its own way draws Baldwin back into the space of late twentieth-century creolist thinking. This play of proximity and distance raises the question of how memory and its affects have after*lives*, layered with signification and rich with sedimentations of pain, melancholia, mourning, play, joy, resistance, refusal, and meaning making. Teasing these out as questions of ontology—what it means to *be* alongside what it means to *feel*—is what it means to think between Fanon and Baldwin on the afterlife of memory.

The arc of what follows consists of tracing out this basic claim: For Fanon and Baldwin, liberation from antiblack racism is tantamount to revolution against the affect of shame. Struggle against shame is no small matter and requires a subtle, nuanced account of the scope and reach of antiblack racism. Antiblack racism is a total project, whether that project is manifest in the plantation, colonial relations, or the simple violent hostility of the (white) society in which Black subjects live. Internalization of feelings of inferiority and shame manifests the total project in the heart of the psyche, troubling all possibilities for Black life from the inside. And yet radical intervention is always still possible; resistance to shame, refusal of the terms of shame, and therefore the promise of transformative action and re-formation of subjectivity remain possible, if exceptionally difficult, work. The terms of that work and what it can draw on from the past form an important difference between Fanon and Baldwin, as well as the conditions of any theory of liberation. And, in the end, this difference raises a particularly complicated philosophical question: Can Fanon and Baldwin account for both the subjectivity that is saturated by shame as a kind of transcendental affect—the condition for the possibility of being—and the subjectivity that is able to gather the resources necessary for revolt and refusal?

This consideration is undertaken in three parts. First, I want to treat the theme of shame in Fanon's and Baldwin's texts with a view toward comparative convergence, with particular attention to *Black Skin, White Masks* and *The Fire Next Time*. Both of those works understand shame as the effect of antiblack racism and locate the affective life and aftereffects of shame in the center of subjectivity; shame precludes senses of the outside precisely because it is the condition of movement in the world. For both thinkers, shame is such a powerful affect because it reveals the *aspiration* of antiblack racism (colonialism in Fanon, segregation and violence in Baldwin) to be a total project, capable of disabling Black subjects at the core of conscious life. Black subjectivity in an antiblack world enters interracial space with shame as an antechamber, disabling the Black subject from the outset. This is the affective foundation of a robust pessimism. While there are limits to such nihilistic aspirations (systems are never closed, whatever their pretensions), antiblack racism remains a force of total transformation; what it requires to move outside of, then beyond, shame is of the most exceptional and remarkable character, even in its everydayness. So, in the second section below, I raise just this issue of moving outside, then beyond, in the context of a preliminary consideration of the question of home. What is home? And how is the affective life of home framed by the force of shame and its overcoming?

The third and final section puts the issue of transformation most directly by reintroducing the meanings of revolution and refusal. For Fanon and Baldwin both, liberation from shame and its long shadow is a revolutionary act, or perhaps an act of refusal that revolutionizes, one that uproots the totality of the racist lifeworld in order to make another subjectivity possible. Home, that site of both violence (racism's reach as a total project) and fragments of resistance (survival and cultural formation on the margins of racist regimes), names a point of both convergence and divergence between Fanon and Baldwin. For both, the question of home is paramount in antiracist struggle, and yet, as we will see, Fanon's eschewing of history and memory contrasts with Baldwin's retrieval of the cultural complexity of resistance and refusal in ways that are absolutely decisive for theorizing shame as the affective site of oppression *and* liberation. *How* we belong in the world makes sense of what affects animate our being in the world. The *how* of belonging and nonbelonging—that is, how such relations are imagined, conceived, and practiced—serves as an indicator of the afterlife of memory. Does memory live as abjection in social and cultural production and reproduction? Or does memory carry with it something transformative, something of the terms of refusal, and therefore a way of understanding subjectivity otherwise than the atmospheric affect of shame?

This comparative consideration of Fanon and Baldwin underscores a crucial question in theorizing liberation: What is the meaning of the past and how does that meaning inform an imagined future? The temporality of liberation—revolution, really, but also refusal—departs from the present and any diagnosis of the affective core of racial oppression, which, in this case, centers on shame. The scope of antiblack racism is here articulated from the center of subjective life, where the total project of persecution comes to live in the psychic life of the body. What remains for meaning making in the midst of that persecution? For Fanon, nothing is worth retaining, which lays the groundwork for his apocalyptic conception of revolutionary action and decolonization. For Baldwin, there is so much that remains outside the white gaze, in the interstices of interracial life, which in turn cites an alternative inheritance that places African American subjectivity in the mode of refusal. In that difference, a deep theoretical difference around the meaning of home and the geography of thinking, is a difference that marks an important crossroads in the mid-century Black Atlantic theory. In our imagination of the future, what and who is history *to* us? And what and who are we *from* history? And, in the end, what sort of revolutionary action, what sort of refusal, is necessary to say yes to life, place, and home? What sorts of affects motivate action and what sorts of counteraffects emerge in this other future?

Race and Shame

"Who are they, in truth, those creatures," Fanon writes, "who hide, who are hidden by social truth beneath the attributes of *bicot, bounioule, arabe, raton, sidi, mon z'ami*?"[5] In this bit from "The 'North African Syndrome,"" an essay from 1952 that reckons with the infrahuman experience in the Maghreb context, Fanon embellishes a notion of lumpen proletariat with racial and geographic specificity of colonial violence. That specificity embeds the racial slur inside ethnoracial designation in order to raise the question asked in the opening section: "Who are they, those creatures starving for humanity who stand buttressed against the impalpable frontiers . . . of complete recognition?"[6] We know this motif from *Black Skin, White Masks*, from the moment that opens chapter 5, when a child points at him and says at once "look, a Black man" and "look . . . ," inserting the vilest of slurs. Language itself bears the ugliest of humanity within its everyday speech. Description as racial violence. Pessimism built into the very structure of everyday life.

In that way, Fanon's *Black Skin, White Masks* remains his most incisive, detailed exploration of the meaning and structure of antiblack racism and how it transforms the affective life of Black subjectivity. Affective life arises in the space between the gaze and the Black body. This forms the existentialist foundation of Fanon's early project. As a matter of methodology, Fanon configures meaning making as the interplay of the subject and the social world, what he calls *sociogeny* in the key formulation. Sociogeny is itself derived from the founding insight of existential phenomenology into the structure of intentionality. To *be* is to be in relation, an interval or site of exchange with the world that makes meaning happen in and for subjectivity. Embodied subjectivity—and this is an important contour of Fanon's method—accounts for both the visibility of Black subjectivity and the abjection of the Black body and its forms of life. In this way, *Black Skin, White Masks* owes no small debt to Jean-Paul Sartre's work on antisemitism in *Anti-Semite and Jew* but also develops a specifically Black existentialist position through a deep conversation with the Négritude movement. A note on both to begin.

Black Skin, White Masks begins with an existential-phenomenological schema that readers of Sartre surely find familiar. Subjectivity and embodiment function as inseparable. The subject is not disembodied consciousness but instead an incarnate being who lives in the world as a social being through and through. The subject sees and is seen. This means that subjectivity is what sees the world and what moves within it while simultaneously being vulnerable to being seen, acted upon, and constructed by ideological forces. In a word, a subjectivity that is *situated*. The distinction between being and the social collapses at the moment of the genesis of subjectivity. Consciousness emerges out of traffic through the world, and the subject sits between the space of being in the world and the capacity to resist from outside that world. We cannot say that the body makes subjectivity from the exterior (passivity) or that the subject simply animates the body from the inside (activity). Rather, the embodiment of the subject in its simultaneously passive and active presence to the world situates it in its presence to and presencing *in* the world. As such, the incarnate subject moves to *assert* that presence in the world, to articulate its identity to a world that is far from indifferent while at the same time understanding that the struggle for the articulation of identity is initiated by the subject's fundamental worldliness—for Fanon, a sort of racialized *Geworfenheit*. Affective life is central to this starting point. The forms of alienation peculiar to the colonized (in *Black Skin, White Masks*, it is the West Indian experience of colonization in particular) structure the experience of knowing and being—a racialization, we might say, of Heidegger's founding insights into mood or state of mind (*Befindlichkeit*) and being in *Being and*

Time.[7] The racialization of mood, and so the kinds of anxiety and ontological insecurity that emerge from racialized experience in an antiblack world, inserts the incarnate subject in the history of a place. To be is to be embodied, and the racialized context of the colonial body introduces a specific, nongeneralizable set of affects that create particular experiences of knowing and being: attention to place, attention to how blackness as a social and embodied phenomenon structures meaning and how the sociality of being itself creates an atmospheric mood that then shapes and contours meaning. Fanon and Baldwin stand in proximity around exactly this point—a starting point that becomes a point of resistance and refusal.

Antiblack racism functions as a formative, foundational event insofar as it draws on the social, cultural, and historical abjection of the Black body. Abjection is not just a social relation. It is a social relation and an ontology of the subject at one and the same time. Thus, Fanon looks not just to cultural and political forces as sites of diagnosis but also (and even foremost) to the most intimate sites of subjective life. Fanon's method is so interesting here. *Black Skin, White Masks* is full of autopoetic elements, immersed in phenomenological description through anecdote, responding to key texts, and attentive to how the colonial gaze is omnipresent in the colony, even in the absence of white people, which is key for understanding the work of colonialism. Abjection of the body in the social relation produces a subject structured by *shame*: a sense of disgrace and disrepute at the heart of identity. Shame gathers together a cluster of Fanonian motifs and pathological names in order to ground the moral psychology of antiblack racism in sociogenic affect. Racial judgment—abjection of body and consciousness—is made interior to the subject, exercising hegemony through a forestructuring of autonomy. In this sense, interiority mirrors and enacts the administrative function of external relations—social, cultural, and political constraints—with efficiency and cruelty. Shame disables the subject by installing a sense of inferiority and precarity and, perhaps most importantly, eliminating any sense of enabling memory and history. History and memory become histories and memories of shamefulness and bequeath to the subject the condition of shame and abjection *from the inside out*, which is only deepened by the affirmation of such a condition in a racist world. Institutions reproduce shame as a constitutive *Befindlichkeit* by authorizing and confirming what the Black subject already knows about itself. History and memory therefore function with special power in the colonial relation. With institutions of the colonizer in place, all of which work as Althusserian ideological state apparatuses[8] in constructing identity and reproducing cultural forms and values, the abjection of memory and history deepens and solidifies the abjection of the Black body. There is no noble memory and history. There is no sense of resistance or refusal as companions to the history of atrocity. There is only a story of defeat and subjugation. The body bears this story in and on the skin, which then becomes drawn in as the affective structure of the psyche.

Located in the skin and in the psyche, the affect of shame functions very much like Sartrean guilt: the irreducible consequence of our absolute freedom, made cruelly ironic because shame bounds Black "freedom" as *unfreedom*. This unfreedom is a self-disabling that services the desires of white racism. That is, shame is like Sartrean guilt insofar as it is a condition *before* action that animates the meaning and significance of any action whatsoever. Shame and identity intertwine at every level of subjective life. Indeed, Fanon locates the problem of shame and identity in the most intimate yet most expansive place: language. Language is neither a mere instrument nor an abstract structure with distance from consciousness and world. Language sets the very terms of relation to self and world. "To speak," Fanon writes in a well-known passage, "means being able to use a certain syntax and possessing the morphology of such and such a language, but it means above all assuming a culture and bearing the weight of a civilization."[9] Inside language, there is no place for Black subjects in colonial culture, except as derivative beings or subjectivities carrying a critical asterisk with their identity—French, yes, *but French and Black*. There is nonetheless the compulsion to speak and perfect French in two senses: as the exclusive language of transaction (marginalizing or eliminating creole and pidgins) and in the refined art of diction. Shame is built into the very act of declaring one's being in the world. "At school," Fanon writes, "the young Martinican is taught to treat the dialect with contempt. Avoid Creolisms. Some families forbid speaking Creole at home, and mothers call their children little ragamuffins for using it. . . . Yes, I must watch my diction because that's how they'll judge me. He can't even speak French properly, they'll say with the utmost contempt."[10] Contempt undermines the Black subject from the outside with a gaze both real and imagined, which, in the cruel efficiency of the affect of shame, then regulates and subjugates the subject from its interior. That is, the Black subject is denied access to their vernacular expressive life. This induces in the psyche an existential forgetfulness. Creoles and pidgins, fully coherent languages with names for the world and idiomatic complexity, play, and creativity, are rendered abject at best and absent at worst, and the Black subject returns to a colonial language in which they have no real place. This is a movement of pure loss. Shame is that affective structure that both motivates the movement away from creole (shame in relation to speech and sound) and is the result of the retreat to the colonized space of the Black French speaker (internal experience of inferiority and compulsion to participate in colonial worlds).

If language carries culture and culture imports a system of values and valuation into the psyche, then we should not be surprised when Fanon's analysis turns to the moral dimension of alienation. Alienation conditions the movement away from creole (or creolisms) to French, which splits the heart of the subject's identity. Fanon writes, "Moral consciousness implies a kind of split, a fracture of consciousness between a dark and a light side. Moral standards require the black, the dark, and the black man to be eliminated from this consciousness. A black man, therefore, is constantly struggling against his own image."[11] *Struggling against his own image.* This is the birth of the inferiority complex. Colonialism for Fanon is a Manichean system—a claim that later organizes the argument of *The Wretched of the Earth*—and this system of difference is always more than imposition by physical or political force. If colonizer-colonized relations were reducible to physical and political force, then decolonization would be accomplished at the very moment in which the colonizer leaves colonized land. The psychological work of colonialism, the internalization of the values and prejudices of the white gaze, builds colonial relation into the life of affect. Indeed, inferiority is a *complex* precisely because it takes place in and touches so many parts of the psyche. Language alienates in the colonial relation, and language is situated at the foundations of thinking and being. The event of language, then, is the event of the coming into being of the psyche. Colonialism wounds from the very outset. *To be* colonized is *to be* wounded. The wound does its work in the affective structures that structure relations to thinking, being, embodiment, identity, and so on. Colonization is a total project.

The wound is therefore not just a wound of difference; it is not simply a matter of epistemological confusion and disorientation that might be righted through therapeutic intervention or political progressivism. The wound is principally moral. Moral, that is, in the sense of determining from the outset what is possible in terms of *good* and *bad* (or even evil) but also in terms of the long tale of value and self- and collective worth that attends to the language of race in antiblack racist regimes. Morality and ontology intersect at this very origin point of the psyche. Black subjectivity is morally complicated from the outset, and the social, cultural, and political structures of subjugation and marginalization confirm and reproduce wounded identity at every turn. *A total project.*

And yet subjectivity is also a site of resistance and hope. Hope, a first affective intervention of resistance, is neither simple nor straightforward. Fanon identifies struggle at the heart of consciousness, born from the abyss of nonbeing, but that struggle cannot be articulated in generalized terms. Subjectivity is always in a struggle with itself. The struggle to be moral, present, just, knowing, and so on, all in the face of the anonymity of being and modern life, is the condition of subjectivity in the broadest sense. So, in a certain sense, one can see a generalized existential position emerge at this moment. But Fanon's subject does not struggle against the world as its neutral exterior or against its own competing desires, impulses, and energies within conscience and consciousness. Rather, the Black or colonial subject in Fanon struggles against the *image* of himself—an important reiteration of Lacanian specularity. The inferiority complex installs a measure inside the psyche against which the Black subject always falls short as a moral creature. And so, ontologically, falling short of authentic being *in* and *of* the world. The inseparability of language and the imagination make subjectivity morally fraught at its very foundation: inner life, feeling, self-knowledge. Such inseparability stalls Black subjectivity inside the psyche itself, before the subject engages with and resists the world, and thus internalizes the subjugating dynamics of colonialism *as a precondition of being a being in the world*. This is dense and dispiriting stuff that follows directly from the opening claim of *Black Skin, White Masks* that language is how one inhabits the world. Colonial *meaning* is the condition for the possibility of habitation. We set up our home in language. In that home, in that language, a specular image is produced that wounds or amputates Black subjectivity in the heart of what it means to be. "I hailed the world," Fanon writes, "and the world amputated my enthusiasm. I was expected to stay in line and make myself scarce."[12]

From its very beginning, Baldwin's work takes up the same sort of issue of affective structure and the internalization of antiblack racism. It is how he warns his nephew about the world. It is how he recalls his own specular formation. It is how he rejoins the discourse of subjective fracture that begins, in many ways, with Du Bois's description of double consciousness in *The Souls of Black Folk*.

To be sure, Baldwin works in the context of the United States and thus, strictly speaking, not on colonial terms. This is a difference that makes a difference. The meaning of interracial space for Baldwin is tied to immanent institutional terror: the ghetto, the police, the white mob, and all cognates. The colonial situation requires intervention in the psyche in order for subjugation to work; administration from abroad is largely about the transformation of intellectual and affective space in order to make whiteness present in a world with few white people. And yet affective dimensions of antiblack racism function in largely the same terms for Baldwin as for Fanon, installing a set of complexes that, just as much as external legal and political structures, set the terms of both antiblack racism and visions of Black liberation.

Baldwin's *The Fire Next Time* begins where his early work so often begins: the travails of childhood, the cruelty of poverty and violence, and the damaging illusions of comfort and liberation. Poverty and violence do double work. On the one hand, they produce structures of subjugation that reproduce themselves through the repressive state apparatus. Racism functions through institutional cruelty and direct physical violence (the mob, the police, the court system) as an external practice of aggression and harm. On the other hand, and here Baldwin echoes Fanon's foundational insights, poverty and violence reproduce the basic ideological structure of racism: inferiority as a sociogenic structure. Inferiority does sociogenic work insofar as it is the ideological cornerstone of an antiblack, racist social world that reproduces itself in institutions and experiences of self, entwining those two sites of reproduction to the point of inseparability. Politics is existential is affect is phenomenological. Lived experience folds into political reality, doubling the effect and affect of antiblackness. Baldwin's earliest essays remember Harlem, and he comes back to this site time and again as a citation of abject suffering and moral outrage. The suffering of Harlem generates affects of shame. The moral outrage sketches a path of resistance and refusal. What lines of flight from inferiority are possible? This is always Baldwin's question. Resources for responding to this question are fraught precisely because of the affective effects of antiblackness. For Baldwin, the church is never enough and the Nation of Islam is always too much, which leaves Baldwin with the existential condition of Black life. He writes, "In the same way that we, for white people, were the descendants of Ham, and were cursed forever, white people were, for us, the descendants of Cain. And the passion with which we loved the Lord was a measure of how deeply we feared and distrusted and, in the end, hated almost all strangers, always, and avoided and despised ourselves."[13] Religion provides comfort by paradoxically affirming the very terms of inferiority, but with the twist that Christianity can provide: the meek are the chosen and most beloved by God. But here Baldwin addresses the cruel side of this: to love God in this way is to say yes to self-hatred. His Nietzschean moment.

The Fire Next Time turns from Christianity and the Black church's perhaps unwitting affirmation of the affect of inferiority to the opposing cultural force of the mid-1960s: the Nation of Islam and its emphasis on Black superiority. But for Baldwin that turn cannot remedy the pathology of interiorization of antiblackness. Rather, and to put it in Fanon's terms, the Nation's reversal of racist terms only confirms the terms of antiblack racism by reifying, in a Black power gesture of superiority, the Manichean structure of raciological thinking; the Nation merely reverses the terms of inferiority. The dualism of the antiblack world and the conflict built into the distinction remain untouched and affirmed, a logic not unlike the Négritude movement's work across the francophone Atlantic world. Fanon's critique of the Manichaeism of Négritude in many ways matches Baldwin's critical hesitations around the Nation. While the revaluation of values in the Nation's ideological reversal labors in some measure against the affective elements of the inferiority complex and, in perhaps the best feature of Black nationalism, promises to challenge the ideologically laden structures of poverty and violence (through community revitalization and focus),[14] the Manichean structure of social relations remains intact. Baldwin's critique is that this radical intervention is not radical *enough*. Radical critique, critique that uproots the affective structures that issue from racism and raciological thinking, ought to reconfigure the foundational social forces of race and relation. To surmount an antiblack world, something more than a revaluation of values is necessary.

Radical critique requires an existential and specular understanding of harm. Baldwin, like Fanon, begins with the existential situatedness of the subject. That situatedness produces the inferiority complex or, in Baldwin's phrasing, *self-hatred*. The interiority of self-hatred is a symptom of the existential condition of irreducible nonbelonging. Baldwin writes, "The universe, which is not merely the stars and the moon and the planets, flowers, grass, and trees, but *other people*, has evolved no terms for your existence, has made no room for you, and if love will not swing wide the gates, no other power will or can."[15] This passage points us in two directions: the diagnosis of the terms of alienation and the metaphysics of cure. I want to pause the question of cure in Baldwin, as that takes us afield of the question of affect, but the terms of alienation are here set out in the very same terms we find in Fanon. Has the world evolved terms that can affirm Black existence? This question recalls Fanon's reflection on moral consciousness, where he notes, like the Négritude thinkers before him, that blackness is fated to abjection in the world *as we know it*. Without words for and generated by a Black world, a world in which blackness is neither abjection nor nonbeing but something *otherwise*, the world we *know*, the interracial world, only generates affects of inferiority, self-hatred, and shame. Against this, the accumulation of words for Black and blackness, words that describe or *would* describe the world as a world of *life* and not social death, is akin to the accumulation of senses of cure. In his early essay "Everybody's Protest Novel," Baldwin writes, "It is the peculiar triumph of society—and its loss—that it is able to convince those people to whom it has given inferior status of the reality of this decree; it has the force and the weapons to translate its dictum into fact, so that the allegedly inferior are actually made so. . . . We find ourselves bound, first without, then within, by the nature of our categorization."[16] The difficulty here lies in the contingent character of the interior life of subjectivity. We are not composed of disembodied consciousness. We are material creatures, embodied and social, which intertwines our fate with that of others—both comrades and oppressors. Our materiality, our embodiment and sociality, roots our sense of being in sociogenic movement and principles. The sedimentation of history and memory is written on the body. One lives in a world with others. If that world with those others is populated by terms that are incompatible with certain forms of creaturely, incarnate being, then the consciousness returned to the Black subject through the process of sociogenesis is alienated from its origins and from the interior. The is foundational affect. The stakes could not be higher. The interiorization of antiblack racism and the affect of shame—the sense that existence itself is a humiliation and indignity—produces the inability to say *yes* to life. It is not that the Black subject says *no* to life in Baldwin's text. That would be a reactive consciousness that has within itself the capacity to negate negation. Rather, in this reading, *being Black in an antiblack world is defined by the incapacity to affirm being*. Again, Baldwin's anticipation of Afropessimism emerges in this key conceptual moment. "For black is the color of evil," Baldwin writes, "only the robes of the saved are white. It is this cry, implacable on the air and in the skull, that he must live with."[17]

If blackness has no place in the world and the world generates only the affective structures of shame, guilt, and self-hatred, then what are we to make of place? Is there a sense of home for Black subjectivity between Fanon and

Baldwin? What sorts of revolutionary acts and transformations are necessary for a sense of home and place to emerge?

The Ambivalence of Home

To appear as Black in conditions of antiblack racism is to appear inside a framework of alienation and shame. Fanon concisely describes this in one of his psychiatric reports:

> SECOND THESIS—*That the attitude of medical personnel is very often an* a priori *attitude. The North African does not come with a substratum common to his race, but on a foundation built by the European. In other words, the North African, spontaneously, by the very act of appearing on the scene, enters into a pre-existing framework.*[18]

Preexisting frameworks are ideological in every sense and saturate the psyche in each and every corner of affective life. Surpassing or overcoming this saturation is the work of revolution and refusal. If alienation and shame express the unimaginable price of what makes the relation of Black people in an interracial world possible, a world made "on a foundation built by the European," then the questions arise: How is one to address this alienation and shame? How can harm be reversed? What would reversal mean, what are its stakes, and what is the desired world and space thought otherwise? How is the legacy of harm transformed by the work of vernacular cultural formation into something world making, place making, and the world made otherwise? Put simply: Between Fanon and Baldwin, what is the future?

Were the problem *simply* the interiority of the psyche, one could imagine self-help and self-affirmation as the alpha and omega of transformation. But Fanon and Baldwin begin in that difficult space of the existential subject. One comes into being in and of the world *as it is known* and *how it knows us*, so the transformation called for in antiracist struggle is, like the project of antiblackness that produced that world, a total project. This is a project oriented toward finding a place in the world unbound by the racist categories of history, a place with words, affects, and social-political space for existence. Utopian? Perhaps. But certainly radically revolutionary.

We arrive here at a first iteration of the question of home. The question of home for Fanon and Baldwin is enmeshed in affective life and, grounded in a sense of being in the word and world, is only possible after a transformation of the dynamics of the interiorization of antiblack racism. That is, home is composed of a precarious and perhaps impossible set of historical experiences—not by roots or legacy (the Middle Passage, the plantation, colonialism, and ghettoization wreck those relationships), but rather in and through the experience of loss, alienation, and the emerging struggle of the movement against antiblack racism. Home is therefore not a *settled* place. To be at home is paradoxical: to be either not at home or in the between space of *making place* in a world that does not want you. In *The Fire Next Time*, we see this most clearly in Baldwin's treatment of his two temptations: Christianity and Black nationalism. The church, as we have seen, does not settle accounts and cannot establish place. The otherworldliness of messianic Christianity tempts because it posits a line of flight from the world, out of the world, and into the value of suffering for eternal life. A sweet revenge at the foot of the Lord. Who would not want to escape a world that offers nothing but hostility and persecution? But Baldwin rejects this line of flight on Nietzschean grounds. Christianity cannot address the existential condition of Black subjectivity precisely because it does not express *rage* (a revolutionary affect through and through[19]) against shame and the inferiority complex but instead sees only a universal character in shame and inferiority: the sinful nature of the human.

Sin is a powerful characterization of the human, one that touches on both sociogenic forces of characterization and a deeper, more abiding name for the human condition. As Nietzsche has shown us in such provocative fashion, the appeal to a sinful nature denies the value of life itself. If life is denied as a value, then suffering in the world is not a spur to rage but instead a constant reminder of the ultimate value and desirability of death—a kind of internalization of social death as spiritual desire rather than abject worldly condition.[20] At the same time, and this is part of the paradoxical thinking that animates so much of his work, the Christian account of sin gives Baldwin a preliminary language for conceiving home in a world that offers hostility and persecution. Sin for Baldwin is a name for being out of place and unreconciled to the world *as a foundation of being* rather than a loss of place *after the fall*. In a gesture of secular reappropriation of Christianity's terms, Baldwin conceives the problem of home as a site of tension, activity, and world making, rather than as a site of comfort and belonging. Baldwin writes in *The Fire Next Time*, "I knew the tension in me between love and power, between pain and rage, and the curious, the grinding way I remained extended between these poles—perpetually attempting to choose the better rather than the worse."[21] This tension between love and power generates a dynamic of becoming. In a certain sense, this is the becoming of subjectivity as such, a relation of self to world that is always negotiation and extension of the subject beyond its grasp and control. And yet, the condition and situation of Black subjectivity fundamentally alters the ecstatic structure of affective life precisely because the meaning of home is at stake. To wit: If we presume a sense of belonging, then the tension of subjectivity in ecstatic affective life is initiated in the loss of or threat to a sense of home. If we begin with the alienation produced by antiblack racism, then ecstatic affective life, as its originary condition, is suspended between the reactive structure of rage and pain—our fundamental objection to persecution and hatred—and the aspirational structure of a *wanting to belong* and *desiring a place*. Baldwin is always careful to describe and prescribe this wanting and desire without an appeal to white ideality. He has no desire to integrate into a burning house. This is a strength of his theoretical work and a large part of its real complexity. The desire to belong *in this place* and not an elsewhere (a world to come, nostalgia for lost Africa), but also the desire for that belonging to be thought otherwise. Baldwin's descriptive distinction between elsewhere and otherwise is paramount.

Just a handful of years prior to *The Fire Next Time*, Baldwin evoked the simultaneity of pain and home in "Princes and Powers." Set between two poles, how could a place defined by unprecedented mass displacement, centuries of enslavement then segregation, and the accumulation of so many cruelties be called *home*? "Princes and Powers" asks this question at the 1956 Congress of Negro Writers and Artists in Paris, where leading figures in the Négritude movement offered justification for an emerging version of a Pan-Africanist thought. And in this frame, the Négritude writers can be read as theorists of *homelessness*. If the slave trade and colonialism decimated Black people, and that decimation is written across every aspect of Black life (language, culture, religion, the arts and sciences), then what could be the meaning of diaspora? Is diaspora merely a historicogeographical note in a terrifying history? Are Black people bound to Africa simply as a line on a map, a bare and barren geographic place of origin and nothing more? Or is diaspora a name for something deeper, an alternative *life philosophy*[22] that could serve as the foundation for Black identity? The Négritude movement articulates and defends a robust version of the latter. For thinkers like Aimé Césaire and Léopold Senghor, diaspora signifies how Black people are fundamentally lost and set astray in the postcolonial, post–slave trade world, lost, but not without the possibility of retrieval. And retrieval is here largely a cultural movement, a feature that distinguishes Négritude from many versions of Black nationalism from Martin Delany and Marcus Garvey and forward; Négritude's recasting of diaspora and transatlantic Black identity was never a project of physical relocation and land reclamation. Black *culture* is lost in the domination of the white world. That cultural meaning has no real place in the wake of that domination.

Fanon draws on so much of this diagnosis in *Black Skin, White Masks*, in particular in his phenomenological analysis of diction and alienation. Language alienates as a psychic phenomenon and also in terms of estrangement from culture and civilization as rooted points of origin. Revolutionary action begins in the movement against this estrangement. In "Princes and Powers," Baldwin sees the very same set of virtues in Négritude: an irrefutable diagnosis of the experience of blackness in an antiblack racist world, the rage and grievance leveled against those who have caused unspeakable pain, and a sense of shared identity in this shared experience, rage, and grievance. But, like

Fanon, Baldwin does not ultimately appeal to the cultural subconscious of an Africanist life philosophy; Black culture, that sense of connection and fecund relation that would generate the feeling and meaning of *home*, cannot—and even should not—be revitalized by its re-Africanization. If retrievable traces of Africa are lost in the centuries of the plantation and its colonial aftermath, then what remains after so much pain and suffering? How can the Americas be anything other than sites of abject suffering? What is the remainder that promises a making of world and worlds?

The relationship between home and memory is critical here. Home and memory thread together a whole variety of Négritude positions developed at the 1956 Congress as well as, ironically, forming the basis of Baldwin's own rejection of the Négritude theorists. *The present is untenable.* The untenable character of the present forges a common identity among Black subjects, all of whom *know the experience of* and *affectively relate to* the rage and grievance that motivates the Négritude movement, Fanon's existentialism, Baldwin's version of the same, and indeed any Black liberation movement whatsoever. This futurity emerges as *the* problem for thinking. But the future cannot be thought without an engagement with the past, whether an engagement that retrieves or an engagement that destroys history in its spiritual forms. If for Négritude thinking the future is a kind of memory project, a retrieval of the spirit of a past crushed and suppressed under regimes of domination, then we can say that the future is a *felt* aesthetic imagination that draws on the *felt* aesthetic past. Négritude wants *inspiration*: to breathe life into the psyche of a withering diaspora. Thus, Césaire and Senghor infuse their poetry with images of a new virility and life impulse that both transforms the untenable present into a livable future and calls upon a past purged of pain and loss, rehabilitated as a forgotten, then remembered, force of life and reproductive capacity. Memory connects to two possibilities. First: the connection to the immediate past as the material subjugation of Black bodies connects to impotence, despair, and hopelessness. This is the past as the present. Second: the connection to the past as a spiritual life force connects to a retrievable life philosophy that makes another, altogether virile and potent future imaginable. This is the past as the future.

Strange temporalities indeed. Yet, the world after catastrophe always calls for new conceptions of time, memory, and creation. Catastrophe does its cruelest work in disabling the past as a resource for the future, which, in turn, creates conditions of cultural dependency and persistent alienation for the colonized. For Négritude, the suppressed but never fully extinguished life philosophy of African "civilization"—which Césaire famously distinguished from "culture" at the 1956 Congress[23]—undermines conditions of spiritual death. Social death is delinked from Black life in this strange temporality. A liberatory temporality. The future need not despair.

Baldwin rejects this story of diaspora. Baldwin's review of the 1956 Congress contemplates the intersection of the familiar and the strange among the conference participants, noting varieties of shared experience, but much more underscoring points of difference. Notes of shared experience in "Princes and Powers" recall Baldwin's famous remark in "Many Thousands Gone" that Bigger Thomas lives in the skulls of all Black people. And yet there are key points of difference in the experience of blackness, especially concerning the relationship between pain, memory, and home. Whereas the pain of history compels Négritude toward another past, a past animated by an Africanized vitalism that saturates aesthetic sensibilities, Baldwin is moved to a different kind of reckoning with the past. Just as he had argued in "Everybody's Protest Novel," "Many Thousands Gone," and other essays that Wright misunderstands the formation of folkways and traditions out of the terror of antiblack racism, Baldwin, when he revisits the idea of land, home, and relation in the United States, wonders if in fact the Négritude writers, with their memory project of life philosophy and its essential blackness, are capable of thinking the experience of home *in* the Americas. Not home as a line of imaginative or land-reclamation flight. Home *in this place*.

To begin, Baldwin places Black people at the heart of the logic of home-making in the United States, rather than, as Fanon does, placing Black people outside the national and cultural rhetoric of colonial identity. Whereas for Fanon the Black subject is lost in the colonizer's world—disoriented by the weight of a total project of domination—Baldwin's negative dialectics of race establishes the dependency of white Americans on Black abjection. This exceeds Fanon's and Césaire's famous claim that the colonizer is also harmed by colonialism; Baldwin does not appeal to another humanism or an unfathomable future. Racial meaning is described, critiqued, and exited *inside* and *on the margins of* one and the same lifeworld. In its dialectical dependency and the swirl of abjection and violence, there is possibility and meaningful cultural formation. Sociogeny is not a total story of a totalizing project. This is something Fanon does not contemplate. In "Racism and Culture," his contribution to the 1956 Paris Congress, he dismisses pidgin, creole, jazz, blues, and other cultural aesthetics as nothing more than mirrors of an antiblack world. Baldwin's exit to the margins of the antiblack lifeworld narrates the Americas otherwise. "It was a society," Baldwin writes of the United States, "in which nothing was fixed and we had therefore been born to a greater number of possibilities, wretched as these possibilities seemed at the instant of our birth." Birth and possibility—this pairing shifts the meaning of exile and its descendants, infusing a sense of home into and against any notion of diasporic identity. Baldwin writes:

> The land of our forefathers' exile had been made, by that travail, our home. It may have been the popular impulse to keep us at the bottom of the perpetually shifting and bewildered populace; but we were, on the other hand, almost personally indispensable to each of

> them, simply because, without us, they could never have been certain, in such a confusion, where the bottom was; and nothing, in any case, could take away our title to the land which we, too, had purchased with our blood.[24]

There is much to be said about this remark, which is drawn out in detail in chapter 5 of this volume. But it is important to offer some treatment here. Baldwin does two interesting things in this passage. First, he invokes the very terms that provoke Fanon to reject history and its possibilities: *wretched* possibilities. Second, with the notion of land, coupled to the suffering and struggle named by *purchased*, Baldwin simply *asserts* home. There is no gesture toward an elsewhere or a fantasy of unconquered Africa. Wretched possibilities produce alienation, to be sure, but, in this interestingly transformed language of sin—the Americas are not pure, pain and rage are intertwined like goodness and fallenness, and the history of suffering purchases a *title* to the land.[25] Presence is not exile. Suffering is not homelessness. Rather, the indispensability of one to the other places Black subjectivity at the center of American identity, especially in the place of abjection. The question then remains: What would it mean to uproot and dismantle the structures that produce only wretched possibilities?

In "Racism and Culture," Fanon argues that antiblack racism is not merely an affective disorder but also a complete and total cultural phenomenon whose eradication demands address on all levels. The programmatic character of "Racism and Culture" means it can (or even ought to) be read as a prelude to the more systematic, detailed elaborations of problems of national culture, political renewal, and the new humanism in *The Wretched of the Earth*. What "Racism and Culture" does particularly well, however, is gather into concise form many of his earlier considerations of the relation between revolutionary action, affective disorders, and conceptions of belonging. But all of those considerations come back to the problem of time. Home never belongs to the present *or* the past for Fanon. There is only the future. The wretched possibilities and suffering under racist regimes and economies produce a disjointure of time. Fanon writes in the opening to *Black Skin, White Masks*:

> Every human problem cries out to be considered on the basis of time, the ideal being that the present always serves to build the future.
> And this future is not that of the cosmos, but very much the future of my century, my country, and my existence. In no way is it up to me to prepare for the world coming after me. I am resolutely a man of my time.
>
> And that is my reason for living. The future must be a construction supported by man in the present. This future edifice is linked to the present insofar as I consider the present something to be overtaken.[26]

The present is overtaken *by the future*, the victory of imagination of possibility over lived actuality. This interesting temporality is Fanon's novel contribution to the mid-century moment. The present offers so little, and yet the future must be thought on the basis of that present—the present as pure negation, rather than roots, titles to land, and the gift of home in wretched places. In this sense, *Black Skin, White Masks* is altogether programmatic, suggestive, and in beautiful ways the product of an existential daydreamer. The present is wished away in flights of critical theory fancy. The rhetorical bookends of *Black Skin, White Masks*—the introduction and the conclusion—read like prayers of exhortation, worry, and demand. *Vexation.* Fanon frets over the obstinacy of the inferiority complex. At the same time, he sees the emerging postcolonial moment as an opening inside the psyche, a break between the present and the imagination and thus the possibility of a resolute *no* spoken to the colonial condition in search of that *yes* Fanon says "resonates" from "cosmic harmonies."[27] A lovely daydream, to be sure, and it is that dreamy character of a liberated imagination that gives *Black Skin, White Masks* its life and vibrant revolutionary character.

To what end, then, is all of this dream and imagination? It is perhaps enough to say that Fanon wants the liberation of Black people or the colonized in general. That is the answer we get in *Wretched of the Earth*. What does liberation entail? *Wretched of the Earth* offers a systematic study of institutional structures, their limitations, and necessary political transformations, but even that book ends with a dreamy notion of humanism uncoupled from the history of colonialism that includes the fantasies about precolonial culture and social organization. Toward what does the new humanism point us? Anticipating the work of *The Wretched of the Earth*, Fanon closes the introduction to *Black Skin, White Masks* with an evocation of home: "As those of an Antillean, our observations and conclusions are valid only for the French Antilles—at least regarding the black man *on his home territory*. A study needs to be made to explain the differences between Antilleans and Africans. One day perhaps we shall conduct such a study. Perhaps it will no longer be necessary, in which case we can but have reason for applause."[28] We get that study just a few years later in Fanon's 1955 essay "West Indians and Africans," which contains its own reflections on home in terms of belonging, land, and the divergence of West Indian and African experiences of colonial domination. But in *Black Skin, White Masks* Fanon lays claim to a specific geography of experience. The *validity* of the observations and conclusions is rooted in connections and disconnections specific to the Black Martinican subject. Imagination of a Martinican home, perhaps. Dream and imagination form the counternarrative and produce the counteraffects to shame: ecstasy, the joy of time with a future, and all forms of pleasure in friendship and belonging. Fanon's rhetorical tone tells a lot of his story.

Home *territory*, however, is a complicated matter. Recall that Fanon rejects Négritude precisely in terms of its location of home; Fanon speaks for the

French Antillean only, the one who is both Antillean and French, and so not an African who is ultimately lost in the Antilles and France. We catch sight here of the crucial difference between the affect of shame in Fanon and the affect of mournful life in Négritude. We can here see the beginnings of Fanon's outright and uncomplicated rejection of nationalism in *Black Skin, White Masks*. The implication of the Antilles in France and France in the Antilles produces all of the anxieties and pathologies of the colonized. And yet Fanon, in a manner similar to Baldwin, will at times identify this paradoxical implication and reversible relation as home. Late in *Black Skin, White Masks*, Fanon writes, "What's all this about black people and a black nationality? I am French. I am interested in French culture, French civilization, and the French. We refuse to be treated as outsiders; we are well and truly part of French history and its drama. . . . I take a personal interest in the destiny of France, the French nation, and its values. What am I supposed to do with a black empire?"[29] This is a complicated passage. It comes near the close of the chapter on blackness and psychopathology, which details the vicissitudes of racial thinking. And in those multiple paths of race and strict racial identity, Fanon shows his rhetorical flexibility. The bleak and troubling account of blackness in a French context that begins the book—an account that diagnoses, then defends, Black subjectivity against the forceful imposition of French culture—gives way to an evocation of mutual entanglement. Fanon shifts registers because he sees the consequences of rendering Black subjectivity completely *other* in the colonial relation. There is no place for Black nationalism (what he here calls *a black empire*) in Fanon's work because, for all of its brutality and cruelty, French *is* the language of the French Antillean. The problem is rather with the absence of recognition in the colonial construction of language and diction. The final chapter of *Black Skin, White Masks* explores how the failed struggle for recognition signifies as loss precisely because the subjects in relation are already inextricably entangled. We might say that the French language is *home* for Fanon, even if that home is alienating. Home as homelessness that is home. This is the paradox of navigating place in an antiblack world.

If we press Fanon closer to Baldwin in this moment, then we begin to see the complexity of theorizing the notion of home in the Americas more broadly. The Americas tell a terrifying history and produce a world with no words or comfort for Black subjectivities. And yet Black people survive and create. Abjection has its limits, and resistance and refusal are as much a part of the story of the Americas as suffering and violence. When Fanon and Baldwin turn to the question of home, it is noteworthy that they hew it close to the affect of shame. The inferiority complex and the self-hatred it produces make home a precarious, complicated, even bloody affair, but it is nonetheless home. That connection to place, which is as much a connection through disconnection as anything else, is saturated with the sadness of memory and history in both the past and the present. But such a connection further motivates the question of the future: If this place is home, then what sort of revolutionary action is called for in the name of a liberation of a home that is already ours? To free our possession from the terms of possession.

Love and Humanism

The unimaginable price is for Baldwin a matter of encountering and reckoning with history. "How can the American Negro's past be used?" he asks. "The unprecedented price demanded—and at this embattled hour of the world's history—is the transcendence of color, or nations, and of altars."[30] Encountering history means sitting with the unimaginable price and its affective life. Reckoning with history means transforming our sense of relation in order to breathe. Fanon's early work struggles with the same question of transformation. The diagnostic sensibility of *Black Skin, White Masks* frames every question in stark terms that leave no real room for breath. The terms are so stark that one wonders how Fanon can account for his own subjectivity or the subjectivity of the revolutionary and the breathing of each. Fanon's Black subjects seem just that bound by his deep, ontological pessimism.

How does one speak or think outside abjection? How does one move in the world outside a kind of carnal social death? History is diagnosed as the impossible and ultimately unnecessary burden of a degraded and degrading past for the Black Americas. The heaviness of this inheritance makes breathing itself a desperate matter. How does one reckon with inheritance and so on? Fanon wants to avoid overly pathologizing Black people; no matter the neurotic conditions produced by colonialism and the anxieties of the emerging postcolonial moment, the Black subject is always capable of struggle, defiance, and critical self-assertion. Baldwin interrupts his own nihilism with signs of life, articulations of being, and ways of knowing that exceed the anxious pathologies of interracial life. How is that capacity possible?

The terms of critical self-assertion remain largely underdeveloped and present only in small, though important, gestures toward another future in Fanon's work. In many ways, this is his limitation as a thinker. The conclusion to *Black Skin, White Masks* raises significant issues concerning history and consciousness, arguing that the Black subject only becomes fully a subject when it eschews historical experience and *becomes*, perhaps for the first time, in possession of consciousness as *a question*. This is Fanon's wildly amazing speculative claim and poetic evocation. We are left with very little sense of how transformation is possible. Under what worldly, existential conditions is it possible for the Black subject to be at home in the world and at home with itself? How is bad faith transformed into an authentic subject? What sorts of cultural and political structures make another subject possible? What is blackness *after*—and so not just in the wake of—colonialism?

We get a detailed answer in *The Wretched of the Earth*, an answer that has become a centerpiece of so much postcolonial theory. Decolonization is the transformative process of moving the colonized toward the sorts of futures hinted at in the conclusion of *Black Skin, White Masks*: beginning again after history, the subject in question, imagining out from under the yoke of colonialism and its Manichean thinking. What *feeling* initiates decolonization? Again, affect is a keystone for understanding transformative work.

The Wretched of the Earth is structured around the affect of grievance. Grievance is in turn structured by memory. This is why key passages in *The Wretched of the Earth* carefully distinguish between the authentic, revolutionary grievance against colonialism and its lingering effects and the intra-African memory of the slave trade with all the companion theories of savagery, inferiority, and the shame of slavery.[31] Sub-Saharan African memory of the internal slave trade survives in the embittered, sometimes cruel, ethnoracial stereotypes of different regions of Africa, where the north is remembered as the greedy, brutal slave trading Arab and the sub-Saharan, Black African is remembered as barbaric and submissive. Fanon eschews this memory in favor of a memory that mobilizes African solidarity: the memory of European domination. The former memory fractures solidarity and divides the continent of Africa against itself. The latter memory remembers the decimation of colonialism no matter region, ethnicity, or color. In that distinction of memory, we see how the outrage of the past and the rage produced by the memory of foreign domination transform the presence of colonialism in everyday life and its psychological structures *away from* alienating ghosts and *toward* what they must be for revolutionary action: occasions for rage and grievance. Affect at this moment shifts Fanon's thinking away from the diagnostic of despair in analyses of shame and toward the mobilization of cultural and political violence in an alternative atmospheric mood of rage and grievance.

How, then, is grievance related to the ultimate aim of *Black Skin, White Masks* and *The Wretched of the Earth*, namely, the articulation and evocation of a new humanism? New humanism is Fanon's imagination of life after colonialism, an emergent sense of the human outside the Manichean logic of conquest and subjugation. Colonial logic splits the world in two. That logic further splits the postcolonial nation into a space of mimicked structures of difference (assimilation) and absolute opposition (anticolonial posturing and cultural formation, atavistic or otherwise). Memory of grievance identifies the source of that logic in two sites: the occupier's repressive presence and the ideological and psychological structure of the colonial system. The latter survives political and economic emancipation; the internal life of the colonized subject generates the affective cluster *shame* that works without the physical presence of white people. Grievance dismantles shame. It is revolutionary affect par excellence for Fanon, a counteraffect. And so grievance functions—or might function—as a force of decolonization. *New humanist memory against colonial memories*. As the precondition of a new humanism, grievance clears affective space of shame, making way for another kind of subjectivity to emerge that identifies, with the lucidity of revolutionary vision, the exact terms of historical transformation. The colonizer is named. In acts of violence, the colonizer is targeted for resistance and overcoming. In this moment, we catch sight of Fanon's final temporality: grievance transforms the colonial past and postcolonial future with a new and radicalized memory. This memory harnesses the present—Fanon's liberat*ing* present, rather than the alienated lifeworld of colonized consciousness—as a revolutionary psychological, epistemological, and ontological force. If we understand how Bigger Thomas lives inside the skull of every African American, perhaps then we can understand the shape and contour of reckoning with our history.

Grievance, then, accounts for revolutionary *motivation*. Motivation is a crucial term for any action whatsoever, but especially so in the exceptionally high stakes of revolutionary cultural, political, and self-transformation. If grievance motivates action, then grievance is charged with sustaining both the possibility and necessity of action. One is motivated when one sees a possible future—in this case, a Fanonian vision of subjectivity and intersubjectivity outside Manichean colonial logic and its grievances, a Baldwinian vision of another country. The desire for the possible future is further motivated by a sense that the past and its present is untenable, atrocious, and fundamentally morally outrageous. The revolutionary does not have time to wait. How could Faulkner be so white that he thinks we work according to *his* time? Thus, grievance manifests a strange and urgent ecstatic temporality, one marked by fracture and continuity at one and the same time. Grievance fractures time precisely because rage—that product of an authentically felt grievance, the Bigger in the skull—blocks the past from being folded into the future. Pain, trauma, and the long shadow of suffering provoke outrage and rejection. And yet grievance, which keeps its intimate companion affect rage alive, also keeps that long shadow alive by making a future out of a painful past and out of the still morally outrageous present.

The ecstasy of the revolutionary lies in this paradox.

It goes by the name "hope."

The lure, for Fanon, is a new humanism. Fanon imagines the world without colonial categories and its structures of thinking, an imaginary that someone like Paul Gilroy has taken to its logical conclusion in the repudiation of race and nationalist racial identities in theorizing a new politics of justice. In *Postcolonial Melancholia*, Gilroy shows us how this repudiation is utopian in the very best sense: an imagination that puts the world of the present out of sorts with itself. At the same time, this utopian shift underscores how the legacy of colonialism—Manichean thinking—saturates the body of revolutionary politics with a certain melancholia. Have we overcome or contested the cornerstone of our oppression? Juxtaposed to mourning in Freud's well-known definition, melancholia is the sadness and immobility of the psyche that results from the inability to locate the terms of psychic harm. One mourns when one names the object lost, then reassembles the self through various modes of working through loss, whether that be replacement, displacement, sublimation, or simple acceptance. Mourning *knows* the lost object. But melancholia suffers from what it cannot do, from what cannot be named. For Gilroy (and here he draws from Fanon's late work) categories of race and the Manichean structures they generate haunt revolutionary politics, and, so long as they go unnamed and operate as ghosts in the revolutionary machine, transformative politics are not really transformative at all. Or, put in the terms of *The Wretched of the Earth*, a new humanism is not possible without contesting the language of race as *identity* and *roots* (the language of Négritude) and transforming it into a provisional, strategic language of race as the basis for grievance, rage, and motivation for revolutionary action.

It is here that we see the limits in Fanon's affective schema. The new humanism is by definition contentless. We cannot imagine the future in any specific terms because it is *the future*. It is not yet here. *Avenir, à-venir*, to come, and not yet. All anticipations of what is to come are rooted in a not yet fully transformed past and present. Our vision of the future is therefore necessarily constrained by the relation between memory and imagination. I think that is the real strength of Fanon's notion of new humanism from its first evocation in *Black Skin, White Masks* to the final gestures in the conclusion to *The Wretched of the Earth*. Fanon understands what it means to think the future as future. Affect is not content. That is, affect is akin to the atmosphere in a room, which one can name and describe without knowing the precise social, cultural, and political structures that will issue from it or be formed by and manifest in it. One can describe the general affective structure of a piece of music—danceable, romantic, sexual, aggressive, sensual, and so on—without knowing what it will mean for the particularization of affects across a room when the DJ plays the song. A political song from the late 1960s Marvin Gaye might provoke fear and anxiety in a room of old conservative white people, sensuality and catharsis in a room of those who know what's up, solidarity and nostalgia for a certain generation, an eye roll or two from a young crowd that knows the song only from infomercials, or just indifference from those unmoved by American soul music. Still, one can say *something* about the song itself and how it sets an atmosphere; affect has atmospheric character, as well as particular renderings of that character in any particular embodied person. If one can *say* that something, then perhaps one can begin to unfold an imagined unfolding of human relations in that atmosphere. We might be able to imagine, however provisionally, the imagined future results of imagination. That is a lot of deferral. But that is also what it means to think futurity radically, without anchoring it in what the past has been and what the present is. What it means for the future to *transcend altars*.

This is where Baldwin's long meditation on love becomes significant and central to any account of revolutionary politics. Fanon's account of revolutionary affect limits imagination to the negative: We can only imagine how we get to the point of imagining the new politics of a postcolonial humanism. What does that postcolonial humanism *feel* like? What is the atmosphere of the intrahuman in the new humanism? The eroticism of Fanon's rage and grievance—the lure and seduction of being able to shed the pain of the past and present—needs the supplemental work of imagining feeling *after*. Baldwin simply calls this love. He concludes *The Fire Next Time* with a famous evocation:

> When I was very young, and was dealing with my buddies in those wine- and urine-stained hall-ways, something in me wondered, *What will happen to all that beauty?* For black people, though I am aware that some of us, black and white, do not know it yet, are very beautiful. . . . Vengeance, I wondered, when that vengeance was achieved, *What will happen to all that beauty then?* . . . If we—and now I mean the relatively conscious whites and the relatively conscious blacks, who must, like lovers, insist on, or create, the consciousness of the others—do not falter in our duty now, we may be able, handful that we are, to end the racial nightmare, and achieve our country, and change the history of the world.[32]

Love and beauty. All that beauty. Baldwin's memory of the cruel, violent hallway also gives him a vision, however fleeting and however traced out, of another future. It is a future in which beauty is sustained by love. Beauty does not make itself in the world. Love, which assures that affective relation is intersubjective rather than merely personal, *creates* consciousness in and in relation to other Black people. This consciousness is needed to root a new humanism in love after the nightmare. Another kind of intersubjectivity. One that is unimaginable in the present—we live in the nightmare—but one we must nevertheless *make ourselves imagine*. After so much violence, love is impossible. Or is it? If grievance is to give way to a new humanism, if the Manichean logic of colonialism and its melancholic effect on the present must die for the sake of another future, then the future must be imagined otherwise. Why not love?

In so many ways, love is the unimaginable after the unimaginable. Who could fathom Baldwin's notion here, that Black people and white people in the Americas could be *lovers*, with all the generosity and gratuitousness the word *love* suggests? Or what would it mean to imagine that centuries-long sedimented affects of shame and inferiority could give way to love of self, to love of memory, to love of a place that signified unspeakable pain for centuries? We can only imagine this sense of love if humanism means something different. That is, we can only imagine love as a postrevolutionary affect when humanism is *new.* A new humanism makes new forms of love possible, inverting and revolutionizing those affects that colonial racism and American antiblackness installed in psyche and institution precisely because love is not possible in what is and what has been. It is only possible *to come*. A future. Unprecedented.

What, then, are we to make of this weaving and unweaving relation between Fanon and Baldwin? In part, as we have seen, it is a question of thinking memory without atavism. Baldwin's distance from any variety of iterations of Black nationalism—whether the metaphysical account of spirit and civilization in Négritude or the at times crass politics of the Nation of Islam—changes the language of remembering and the conceptual schemes by which we might imagine a future. Fanon and Baldwin occupy the same conceptual space here: the new is what makes humanism possible for the future. From grievance to love, the colonial affect of shame becomes—or will become—a bad memory and sad, transcended remnant of history.

And yet, Fanon leaves Martinique for Algeria. What does that mean in this context, especially if we link affect, love, and home? Fanon's departure helps us see the differences between *Black Skin, White Mask* and *The Wretched of the Earth* with clarity. In leaving Martinique, Fanon moves from a diagnosis of the Martinican situation in the early work to the more general account of *the colonized as such*—a global notion—that structures the broad vision of the final reflections of *The Wretched of the Earth*. Baldwin, no matter his exilic travel routes, always remains located in the United States. Harlem begins and ends his intellectual work.

But we are readers, not just reporters. We *interpret* and in interpretation can make unconventional claims on a text, a thinker, and a movement. In that spirit, I wonder what it would mean to claim Fanon back *for* the Americas. Such a claim requires us to imagine Fanon without France and therefore simply as an American—simply *of* the Americas. In his reflections on home, Fanon repudiates any and all pretensions to a "Black empire" in the name of the contentless, dream-laden future of a new humanism. Baldwin reminds us that it is possible to dream a new humanism and to delink the imagination from the sort of total abjection of history we find in Fanon. Indeed, Baldwin reminds us that the imagination has never been fully bound by that abject history. Even the abject past has dimensionality. Baldwin's nuance on the affective transmission of history's pain reclaims more broadly the experience of the Black Americas while most importantly creating a space within which to think both the experience of antiblack racism and home. It is worth recalling here a remark Baldwin makes in "Encounter on the Seine," an early essay in which he takes account of important differences between African Americans and Africans—a remark that anticipates so many of the observations made by Fanon in "West Indians and Africans." Baldwin writes:

> The American Negro cannot explain to the African what surely seems in himself to be a want of manliness, of racial pride, a maudlin ability to forgive. It is difficult to make clear that he is not seeking to forfeit

> his birthright as a black man, but that, on the contrary, it is. Perhaps it now occurs to him that in this need to establish himself in relation to his past he is most American, that this depthless alienation from oneself and one's people is, in sum, the American experience.[33]

In Baldwin's address to the hypothetical African, he formulates becoming black and becoming subject—"struggling to recognize and make articulate"—in terms of the very structure of subjectivity itself. But this is an American subjectivity brought to a certain becoming because of the strangeness of its history, made all the more strange and unprecedented by the conditions of arrival and survival for Black Americans. Depthless alienation is at once the condition of Americanness as such *and* the particular struggle for Black Americans in a place that does not welcome or recognize and only makes abject and subjugates.

In this intersecting moment of Fanon and Baldwin—Fanon's diagnosis of the condition of the Americas is near exactly the same—the divergence that follows can be seen in the cluster of specific affects that gather to the site of alienation. Fanon and Baldwin cast history as a manifold of pain, suffering, subjugation, and transgenerational trauma, all of which set up in the psyche as the affective structure of the inferiority complex. Language, thought, and embodiment all bear the marks of this complex. Memory and history connect the psyche to the past. The interval toward the future, however, marks that alternative affective structure, one in which Fanon's wresting free of memory and history—his Sartreanism brought to affective Black subjectivity—makes hope possible and the imagination of another humanism inspires and motivates. Hope does not need content. Perhaps this relation and desire is more indebted to the pain of history than Fanon acknowledges. It is enough to imagine that this world will someday not be. Baldwin's interval works in a different relation to the pain of history. For Baldwin, the interval develops a counternarrative that resists the characterization of African American history as *total* abjection. African American humanity, Baldwin writes in "Everybody's Protest Novel," "is our burden, our life; we need not battle for it; we need only to do what is infinitely more difficult—that is, accept it."[34] In this moment, we can imagine Baldwin reading the Fanonian interval between past and future as a kind of theoretical protest novel, one that rejects life and, even in the most abject moments of history, denies "beauty, dread, [and] power."

If we read Fanon in that frame, then we can begin to see the stakes of reclaiming Fanon for the Americas and how that reclaiming would alter the register of his abjection of memory, history, and affect. The key element of this reclaiming is the problem of language. How is it possible to *speak* from a position of resistance and refusal? How is it possible to speak as a revolutionary? A radical, transformative theory of language and time, the words and temporality of the revolutionary, has to be able to account for this subjectivity. Recall that for Fanon, creole embodies all the affects of abjection and colonial exclusion. In speaking creole, the West Indian is an outsider in France and too ethnic in the Caribbean. While it is true that diction, the perfection of the *French* version of the French language, is no solution and only deepens alienation, it is noteworthy that Fanon never returns to creole as a mode of refusal or revolution. And yet creole is the language of the Americas. Creole is a vernacular that marks place, siting language *here*, in this space, with a marker that carries with it all that we want from a language: words for things, words for consciousness and its populations, and so words for the connection of self, world, and being. In a late essay on Black English, Baldwin makes this clear while also underscoring the risk such marginal, *wholly American* languages undertake:

> What joins all languages, and all men, is the necessity to confront life, in order, not inconceivably, to outwit death: The price for this is the acceptance, and achievement, of one's temporal identity. . . . It goes without saying, then, that language is also a political instrument, means, and proof of power. It is the most vivid and crucial key to identity: It reveals the private identity, and connects one with, or divorces one from, the larger, public, or communal identity.[35]

We will return to this passage below in real detail, but it is worth pausing here to see how closely Baldwin stays with what Fanon wrote in the opening pages of *Black Skin, White Masks*. Speaking a language is akin to taking on, then inhabiting, a world. However, what Fanon does not see is how the very language he assigns to abject history and the suffering present already opens up a whole world. To be sure, that world cannot be thought apart from the pain of the past—creole is a story of loss, even as it is a lexicon of the world[36]—yet it still gives all of the texture and meaning of the world *in this place, the Americas*. Decolonizing the affect of shame in this moment allows creole to emerge as world making in the afterlife of memory.

In the end, I wonder if this musing on affect, revolution, language, and place is simply a gesture toward and attempt at articulating the very space Fanon wanted to take us in the closing line to "Racism and Culture": life after the colonial relation—a life Baldwin documents in the interstices of interracial life rather than at the center of the world. In Fanon's work, that is the space of a subjectivity freed from the inferiority complex, which means, in the moment of twisting free, that all affects show up in new light. The body's sexuality becomes new, sadness and regret become new, mourning and hope become new—all of the newness Fanon anticipates is only anticipated because it is the future without a past. A future, perhaps, in which love is spoken in vernacular: a language in which it is already spoken, if not yet heard. A hearing to come.

What is this vernacular? What is language? How is the word already a sign of life in a space of social death? If affect is modified in this interval of time, memory, and its afterlives, then what does it mean to speak? It is here that Baldwin makes one of his most important contributions to the Black Atlantic tradition. Let us turn to that.

Chapter 4

Vernacular as Remnant and Life

Language is a critical part of the infrastructure of alienation, estrangement, and all of those other affects that gather to the psyche under an antiblack racist regime. This is a key insight between Frantz Fanon's work and James Baldwin's lifelong concern with the conditions of writing and the writerly self. We are all born into a language. This is part of our facticity. But the reception of that birthed subject is shaped by the racial politics of language and embodiment. The writer reckons with that reception and shape, both in terms of the politics of outrage and in terms of the cultural meaning of their own writing. "Writers are obliged," he writes, "to realize that they are involved in a language which they must change. And for a black writer in this country to be born into the English language is to realize that the assumptions on which the language operates are his enemy."[1] This remark is from a short essay "On Language, Race, and the Black Writer," written in 1979. In that year, Baldwin composed two important essays on what he calls "black English," bringing over two and a half decades of reflection on African American history and memory to bear on the question of language, identity, and cultural meaning. (I will keep "black" in lower case in order to stay consistent with Baldwin's own usage.) Baldwin understands that the question of language is no small matter and cannot in any way be reduced to style or mere aesthetics—although both are part of communicative practices and meaning making. But style and aesthetics cannot be the whole story. Speaking is not using an instrument. Rather, language makes, remakes, produces, and reproduces a world. Language is also a key site of ideological hegemony, where, as we saw in the previous chapter, questions of affect, world, home, and belonging are both negotiated (shifts in questions of "the proper" reflect largely white political cultural formation) and navigated (a sense of place but also resistance and refusal guide speakerly praxis). Language bears everything in it, with it, and through questions of diction, the proper, and so on we glimpse some of the essential structures of interracial, antiblack life. So, when the legitimacy of African American English is contested, a contestation that is common to the point of everyday ritual, an entire sense of knowing and being is at stake. Baldwin therefore takes on the question of language in urgent and provocative terms. What does it mean to speak? What is the relation of language to senses of home, belonging, dissent, and resistance? What does it mean to inhabit a language that has from the beginning been an instrument of the enemy, wielded in the service of oppression, but also transformed by and recalibrated for the oppressed? What can be said when the speaking and inhabitation of a transformed English is contested on racialized terms? In short, how do vernacular languages tell us a story about the traces of life inside a world of social death?

Both of Baldwin's essays from 1979 are angry, defensive, and, in many ways, improvised pieces of outrage and emphatic argumentation. And rightly so. "If Black English Isn't a Language, Then Tell Me, What Is?" and "Black English: A Dishonest Argument" both speak against the racial hegemony at work in the disparaging of vernacular speech—and, as we shall see, vernacular cultural forms more widely. That wider sense of vernacular cultural form will prove crucial in the following reflections. The origins of black English, which Baldwin identifies as memory of and witness to the auction block, link vernacular speech to familiar and complex stories of African-American culture and identity: the Spirituals, the central role of musicality in Black life, and forms of resistance, refusal, and saying yes to life that animate the *sounds* of identity formation.[2] If, as Baldwin puts it, the sound of the choir can tell the story of the auction block, and that story is further borne in and by vernacular speech, then wider questions of identity, place, and home intertwine with history and memory to form a sense of belonging even under conditions of radical persecution and terror.

In this moment, Baldwin in the mode of critic is brought back to many of the issues at play in and haunting the colonial world in post–World War II moments of liberation struggle. Anticolonial thought was from the beginning concerned with speech, writing, and racial authenticity. Like the well-known manifestos from Aimé Césaire, Léopold Senghor, and others in the postwar period, Baldwin's essays on African American vernacular, written two and a half decades after the Bandung and Paris conferences in which a number of *francophonie* manifestos were forged, read with the same sense of moral defense and uncompromising, if at times excessively demanding, love for Black people. Indeed, Baldwin's nonfiction always asks the most difficult questions about race and self, interrogating everything from rage to love, questioning the distinction between the two, and imagining in every instance how the history and memory of African American life is to be theorized, defended, and moved to the center of cultural identity formation. Baldwin's work on language is at the center of wide questions of race and self; he makes it clear in incisive, enraged rhetoric that the dismissal or denigration of African American speech is nothing other than white racism concerned with severing Black people, for a second time, from historical and memorial roots. An historical intervention in the present, as it were, repeating the same atrocity in another context. As with all roots and appeals to rootedness, *self-knowledge* is at stake. That occasion of rage, as with so many other occasions in Baldwin's nonfiction, is also a moment of deeper theoretical reflection on the nature of race, identity, memory, and history. And that reflection puts some distance between him and other mid-century Black Atlantic theorists, especially around questions of home. In that distance from his mid-century companion writers, Baldwin travels a path familiar to post-Fanon Caribbean thought and its revitalization of the question of creole language and creole identity.

In a particularly existentialist register, which is typical of even his earliest nonfiction, Baldwin's work on language evokes something very much like Martin Heidegger's famous turn of phrase "language is the house of Being."[3] This is of course not to say that Baldwin had anything like Heidegger's metaphysical or ontological system in mind when theorizing the relation of language to being. Rather, Baldwin's rhetorical intensity around the question of vernacular speech is located in a smaller and more localized, yet also just as enormous and transhistorical, problem: How is a sense of home, that sense of belonging and being in a place and culture, possible inside a multicentury history of unrepresentable violence? How does language, having paid this unimaginable price, remember what we might otherwise forget? We are always inside that history, even as the interior constraints of history are shown in Baldwin's fiction and nonfiction to be partial and fractured (Baldwin's protagonists are never in full possession of themselves, and his nonfiction is remarkable for its wandering, impressionistic, exploratory character). Constraints are fractured because vernacular speech and culture produce and reproduce a sense of home for African Americans that is simultaneously inside and outside violence. How, then, might we conceive vernacular speech and vernacular cultural forms as speaking *to*, *as*, and *from* sites of not just resistance, refusal, and survival, but also, in the mode of refusal, from sites of world making and being that sustain life in—and then after—the wreckage of History? That is, how could we see in Baldwin's work on language a theory of memory and history akin to what Paul Gilroy's *The Black Atlantic* famously named "countermodernity," an alternative story in which pain and pleasure, everydayness and sublimity, aggression and equanimity, and all of those vicissitudes of speaking life into being are *heard* and *felt* in so-called black English?

Part of the story of Baldwin's account of vernacular speech and how it speaks life into being, against social death and in the horizon of the Auction Block, draws on a key cluster of concepts in the African American intellectual tradition: sound, memory, and the Spirituals. I want to begin here by marking and outlining two signature moments from that tradition in Frederick Douglass and W. E. B. Du Bois in order to deepen the historical resonance of Baldwin's claims. His claims do not come from nowhere. Baldwin's thinking is innovative in that peculiar interval produced by an engaged repetition of the past that wants, in repetition, to say something new. One can recall, for example, how the biblical evocation of "the fire next time" becomes, across a critique of religion and religiosity, a way of linking the persistence of rage to a vision of love that is at once radically secular in its politics *and* preacherly spiritual in its prophecy and existential meaning.[4] Repetition, interval, the new. A similar story is told in Baldwin's theorizing vernacular speech and cultural forms. In that theorizing, Baldwin draws on the irreducibly conflicted relationship between whiteness as standard and black English as a counterspeech, but, as is typical of his unexpected reversals of thinking, such conflict leads Baldwin not to a sense of alienation, but instead to the "paradox: blacks, Indians, Chicanos, Asians, and that beleaguered handful of white people who understand their *history are the only people who know who they are*."[5] To understand African American history is to understand the sound of tradition, something that begins in the past and, in its haunting of the present, animates the realities and possibilities of Black life. And so we begin with what must be repeated in order to return to an account of self-knowledge.

Memory Sound

The auction block become Auction Block. This shift from historical-memorial event and atrocity to critical concept organizes so much in Baldwin's work and companion pieces of the African American intellectual tradition. *Tradition.* This last word goes by many other names and is linked to its own origin point. The Sorrow Songs and the Spirituals as origin. World making, spiritual products, race genius, community bond, ethnic meaning as tradition. Alain Locke theorized exactly this in his broad and expansive theorization of the New Negro. "The Spirituals," Locke writes, "are really the most characteristic product of the race genius as yet in America. But the very elements which make them uniquely expressive of the Negro make them at the same time deeply representative of the soil that produced them. Thus, as unique spiritual products of American life, they become nationally as well as racially characteristic."[6] There is so much about Baldwin's conception of language in Locke's words, in terms of both its link to sound and link to African American memory carried through sound. But most of what we know about his theorization of language is built in Baldwin's own words. Indeed, one of the quirky features of Baldwin's nonfiction is how it rarely cites sources or names influences in any significant way. Most of that is because he wrote in popular venues, where citation practices and expectations are just different than in scholarly writing. And it makes things difficult when we begin to draw a portrait of his readerly background and context. Perhaps we fabricate a bit. Perhaps we identify phrases here and there that lend insight into what is on Baldwin's mind as he writes. For me, what is most insightful and productive is situating him inside a sense of *tradition*. Baldwin's sense of tradition is exactly like the tradition of which he is a part. It draws from music, painting, poetry, everyday speech, witnessing to history, recollection of community memory, and characterization of the uniqueness of African American historical experience. I am reading for absences, yes; as we have seen in chapter 2 above, Baldwin writes about Africa under erasure and that act reveals its own insights. But I am also reading for resonance and membership in tradition. This is a question of *style* and *sensibility*. Baldwin looks to sound in all of its forms, and sound functions as a medium of intellectual work unlike any other. This is what draws Baldwin to think through the Spirituals and the conditions that made them possible.

The function of the Spirituals in the African American intellectual tradition is familiar and has a long history of elaboration, with particularly important moments in the cultural history work of W. E. B. Du Bois and Alain Locke. For both, the Spirituals are the foundation of the tradition. Emerging from sites of mourning, resistance, and pleasure, the Spirituals make thinking possible under conditions of impossibility and thus begin the African American tradition from a rooted, complex space of being and becoming. The sound and content of the songs reckon with and, in their performance, conjure the common grounds of African American historical experience. In that way, the Spirituals root the tradition without an appeal to ancestral land, but instead with memory work in relation to place, setting up a sense of home even in a nation and on a land that has never wanted Black presence beyond the atrocity of slavery and its aftermath. And yet, for all their grounding work for the tradition, it must be said that the Spirituals are altogether enigmatic, complex, and, while the origin of tradition, elliptical in their own speaking to origins. The content of the Spirituals is composed of both lyric and sound. The distinction between those two forms of expression is thin at best and probably best expressed as inextricably bound and interdependent.

The Spirituals also play an important role in Baldwin's conception of language. Black English is for Baldwin a composite of history and being brought to diction, syntax, sound, and expressive life. Black English reckons with racial history in vernacular form—it is a sound with history and memory inside it—and is an expression of having-come-to-self-knowledge. The Spirituals and black English transmit nonalienated forms of life across generations, hewing the present and future close to the past without the affective disabling of Black subjectivity. In this way, Baldwin's turn to language shows us the limits of the hegemony of shame and its related affects. The sound of speaking already tells an alternative story, a story embedded in histories of refusal and world making. Baldwin's elaboration of the origins of black English in slavery and its aftermath—survival and protection—shows the interconnection between history as cruelty and language as identity formation, but always without casting that language and identity formation as pathological. Rather, the insistence on the "sheer intelligence" of Black vernacular language, a phrase he borrows in the black English essay from Toni Morrison, underscores the seriousness of vernacular expression both for the meaning of existence—the world-making force of language—and for cultural formation in the Americas generally and the United States in particular. It is an example of what in the Caribbean context Kamau Brathwaite called "syllabic intelligence."[7]

Let me take two examples in order to prepare the ground for understanding Baldwin's appropriation of the Spirituals and conceiving black English as the vernacular of world making. Consider, for example, how the sound of slaves singing impacted Frederick Douglass. Amidst the sharp rhetoric and horrifying stories of plantation violence in the opening two chapters, Douglass's *Narrative of the Life of Frederick Douglass* is interrupted by a strange and compelling pause in the second chapter. The second half of the second chapter interrupts his depiction of enslaved life with haunting descriptions of slave songs heard across a plantation field. The dramatic context of this interruption is remarkable; the entire tone of *Narrative* changes, just for a few pages, shifting from the righteous outrage of depictions of slave owner violence to a sense of wonder and melancholy at the sound of slave songs sung in the field. Douglass recounts how slaves returning from work so profoundly manifest experience in sound. He writes:

> While on their way, they would make the dense old woods, for miles around, reverberate with their wild songs, revealing at once the highest joy and the deepest sadness. They would compose and sing as they went along, consulting neither time nor tune. The thought that came up, came out—*if not in the word, in the sound*;—and as frequently in the one as in the other. They would sometimes sing the most pathetic sentiment in the most rapturous tone, and the most rapturous sentiment in the most pathetic tone.[8]

The chapter and a half before this and the paragraphs, then pages, that follow through the remainder of the text are noteworthy for their adherence to linearity and clear lessons. He writes with purpose and with a transformative moral lesson in view. Douglass's suffering at each point of the autobiography deepens the pain of slavery; each moment of witness gives depth to rage and despair. *Narrative* leaves no doubt that it is an abolitionist text concerned with communication of the particular violence of plantation life and articulation of the conditions of liberation through violent resistance. The confrontation with Covey, which shifts the arc of the story from suffering toward an emerging freedom, is followed by glimpses of light and increasingly open horizons, all of which culminate in Douglass's freedom from both the literal bonds of slavery and the decimation of subjectivity made through its violence. The singing of the slaves, however, changes everything in terms of his tone and orientation. This passage, like the sound, is unlike anything else in *Narrative*. Space and time break away from the text's linear model, and the aesthetic sensibility of the song and singer is confounded and confounding.

The mixture of sadness and joy, heard in all of its paradoxical power, leaves him confused, curious, and transformed. Douglass is moved by the song, especially the *sound*, but cannot, for once, make sense of what he sees and hears. This is a singular moment in the text. That is, for all the astonishment in Douglass's prose about slavery's violence, for all the clear moralism and outrage one expects from an abolitionist text, the songs of the slaves open up, if only for a passing moment, a massively different horizon in *Narrative*. He instrumentalizes the songs in a brief remark, noting, "I have sometimes thought that the mere hearing of those songs would do more to impress some minds with the horrible character of slavery, than the reading of whole volumes of philosophy on the subject could do."[9] But his instrumentalization is an interruption of a longer pause in the swirl of pain, suffering, and hope the songs bring to word and sound.

What are we to make of this moment? To be sure, unlike the first witnessing of slave master violence—the beating of his aunt, which initiates him into slave subjectivity—or the fight with Covey—the moment of psychic liberation—the songs of the slaves confound Douglass's own vision of himself and the cruel institution of slavery. The slaves sing without didacticism; there is no lesson to be drawn from the words or the communicative action of collective singing. In fact, the slaves sing from and to a lessonless place. Unmediated witness. Unmediated testimony. Unmediated voice. Without a didactic moment, Douglass is left with only the impossible mixture of despair and hope, pathos and rapture, sadness and joy. Even the sound itself does not make sense; Douglass describes the music as disobedient to time and tune, even though the strangeness of the sound does not inhibit or limit the *power* of sound. Indeed, the distortion of rules and the abdication of moral lesson and instruction can be said to imbue the songs with their own special power—a *philosophical* power that transcends the (rightly) uncomplicated moral arc of *Narrative*. The transcendence of the moral arc thereby opens up another dimension of slavery—a noninstrumentalizable dimension, to be sure—that is otherwise absent from Douglass's account of the plantation. And, further, this brings into view how *Narrative* largely eschews the melancholy of slavery, the meaning of the sound of the slaves' song, in favor of the outrage and wound of violence. What that violence leaves behind, the memory of pain and unredeemed suffering, does not appear in the text except in the slave songs overheard in the field. Douglass's lack of clear vision and description when recounting the songs, his absorption in the strange spectacle of it all, is, in its own way, an authentic mode of describing the melancholic site. Douglass's words break off. In that break, something important is said and heard and registered. Melancholia can only *interrupt* a didactic narrative. And so, in a compelling twist, the slave songs interrupt Douglass's autobiography with the very theme of *Narrative* itself: the memory of slavery's pain and suffering. The text against itself, but also the text in perfect harmony with itself. Without lesson and without resolution, the songs stall

Douglass's dialectic of liberation and posit what is for *Narrative* the text's outside and its unassimilable enigma.

In the closing chapter to *The Souls of Black Folk*, Du Bois echoes Douglass's encounter with the peculiarity and intractability of memory in the Sorrow Songs. Like Douglass, Du Bois's account of hearing memory music, of his discerning the *sorrow* in the Sorrow Songs, is animated by a kind of wonder. It is a wonder that draws the listener in, to be sure. That is the character of wonder-as-affect. But it is also a wonder that marks a difference between the memory carried by the song and the capacity of the listener to comprehend the meaning of that memory. In other words, it is a wonder begun in the trauma of slavery. Sorrow is unassimilable to the narrative of uplift that threads the various chapters of *Souls of Black Folk* together. And yet that wonder, that memory whose pain draws the reader and listener back from the looping story of freedom, is inseparable from the meaning of the *place* in which the Sorrow Songs were gestated, then born. Du Bois writes:

> The Music of Negro religion is that plaintive rhythmic melody, with its touching minor cadences, which, despite caricature and defilement, still remains the most original and beautiful expression of human life and longing yet born on American soil. Sprung from the African forests, where its counterpart can still be heard, it was adapted, changed, and intensified by the tragic soul-life of the slave, until, under the stress of law and whip, it became the one true expression of a people's sorrow, despair, and hope.[10]

Thus, Du Bois claims, and this is no small intervention in the question of home and place, that the *Americanness* of the Sorrow Songs comes from their embeddedness in a *particular* history and memory. The songs make place and home through the soul-life of the slave—a kind of founding ghost, perhaps, and certainly a kind of identity forged in and out of shared historical memory. They begin as the Americas begin: pain, suffering, exile without promise of return, and the endless trials of what Du Bois called the color line, the veil, and double consciousness. The Sorrow Songs are a gift, but not one that edifies or even makes sense. Indeed, part of Du Bois's commentary on the songs in chapters 10 and 14 of *Souls of Black Folk* consists of his astonishment at the *sound* of the music, a sound we can identify with memory and its unfathomable character. Du Bois's reflections on the Sorrow Songs always come back to this astonishment and wonder and how sound makes memory's ineffable character present in sound, even as the sound of suffering's memorial asks us (or induces the question in us), What do the songs mean? How has sound become so melancholy, yet crucial for the meaning of present and future? Begun in slavery, the melancholic sound is the sound of the other founding father, the "father" who passes along sadness and hope at one and the same time. In that sense, Du Bois argues, the slave experience is *in* the song. Du Bois writes, "What are these songs, and what do they mean? . . . I know that these songs are the articulate message of the slave to the world. . . . They are the music of unhappy people, of the children of disappointment; they tell of death and suffering and unvoiced longing toward a truer world, of misty wanderings and hidden ways."[11] The temporality of this passage is key. All of the affects and conditions of subjectivity described in this and other passages on the Sorrow Songs trail off into the past. In that sense, the song is a *clue*. The song directs the listener to the trail of the past, draws the one who hears the message and memorial into the moment, but then withdraws into the sorrowful memory it bears. Memory is elliptical. We are never brought to the experience of slavery itself, but only the melancholy of its wake.

The crucial element of the Sorrow Song as memory song is sound. And it is sound that provokes Du Bois's deepest anxiety about the future of memory. Sound in *Souls of Black Folk* is linked to authenticity in ways that are inseparable from the capacity of the song to carry memory of pain, suffering, longing, and hope; the Sorrow Songs are the slave's message to the world, and that message is made ever more precarious with the passage of time. Du Bois constantly reminds us of the threat of caricature, defilement, and imitation. If the songs lose the *purity of sound*, the songs lose the sanctity of memory. Authenticity is therefore not solely a question of performance and the aesthetics of reception (although it is certainly that) but also, and perhaps first, a question of preservation of founding wounds and their strange gift of life to the future. Du Bois writes, "Since their day they have been imitated—sometimes well, by the singers of Hampton and Atlanta, sometimes ill, by straggling quartettes. Caricature has sought again to spoil the quaint beauty of the music, and has filled the air with many debased melodies which vulgar ears scarce know from the real. *But the true Negro folk-song still lives in the hearts of those who have heard them truly sung and in the hearts of the Negro people.*"[12] Every iteration of the Sorrow Songs traffics in imitation. This is the nature of iteration and of performance. The critical issue is how imitation is able to summon and evoke the ghostly past. That is, Du Bois's question is how can we discern the *haunted aesthetic* of the Hampton and Atlanta University singers and, in that discernment, understand both the potential of authentic performance to call forth memory and the potential of caricature to pervert memory, identity, and the sanctity of both. Du Bois therefore marks an important distinction here between authenticity and mass-produced, mass-consumable musical expression. Caricature appeals to vulgar ears. But the authenticity of the Sorrow Songs is ensured in part by the performance and in the main by the listener: the Negro people. This is a key moment in *Souls of Black Folk*, for it tells the story of memory, history, and sound without naivete about the modern world. Mass production and mass consumption transform the aesthetic character of any given object—the *mass* of mass consumption requires the leveling of cultural production. Du Bois worries about the future of memory in this moment, and yet that concern is eased through an appeal to his notion of race and racial identity. The common spiritual striving of Black people, which ranges in his early work from essentialist claims about blood to the promise of shared history and culture, ensures that the song will be *heard* and that the *sound* will carry somewhere. Transmission of pain and memory, then, has a future, even as caricature and vulgar ears remind us that every cultural production is exposed to mass production and its perversions.

What are we to make of Douglass's and Du Bois's encounter with the music of slavery? For both, it is a moment of profound disturbance. The songs in both *Narrative* and *Souls* interrupt stories of resistance and liberation with memory and trauma and its ghosts. This disturbance then evokes a kind of devotion—for Douglass, the memory of the moment stands as a sacred space of pain that exceeds the abolitionist program of the text, and for Du Bois it situates Black subjectivity in the strange, haunting interval between the painful past and the future of the color line. Douglass and Du Bois tell compassionate ghost stories: concerned about the ghost, worried that the ghost will wander rather than be summoned and loved, but also wary of any attempt to inscribe the ghost into logics of comprehension and description. The songs come *to* Douglass and Du Bois, and their appearance in the text is always marked by a kind of astonishment at the ineffability, yet affective communicability, of what is brought to presence in sound. In that sense, we can call the presence of the Sorrow Songs in both texts moments of the sublime. The sublime has a specific history in white Western philosophy, to be sure, and it is often used to mark the limits of the intellect. God, nature, infinity, perhaps even the soul—those moments of the sublime that underscore human finitude in noting, through the boldness of the examples, the limits of knowledge. The excess of pain and memory in the Sorrow Songs, however, does not dazzle or astonish in that same manner. Rather, as Douglass and Du Bois both argue, the intensity of the slave experience astonishes with the unthinkable and unsayable of centuries of cruelty and suffering without pause. That is, rather than astonishing us with the power of what exceeds human finitude and thinking as a kind of exaltation, the sublimity of the Sorrow Song evacuates the world of meaning and redemption, leaving the sadness of memory of suffering in sound and word. And yet that evacuation is itself the condition of being and another kind of future. A strange double, yes, but such doubling is sustained by the sublime's power to disrupt and reorient according to its own logic. Human finitude is marked, underscored, and moved to the center of the world in order to make another order possible or thinkable, even in its unthinkability. The irrevocable paradox of the Sorrow Songs—the sadness that is joyful, the hope that is impossible—makes the Americas possible. Memory of possibility is sound itself. Sublimity marks the intensity of the founding of vernacularity, the unspeakable and unimaginable made into speech and form and thought. *Language.*

Let me now shift to Baldwin's intervention. Baldwin's conception of language draws precisely on this location of memory inside sound, writing Douglass's and Du Bois's accounts of sound into the medium of vernacular expression. In the short essay "Of the Sorrow Songs: The Cross of Redemption," Baldwin evokes the spirit of Douglass, Du Bois, and Locke while adding important depth to his understanding of language. He recalls and claims the genealogy of black English, forged on the Auction Block (functioning as a critical concept and ghost in sound), and then links language to musicality and music's ability to transform the meaning of time. It is this temporal transformation that means everything. If time can mean something other than the transmission of abjection and pathology—something against which Frantz Fanon struggled mightily—then perhaps memory of the past, borne as it is by vernacular language and expressive culture, is a ghost that can be welcomed rather than fled, a friend rather than an enemy of the future. It is worth quoting this passage again in full, which was given some treatment in a different context above in my opening chapter but returns here with new significance. In "Of the Sorrow Songs," Baldwin writes:

> It is out of this, and much more than this, that black American music springs. This music begins on the auction block.
>
> Now, whoever is unable to face this—the auction block; whoever cannot see that that auction block is the demolition, by Europe, of all human standards: a demolition accomplished, furthermore, at that hour of the world's history, in the name of "civilization"; whoever pretends that the slave mother does not weep, until this hour, for her slaughtered son, that the son does not weep for his slaughtered father; or whoever pretends that the white father did not, literally, and knowing what he was doing, hand, and burn, and castrate, his black son—whoever cannot face this can never pay the price for the "beat" which is key to music, and the key to life.
>
> Music is our witness, and our ally. The "beat" is the confession which recognizes, changes, and conquers time.
>
> Then, history becomes a garment we can wear, and share, and not a cloak in which to hide; and time becomes a friend.[13]

Musicality is critical for both functions of vernacular. In turning to the particularity of the Spirituals for theorizing musicality, sound, and culture, Baldwin marks his approach to language as distinctively African American, gaining a good bit of distance from visions of African diasporic unity and generalized racial identity. That is, as we will see later, the conquest of time, which makes time a *friend*, and speaks to the particularly of an African American ghost as carried by the sound and form of speaking and expression. While one could argue that this relation to a ghost in sound is characteristic of orality in multiple traditions across the Black Americas, Baldwin's claim is not concerned with a shared morphology or "aural syntax," as it were, but instead with how the specifically African American experience of the Auction Block, folded into the Black church and the Spirituals, founds an expressive medium that marks *this place* with *this memory* and *this culture*. With that specificity, Baldwin is able to articulate a kind of counternationalism—a sense of home, really—that works against the pan-African current of the time in Black Atlantic theory as well as, more locally for Baldwin, against the cultural nationalism of the Nation of Islam and related movements. Fanon's claim that to speak a language means inhabiting a whole world then returns to Baldwin and is retooled with an affirmation of—rather than distance from—vernacular cultural forms. This affirmation, which makes for an intense defense and elaboration of black English in all its aspects, sees the truth in Fanon's claim that language has a history and that such history determines how identity is made (or unmade) in acts of expression (personal, interpersonal, and cultural), and yet, because Baldwin does not see abjection in the history carried by vernacular forms, Fanon's insight is upended and works as a *productive* account of Black culture and not just critique and testimony to alienation. The Spirituals are history and memory in sound and word. That specific history and memory makes a certain language. And that language makes a certain sense of home, not only "no matter or despite the brutality and pain," but also because "sheer intelligence" emerges from brutality and pain. This is the ghost in language that for Baldwin makes saying yes to life possible, necessary, and joyful.

Vernacular Sounds

In "Letter on Humanism," a letter written to French theorist Jean Beaufret in response to the claim that his book *Being and Time* did not contain an ethics, Heidegger famously remarks that "language is the house of Being."[14] This is a signature moment in Heidegger's work, one that (roughly) shifts his work from the relationship between subjectivity and ontology to the more searching, and certainly more peculiar, question of the intertwining of language, truth, and Being. This is without a doubt a very mid-century *European* problem. But Heidegger also underscores something very important that travels with important insight across national and racial geographies: Language and what it means to be are inextricably linked.

For Heidegger, the question of language and Being begins a long story about the special relationship between German and ancient Greek, the special character of the Greek language and its ability to reveal certain things about the world, the special capacity of German to reactivate so much of that specialness of ancient Greek, and so also a long story about the special depth of German nationalism. A philosophical nationalism, of course, but nationalism nonetheless. So much specialness. So very German. If we despecify Heidegger's remark for a moment—bracketing the particularities of his own work on language and Being—then we can also catch sight of a crucial insight that also lies at the heart of the Black Atlantic with a decisive colonial twist: Being is inconceivable outside of how speaking, writing, and expression manifest. The question of *how* is pointed and crucial. Inside the question of the capacity of language to be tweaked, transformed, or wholly overturned lies the question of the possibility of liberation. The violent effort and effect of colonialism is to simultaneously maintain the link for the colonizer between language and home in order delink, in the production of alienation at the level of the psyche, of knowing and being, colonized subjects from language and therefore from any sense of home. Language and liberation share an intimate space in this moment, to the point of absolute inseparability.

This is the question that drove so much of the Négritude movement and its obsessive rewriting of the French language in Césaire's and Senghor's poetry. Rewriting as the question of another kind or mode of being in language. This is the existential moment for Négritude poets, reshaping Heidegger's insight for the sake of liberatory vision. The meaning of existence and the task of liberation from the alienating effects of colonization is a cultural project, one that turns on a transformation of the colonizer's language. Making French *Black* liberates Black colonial subjects. Fanon, for all of his criticisms of the Négritude movement and sensibility, underscores this same claim in his own particular existentialist context in *Black Skin, White Masks*. That context prompts Fanon to make two key remarks on language. First, in the opening page of the opening chapter, "To speak means being able to use a certain syntax and possessing the morphology of such and such a language, but it means above all assuming a culture and bearing the weight of a civilization."[15] And then, further in that same chapter, "To speak a language is to appropriate its world and culture. The Antillean who wants to be white will succeed, since he will have adopted the cultural tool of language."[16] Language carries culture and civilization—a *world*—in word and syntax. The world carried is antiblack. The house of Being in Heidegger becomes, in the Black Atlantic context, the house of the colonization of the human, of being, and therefore of Being. To speak is to be inscribed in a language whose history and roots set the terms of alienation or home. Antiblack racism, for Fanon and so many other mid-century Black Atlantic theorists, makes the very act of speaking a moment of subjugation and absolute loss. Immanent nihilism and pessimism. For all of the differences between them, the early Fanon and Négritude thinkers share this fundamental claim about language and alienation from the very possibility of being: Roots are set in what cannot be home for the colonized, which in turn makes a home for the colonizer in the language of subjugating. Everyone is implicated in the act of speaking the language of subjugation.

For all of his attempts to differentiate himself and African American cultural life from mid-century diasporic thought, especially in "Princes and

Powers," Baldwin nevertheless makes a similar sort of claim when he begins a defense of black English. Alienation in language is a sort of horizontal solidarity in the Black Atlantic world, a shared beleaguerment in language that does not require any essentialist claims about race and identity. Something important about being Black in an interracial world is displayed in the cultural politics of speaking and the generation of words for things, self, and world. Something about how the hegemony of the white gaze is manifest, as a ghost of subjugation, in notions of the proper. But it is also important to see how the vernacular speaker manifests otherwise by evoking histories of refusal in marking distance from properness and its claims about diction. *This* speaker is also revealed in language. Being otherwise is housed in language. Baldwin writes in "If Black English Isn't a Language, Then Tell Me, What Is?" that "language, incontestably, reveals the speaker. Language, also, far more dubiously, is meant to define the other—and, in this case, the other is refusing to be defined by a language that has never been able to recognize him."[17] This passage recalls Fanon's long reflection on the problem of diction in *Black Skin, White Masks*, a reflection that circles around the terrifying claim that the destiny of the Black person is to be white, confronting the impossibility of the actualization of blackness in standard, proper French. Fanon never quite responds to this dilemma in terms of a liberatory vision of language. Pidgin and creole, the two vernacular moments in the Caribbean context, are derided by Fanon as degrading racialized performances for white people. This is a serious issue in his thinking and the lack of resolution of it is an Achilles' heel of sorts for his work. It is true that *Black Skin, White Masks* opens with qualified praise for Césaire's "Notebook of a Return to the Native Land," but Fanon never quite affirms or articulates an approach to language as liberation strategy. Instead, Fanon leaves his work on language in the between space of pessimistic diagnosis and the optimism of a new humanism.

This impasse is no small matter given the role of language as the house of the being in a Black Atlantic sense. Baldwin's advance on Fanon, and I do think it is a profoundly important one, is to see in the evolution of vernacular(s) resistance to alienation and the construction of a medium in which the oppressed can see and know themselves. If language is how we inhabit a world, then what would it mean for vernacular expression to be a whole world unto itself and to perhaps be a home? Baldwin writes, "People evolve a language in order to describe and thus control their circumstances or in order to not be submerged by a situation that they cannot articulate. (And if they cannot articulate it, they are submerged.)"[18] Without language, being is submersion—an interesting twist on the Afropessimist thesis that *being* is antiblackness and that Black (Being itself, blackness itself) or black (expression of a being) is the companion antipiece of a metaphysical *nothing*.[19] In this case, submersion drowns being in the wave of antiblack racism, wherein whiteness occupies Black being from the inside and outside—the effect of standardized word, syntax, and diction documented in Fanon's early work.

But as Baldwin notes, language evolves in order to resist this submersion. Black vernacular—the pidgin and creole Fanon so casually derides—*articulates*. It articulates survival, yes, but it also articulates what comes after survival: the formation of identity and culture. Thriving. Making. Imagining. Joy. Mourning. Play. Intellection. Melancholia. Rage. Pleasure. What does this evolution look like? A long passage from "If Black English Isn't a Language, Then Tell Me, What Is?" is worth quoting in full:

> Black English is the creation of the black diaspora. Blacks came to the United States chained to each other, but from different tribes. Neither could speak the other's language. If two black people, at that bitter hour of the world's history, had been able to speak to each other, the institution of chattel slavery could never have lasted as long as it did. Subsequently, the slave was given, under the eye, and the gun of his master, Congo Square, and the Bible—or, in other words, and under those conditions, the slave began the formation of the black church, and it is within this unprecedented tabernacle that black English began to be formed. This was not, merely, as in the European example, the adoption of a foreign tongue, but an alchemy that transformed ancient elements into a new language: *A language comes into existence by means of brutal necessity, and the rules of language are dictated by what the language must convey.*[20]

This passage raises a number of questions, including the relationship between sound, memory, and the Spirituals—something that as we have already seen links Baldwin's work on language to the foundations of the African American intellectual tradition. Let me postpone that matter for a moment and first pose the existential question raised by Baldwin here. Being itself is made possible in the moment of brutal necessity. This is a necessity that *is* and is *made possible* by the refusal of nothingness and the abyss of submersion. The moment of brutal necessity is terrifying and repeated for two and a half centuries, so the question of vernacular raises the very real problem of the relationship between painful origin and the culture that is made out of that origin. For Fanon, the painful origin is too much and becomes a ghost that drags down the present with the terrifying past; survival, for him, meant producing relationships to language—pidgin and creole, then folded over into cultural forms like blues, jazz, and spirituals—that repeatedly degraded rather than liberated Black people in every utterance. But Baldwin, borrowing Morrison's turn of phrase, instead calls vernacular language a whole world (and not a "dialect," which would subordinate black English to white English) that is marked by "this sheer intelligence." An *intelligence*—that is, a way of thinking, expressing, and making a world. Or making a series of worlds, diverse from the beginning, in the world of black English and the various histories and memories of which its varieties are composed. To inhabit the word, syntax, and sound of *this* English—or *these* Englishes, Frenches, all the other European languages and the creolized versions of them—is to be more than Fanon's alienated subject. It is to be outside the zone of nonbeing, the nothing, that the white gaze and its hegemony wants to make out of and against Black life.

The cultural question raised by the Négritude movement takes on an interesting twist here. Whereas for Césaire and Senghor culture signified a world to come and was thus a question of the future as such, for Baldwin it is a question of simply theorizing what is already there, not as the remainder, but as the fully realized production out of history and memory. That is, Baldwin takes the vernacular example on its own terms, neither projecting it into a distant future nor framing it with the abjection of Black diasporic history. This is absolutely crucial. It pushes back against so much of Black Atlantic theory in the middle of the twentieth century, which turned on an interpretation of the past as abject and which, in turn, rendered the cultural inheritance of that past abject as well. Fanon's remark that blues and jazz were produced for the pleasure of the white gaze—"offered up for the admiration of the oppressors"[21]—and not out of a sense of resistance, refusal, survival, or pleasure, neatly embodies this abjection of history. Baldwin's turn to the vernacular as such, his encounter with and appreciation of black English on its own terms as expressive of a sense of *home* outside the hegemony of white America's sense of belonging locates the crucial concept of creation in the past and documents its presence in the present. *Pace* Négritude, then, the colonizing language—the language of atrocity and alienation—does not stand in need of change because *it has already been changed*. In that having been changed, there is a sense of a house of Blackness, so to speak, as knowing and being. A whole world, not *to someday inhabit* but that is *already inhabited*. So, in "Black English: A Dishonest Argument," Baldwin writes plainly, "The black American *has* no antecedent. *We*, in this country, *on* this continent, in the most despairing terms, created an identity which had never been seen before in the history of the world. We created that music."[22] Music, language, identity. Or, in a word: being. Being, perhaps, as direct description, but this is a description that requires a certain eye and ear. The sort of description that attends to the doubled structure of a vernacular born out of survival, resistance, and pleasure.

This turn to creation, evoking the need to break out of, while also being ensnared in, the assumptions of an enemy's language, marks Baldwin's departure from dominant cultural nationalist currents of mid-century Black Atlantic theory. It also recalls the opening lines of one of his early essays collected in *Notes of a Native Son*. "It is only in his music," Baldwin notes in "Many Thousands Gone," "that the Negro in America has been able to tell his story," but he qualifies this with the subordinate clause "*which Americans are able to admire because a protective sentimentality limits their understanding of it*."[23] This last bit echoes Du Bois's worry about reproduction and performance of the Spirituals. But for Baldwin this is not a question of the degradation of history but instead of the capacity to *be* the kind of subject capable of hearing and, in that hearing, knowing the knowledge transmitted, the memories preserved, and the history inherited. Words in worlds made by and for Black people. Baldwin's defense of black English moves beyond the aesthetic in this moment. It is a matter of being, knowing, and home. Epistemology and ontology.

What, then, is the key to discerning the seriousness of the story of "the Negro in America" outside the sentimentality that distorts and makes African American music and language digestible, common? That is, what is the sheer intelligence of vernacular? Baldwin's claim here is simple: the link between memory, history, and language. The capacity of language to carry the past inside of its meaning in and as sound, negotiated in part by its link to the documentation of pain in the Spirituals we find in Douglass, Du Bois, Locke, and others, folds intelligence into description, doubling the resonance of black English as at once sentimental *and* revolutionary. Baldwin writes:

> The language forged by black people in this country, on this continent, *as the choir just told you* [my emphasis], got us from one place to another. *We* described the auction block. We described what it meant to be there. We survived what it meant to be torn from your mother, your father, your brother, your sister. We described it. We survived being described as mules, as having been put on earth only for the convenience of white people. We survived having *nothing* belonging to us, not your mother, not your father, not your daughter, not your son. And *we* created the only language in this country.[24]

The only language in this country. With that note, Baldwin roots the story of language in its orphaned moment, a moment in which the choir can *tell*—speaking with sheer intelligence—because sound functions as the element and embodiment of the transmission of memory. This moment of description means everything for the present and future of language. History and memory here bear on the word, making the bass and treble and tremolo of utterance happen and therein give the word shape and contour. So, when Baldwin writes that "language comes into existence by means of brutal necessity" and that "the rules of language are dictated by what the language must convey," brutality and conveyance hinge on this moment of an orphaned birth. Sound as life itself.[25]

It is crucial to underscore, however, that Baldwin's orphan narrative is no melancholic or abject story. He resists the apocalyptic and nostalgic tendencies of mid-century Black Atlantic thought with a simple appeal to the vernacular of home. This phrase is important. In his appeal to vernacular, Baldwin sees black English's deep roots and how sound as site of memory of resistance and cultural formation builds history into speaking. There is no need for what Césaire calls "the end of the world" in "Notebook" or for Fanon's declaration that he is not a prisoner of history in the conclusion to *Black Skin, White Masks*. History is already enough for beginning again for Baldwin precisely because the history of violence is already also a story of survival, resistance, pleasure, and world making. Vernacular houses being. And that being cannot be reduced to alienation and abjection. Baldwin of course has plenty of outrage; his famous claim that every Black man has a Bigger Thomas inside of his skull plenty clear on that front. But at the same time Baldwin will always insist on a sense of home as both a right and its own sort of fact of blackness. In that insistence, Baldwin locates the question of language and being in a precarious yet rooted sense of place and belonging as the vernacular of home, as home's vernacular, and how being itself is sustained by speech. As the choir just told you, in the only language of this country, the past is remnant in our sound and word. This quirky conception of language and being is what Marisa Parham describes in *Haunting and Displacement* as "living with a painful absence, with a phantom limb. Yet even if one might not be able to control one's environment, cannot alone end racial violence, or steel against the news of other people's deaths, there are indeed ways we seize tiny bits of control, make small spaces of balanced relation find some distance so that we might live with, as Karla Holloway puts it, 'grace, hope, and resilience.' "[26] Grace, hope, and resilience give content to that much too broad and even quasi-abject term "survival." To have passed on—evoking Holloway's work—means both that death is at the center of cultural formation and that cultural formation is not pathologically linked to death and its attendant sufferings. Rather, the *grace* of passing on manifests in the sheer intelligence of what comes out of testimony to the Auction Block. Testimony seizes control precisely when the loss of control is staged as the market and traffic in Black bodies. Neither melancholic nor mournful, Baldwin's vision of black English as what is passed on in the mode of grace, hope, and resilience is that which has sustained and sustains life. Defense of vernacularity is therefore at once a memory project honoring what has come before and laying claim to the roots African Americans, even in the swirl of persecution and marginalization, have and insist upon in *this place*. A sense of belonging. A sense of speaking. A vernacular of home.

Perhaps ironically, or maybe just appropriately, Baldwin situates his encounter with this sense of language in the experience of exile. Reflecting on his time as a writer abroad, Baldwin steps away from the standard tropes of exile (alienation, loneliness, comparison, etc.) and recalls instead *hearing* black English for the first time from another space. In "On Language, Race, and the Black Writer," he writes, "In order to deal with that reality [the reality of language as an enemy], I left the United States and went to France, where I was unable to speak to anybody because I spoke no French. I dropped into a silence in which I heard, for the first time, the beat of the language of the people who had produced me. *For the first time, I was able to hear that music.*"[27] Exile clears the space for Baldwin to hear. And while in this essay Baldwin reproduces one of the standard tropes of race and exile—that one understands place from a distance, by way of contrast in feeling and senses of nonbelonging—it is also important to note how intimately he links sound, music, language, and identity formation. The speechlessness of arriving in France without French language skills, along with the perspective on place afforded the exilic writer, opens Baldwin's ears to the world-making force of vernacular language and culture. It is a question of production. Language, that house of being, produces a people. In producing a people and a way of being in sound and speech, vernacular makes a sense of home.

✦

In one of the better-known passages from *Invisible Man*, Ralph Ellison reflects on the meaning of Louis Armstrong's music. With this short reflection, Ellison, a lifelong fan and defender of Satch's music, moves from an appreciation of Armstrong as a musician and the question of voice to a larger question of how we are to locate the meaning of African American life, its expression, and the remarkable world that emerges from—or perhaps *as*—a people of the margins. The reflection is at once epistemological—a question of how Armstrong's music is an expression of a form of knowledge and way of knowing—and ontological—a description of being in an antiblack racist world—and therefore cannot be reduced to a sort of "art from the ashes" model of suffering and its expression. Ellison locates knowing and being in the aesthetic expression of the between as falling through, which is neither some sort of interstitial nor an interval space in search of another place but is rather the breaks and cracks *as such*, simultaneously inside and otherwise than being, and in which African American history and memory paradoxically sets roots, conceives space and place, and makes belonging and home. The breaks and cracks are intended in an antiblack racist world to be where a Black person falls in order to never be heard from again, to be rendered voiceless and therefore outside meaningful registers, and so, in the title of Ellison's book, *invisible*. But Armstrong's music makes sound from the cracks and as the invisible, an expression that *knows* and that *is*. Ellison writes:

> There is a certain acoustical deadness in my hole, and when I have music I want to *feel* its vibration, not only with my ear but with my whole body. I'd like to hear five recordings of Louis Armstrong playing and singing "What Did I Do to Be so Black and Blue"—all at the same time. . . . Perhaps I like Louis Armstrong because he's made poetry out of being invisible. And my own grasp of invisibility aids me to understand his music. . . . Invisibility, let me explain, gives one a slightly different sense of time, you're never quite on the beat. Sometimes you're ahead and sometimes behind. Instead of the swift

> and imperceptible flowing of time, you are aware of its nodes, those points where time stands still or from which it leaps ahead. And you slip into the breaks and look around. That's what you hear vaguely in Louis' music.[28]

The language of African American life is in these breaks and cracks. Born from the experience of not just being Black and blue, but also asking *why* this should be, African American expressive culture demands that it be understood in this peculiar, enigmatic nonspace between spaces. Understood on its own terms and thus not measured by and set in comparison to the (putatively) seamless and open space of white culture.

I want to evoke Ellison here in order to return, by way of conclusion, to Baldwin's remarks on the Sorrow Songs and sound. The relationship between Baldwin and Ellison, which always seems to involve that other great writer of the period, Richard Wright, is too much for this brief concluding remark, but it is worth saying that Ellison's remark puts in concise terms what Baldwin articulates across a long series of essays on the language of vernacular culture. For Baldwin and Ellison, it is not enough to say that African American language is a language worth valuing or that it is pragmatically important in terms of pedagogy and cultural respect. Those are the sorts of terms on which, say, the Ebonics "debate" of the early 1990s was premised. Those are actually quite different questions. Baldwin, insofar as he moves away from straightforward political debate, deepens his account of language by seeing in vernacular speech the sound of memory and history, the *knowing* and *being* that comes from asking, in Armstrong's famous song evoked by Ellison, "what did I do, to be so black and so blue?" Why has this come to pass?

What and why indeed.

The *why* of a language rooted in blackness and blueness captures so much in a single word. In asking *why* blackness makes a world blue, all of survival, refusal, and resistance are built into the first word of vernacular language and cultural formation. To make that question into sound is to transform resistance into the possibility of pleasure, both in the sense of the pleasure of sound (what could be more beautiful and pleasing than the sound of the choir's telling or Satch's trumpet and vocals?) and the pleasure of outwitting the enemy in his own language (the doubling of speech and signification). Sound and language slip into nodes, as Ellison puts it, and look around. And what is this looking around, this being settled in a node or break, if not marking place as home? I am here and I see myself, I see you, even though you tried to keep me underground and keep me lost in the breaks. The complication and complexity here lie in conceiving home in a place so violently hostile from the beginning to the very idea of blackness. How can Baldwin posit the United States as home when the nation's name names such terrifying space? What keeps him from the nostalgia for a civilizational past or messianic hope for a wholly new future—those signature gestures of Césaire and Fanon and their Black Atlantic theory moment—in the face of such terror? The relation between language and being changes everything. If language is the house of being, and, as Baldwin argues, vernacular speech and culture welcomes and creates a people, then the terror of antiblack racism reaches a certain limit. Racism's reach is not total. Baldwin refuses to concede to the abjection of blackness in language. If there is resistance to language as another language altogether, then the scope of antiblack racism is limited by the cultural formation of Black people *by* Black people. Not by direct political struggle or conflict but by the uncomplicated assertion and defense of difference. Language is how we inhabit the world. The defense of black English is a defense of a world and the right to inhabit it. It is, as Baldwin puts it, a matter of *self-knowledge*. To speak vernacular culture is to know both *that* you are and *who* you are.

Language as knowledge and being.

Language as a whole world.

What, then, is *home*?

Chapter 5

The Unimaginable Price of Home

Baldwin's family plays such a central role in his nonfiction. It is through stories of his father that we gain access to the nihilism of Harlem life. It is through children that we gain a sense of Baldwin's affection for play and renewal of life, and his brother David—this life that is so exemplary for moral lessons. I am thinking of this passage from the late essay "The Price of the Ticket" in which Baldwin reflects on David's relation to nation, place, and home:

> My brother, describing his life in uniform, did not seem to be representing the America his uniform was meant to represent—: he had never seen the America his uniform was meant to represent. Had anyone? Did he know, had he met, anyone who had? Did anyone *live* there? Judging from the great gulf fixed between their conduct and their principles, it seemed unlikely.
>
> *Was it worth his life?*[1]

What are we to make of David Baldwin's American life? One of the signature features of Baldwin's middle and later nonfiction is the persistent moral appeal to the worthiness of something, of anything, to a life. Not just any life, but always a Black life or even Black life in general. Were these principles, this Americanness, worth a life? Were they worth David Baldwin's life? What does racism make of his and of Black life in general? Who and what are Black people in this nation-place, a place so concerned with, even comprehensively committed to, producing Black suffering—the decimation, then elimination of life? For Baldwin, this form of the question—an unanswerable, even almost unutterable, question—is asked without hesitation and set out in the starkest terms.

I am thinking here too of the letter Baldwin writes to his nephew that serves as an introductory companion to the Vintage edition of *The Fire Next Time*, in which the nephew will read this characterization of racial reality in the United States:

> This innocent country set you down in a ghetto in which, in fact, it intended that you should perish. . . . You were born where you were born and faced the future that you faced because you were black and *for no other reason*. The limits of your ambition were, thus, expected to be set forever. You were born into a society which spelled out with brutal clarity, and in as many ways as possible, that you were a worthless human being.[2]

Baldwin's theoretical work will always *begin* here, in this messy and messed up space. It will never *end* with the perishing of worth and life, for Baldwin is always in some measure a theorist of hope even in moments of profound nihilism and pessimism. But this first moment, this first messy and messed up frame, challenges and haunts all that comes after the setting of limits. Social death is the beginning of Baldwin's thinking; even in the surmounting of death's totalizing claims, it is the ghost that survives reconfigurations of Black life and its possibilities. Baldwin's nonfiction has a haunted character to it that is often underappreciated, yet it is also a writerly characteristic that neither contravenes nor neutralizes his more joyful and ecstatic moments of reflection. The brutal clarity of antiblack racism recurs in Baldwin's work, not as a balance to hope, but as constitutive of hope itself. Aporetic, paradoxical. This is Baldwin's terrifying honesty. Honesty, that is, because Baldwin will never *think* outside the machinery of violence and cruelty—what could be crueler than a child's life intended to perish?—because questions of knowing and being are rooted in that machinery, even as they express resistance and persistence. Whatever the messianic language and whatever the appeal to the fundamental humanity of African American memory and history, Baldwin keeps the ghosts present and alive. Those ghosts sustain life with their sadness. The ghosts make sweetness, pleasure, and sublimity possible in their wake or as their companion narrative. We can think here of how Baldwin, like Du Bois, Locke, and others before him, described the Sorrow Songs. "This music begins on the auction block," Baldwin writes in the late essay "Of the Sorrow Songs," and bequeaths an aural syntax intimate to memory and history, painful yet not death. "For," Baldwin continues, "the 'beat' which is key to music, [is] the key to life."[3]

In posing the question of home in Baldwin's nonfiction, we must always attend to the particularities and peculiarities of this deep African American context. That context: the knowing and being and sense of belonging created from what Marisa Parham describes as "a population generally familiar with the facts of living too hard and dying too soon."[4] A too-soon death is not simply a social phenomenon or tragedy, but instead the condition of American identity, memory, and history. We might call this Baldwin's engagement with finitude, but it is finitude as a social and historical condition, not simply the human condition as such. Therein lies the nuance: Baldwin labors in that strange space between the human condition and the specificity of racial difference and its histories. It is also where Baldwin's at times messianic optimism takes root. Baldwin is an optimism who is less concerned with diagnosis and a sense of cure and more engaged with the strange double life of African American humanity: to be at once intended to perish and at home in that same place. Aporetic, paradoxical. What, then, is this thing called home?[5]

Let me begin by setting out three interrelated contexts.

First, the place of the question of home in Baldwin's work. In the previous reflections, we have seen how Baldwin's reflections on racial identity, memory, history, and language tell a deep and complex story of Black vernacular culture. What is the purchase of this story of Black vernacular culture? Is cultural production an end in itself or the sign of a wider sense of knowing, being, and belonging? That is, how does Baldwin link concerns with cultural production to the question of belonging, community, the interhuman, and shared space—the question of home? Across his nonfiction, Baldwin describes vernacular culture in both ethical and political terms. The ethical dimension is rooted in a certain ontology of African American memory and history; vernacular speech and other cultural productions (music, religion, gesture, cuisine, mourning rituals, speech, etc.) embody history as survival, resistance, refusal, and pleasure. This creates a complex interplay that defines what Baldwin simply calls "humanity." Respect for and productive engagement with the (often aural) syntax of vernacularity signals an ethical relation, one that sees radical otherness at the heart of vernacular culture (the unimaginable price paid by the shared African American past) and the playful vitality of the remains of history (the fecundity of pain, the obstinacy of life after disaster). The political dimension is more complex. Baldwin's political articulation of vernacularity deploys a series of questions familiar to readers of his nonfiction, including the relationship between tradition and community, race and representation, hate and love, and, in the end, the problem of how to reckon with the promise of a nation so dedicated to the intention to perish. The meaning of home, then, is ethical and political and is embedded in the central concerns of his nonfiction from the Paris essays forward. This leads to the second context.

A quick note on scholarship. Lawrie Balfour in her book *The Evidence of Things Not Said* and also James Miller in a key related essay argue that Baldwin's work on Americanness and identity ought to be interpreted inside the question of citizenship. Balfour is certainly right when she writes that Baldwin "exposes the links between degrading assumptions about black Americans and the depreciation of their claims to the fruits of citizenship,"[6] which is in many ways a translation of the existential question of home into the language of political justice. On this argument, Baldwin's return to the question of what the *American* in *Black American* means is a matter of promise—the sort of relation to national history that allows him to say in "Princes and Powers" that African Americans "had been born in a society, which, in a way quite inconceivable for Africans, and no longer real for Europeans, was open and . . . free."[7] That is, Balfour and Miller, as well as George Shulman in key parts of his fabulous *American Prophesy*, situate Americanness in relation to the founding and guiding principles of the nation, constitutive of even our fraught sense of shared and unshared place where those principles function, not as racialized ideological tools or expressions of white supremacy, but as promissory notes for which Baldwin demands redemption. Miller argues with real precision that Baldwin's relation to that promissory note is what makes it possible to overcome the dialectical formation of race and affirm a sense of African American identity outside the work of abjection. Redemption in this context becomes the moment of recognition, which then becomes a question of making good on a promise, rather than, say, redemption as a religious invocation of the end of history and the beginning of something new. In this way, we can see how Balfour, Miller, and Shulman offer antimessianic readings of Baldwin. The dialectic of race, racism, and racial identity, guided by the politics of citizenship as recognition, is thus oriented by a moment of mutuality. *Sublation as democratic belonging*. Not in a future deferred and delayed, not in a future that interrupts the governing order with the force of another law, but in a future that is embedded in the present as the promise of the nation.[8]

I want to push against that a bit here by emphasizing the third context: the existential meaning of the question of home. This is in part drawn from the emergence of Afro-Caribbean intellectuals in the Black Atlantic tradition just after the Second World War in which questions of home were seated in the psyche and affects. Belonging to or in a place, that sense of landscape and *Umwelt* that negotiates matters of life and death in conceptions of social and memorial space, lies at the heart of what it means to be. Alienation from landscape, the inferiority complex, the melancholic condition of not yet life in diasporic spaces—all of these motifs, taken up by Aimé Césaire, Frantz Fanon, V. S. Naipaul, and others—put the question of home in the most intimate place: what it means to be and what it means to imagine what it means to be. I want to claim here that Baldwin's conception of home is seated in that same intimate place, but with a crucial difference. African American life is neither a story of abjection—this is no small part of his critique of Richard Wright, of course—nor is it a story of a people welcome in the stranger's still strange land. The question, however, is what that unwelcome means and what it would mean to demand recognition in the stranger's strange land—even a demand rooted in that land's self-description as free, equal, and committed to the *demos* in the best sense. To be plain: If home is more than recognition, citizenship, and belonging in a multiracial space—that is, if home is an *existential* question—then we have to take vernacular culture seriously and ask if this deeper sense of home operates as an antechamber or moment of refusal of, even resistance to, political questions of citizenship in a shared world. Baldwin will never tire of saying he has no desire to be white or to be a part of the white world. Something more must come to pass. Vernacular culture roots African American life in a sense of home that, for all its muddiness, does not need white people, their contributions, or their recognition. It is already a whole world unto itself. It is a space opened up by generations of refusal and the fecundity of that work. This is Baldwin's counternarrative to mid-century Black Atlantic anxieties about home, but, as always with his work, it is also the complexity of how he understands the memorial and historical construction of the place of African Americans in the American imagination and history. A doubled relation, both alienated *and* at home. A home drawn from an unimaginable debt to ancestors who paid so unimaginable a price.

Black Atlantic, Alien Nations

Aimé Césaire's "Notebook of a Return to the Native Land" tells a Caribbean origin story. an origin story of great complexity. And in that origin story, the terms of so much Black Atlantic theory are set for multiple generations. In telling an origin story, the event of Césaire's poem is its own kind of origin story—a story of Black Atlantic poetics and critical theory that breaks with so much of the African American tradition(s), as well as colonial-era West Indian and African approaches to theoretical questions of time, space, meaning, language, knowledge, and being. Négritude's revaluation of colonial racial values shifts terrain in radical ways, provoking critical response, of course, but also drawing in even critics to the notion of a beautiful blackness.[9] And so in "Notebook" we see Césaire both begin and begin *again* through a repetition of colonial abjection. In that repetition, discerning the difference at the heart of the white gaze and its institutions is crucial. Césaire begins again because, for the Black Atlantic, he puts the entirety of history and History into a poem and then through that traumatic retelling negotiates the passage out of abjection into another kind of future.

"Notebook" is an origin story beginning with how the title itself evokes a first beginning: birth. The *pays natal* evokes land and birth at one and the same time, asking, perhaps, how Black people in the Americas could lay claim to something like birthright. Césaire wants to know whether and how it is possible to see in the land and landscape of the New World something resembling life itself. Not just space or the bare and banal geography of a map (although that too surely belongs to the inhabitants who struggle—or should struggle—for independence), but a *place*, with all that term might imply. Place as familiar. Place as earth and land and landscape. Place as filiality. Place as existential event. Place as home. To be sure, the abject Americas are not the land of birth for Césaire, which he makes plenty clear in the opening pages of "Notebook." What does this mean? It means that to understand birth land and place is to rethink the meaning of place—in an apocalyptic tone. Beginning with the repeated phrase *au bout du petit matin*, he writes, "At the end of the wee hours, the extreme, deceptive desolate bedsore on the wound of the waters; the martyrs who do not bear witness; the flowers of blood that fade and scatter in the empty wind like the screeches of babbling parrots; an aged life mendaciously smiling, its lips opened by vacated agonies; an aged poverty rotting under the sun, silently; an aged silence bursting with tepid pustules, the awful futility of our *raison d'être*."[10] In many ways, the entirety of "Notebook" is contained in this and other structurally similar descriptions that commence the poem, insofar as the poem unfolds as a response to the torpor and dejection that fills the opening pages. Césaire's description of the Martinican *landscape*—and implicitly, of the Black American one, broadly conceived—as "the awful futility" is linked here to the rationality and the possibility of being. Something about the bearing of memory and history on the landscape of the Americas makes it an impossible place to live, think, and *be*. Rather than ecological space as neutral container or radical otherness with its own life, Césaire conceives landscape, much like René Ménil and Suzanne Césaire in the same moment, as a bearer of social and political memory, a place that is both haunted by the abjection of blackness and a site of representation and reproduction of that abjection. Place itself is the problem. The materialization of the trauma of history is reflected in the shift in the opening of "Notebook" from *Au bout du petit matin* to *Et dans cette ville inerte*. The inert townhouses, like alienated language itself, are both the home and the being of the colonized.

Landscape, then, is the *impossibility* of home. Bedsores and wounds. The abjection of the Black Americas, here put in the starkest of terms in Césaire's great epic of the West Indies, functions as a diagnostic moment in his long story about the necessity of radical reinvention, revolution, and reconception of the very meaning of the human. The human, humanism in its European register, is not written to the measure of the earth and its varied peoples, per Césaire's diagnosis and plea in *Discourse on Colonialism*.[11] How does Césaire imagine that new humanism made to the measure of the world? The pivot point in "Notebook" could not be more dramatic or severe. And for good reason. Césaire writes:

> What can I do?
>
> One must begin somewhere.
>
> Begin what?
>
> The only thing in the world
> worth beginning:
> The End of the world of course.[12]

Now, "Notebook" is best known, rightly, for Césaire's utterance of the term "Négritude"—"my negritude is not a stone"—which then becomes the name of arguably the most important pan-African, transatlantic cultural movement of the mid-twentieth century. But I would argue that this apocalyptic[13] moment in the poem is just as important, if not immensely more impactful. In theorizing beginning as possible *only* at the end of the world, Césaire faces and reckons with the truth of colonialism as a total and centuries-long project. If the world is made out of the hegemony of the white gaze and European power, and Black people are rendered socially dead in that hegemony, then what of the world could possibly be worth saving? The apocalyptic tone and turn is also where Fanon's work moves close to that of Césaire. For both, the Caribbean landscape, in both land and psyche, is alienated and violent.[14] Fanon's Martinicans are "an ironic people," he writes in the 1955 essay "West Indians and Africans," by which he means a people incapable of speaking a world into being. Colonialism diminishes, if not outright disintegrates, sincerity and will. The abjection of the land in Césaire gets its early Fanonian twist here. Abjection in language, that peculiar homelessness in speech and speaking Fanon documents in the opening chapter of *Black Skin, White Masks*, renders inhabitation impossible. If language is the house of being, there is no house or home under colonialism—Césaire's efforts at making French speak blackness notwithstanding.

What drives Césaire's Négritude is not simple nostalgia. Nor is it a particularly fantastical vision of Africa. These are caricatures of Négritude, even if they are rooted in some of his more bombastic claims about identity and civilization. Rather, and this is something that for all their differences couples Fanon to Césaire's animating sentiments, the turn across the Atlantic toward the continent in search of a sense of home is rooted in a key claim: the impossibility of beginning in the New World *as such*. Abjection is not simply a *feature* of the New World, but rather a *critical element* of an ontology of place that is antiblack. Césaire's Afropessimism. With Fanon we see something similar in terms of the turn toward a *proper* place. He leaves the Caribbean in pursuit of revolutionary authenticity in North Africa. For Fanon, the turn is not to Africa as a legitimate and legitimizing racialized identity—the sort of civilizational force discussed in Césaire's critical work—but instead to the Global South broadly, its revolutionary atmosphere, and the unprecedented identity that is yet to come. Césaire the ancestral thinker, Fanon the thinker of pure futurity. Fanon's *The Wretched of the Earth* concludes with a provocative vision of this future under the rubric of a new humanism. "For Europe, for ourselves and for humanity, comrades," Fanon writes in the last line of *The Wretched of the Earth*, "we must make a *new start, develop a new way of thinking, and endeavor to create a new man*."[15] Ancestral thinking makes a new humanism in the recovery of African humanity. Thinking pure futurity makes a new humanism out of the thought and praxis of the unprecedented.

Imperatives for the new are not merely revolutionary slogans. Rather, imperatives for the new—whether realizable in the action of poetry or revolutionary violence—draw on a vision of how the past bears on the present, embedding that vision in new epistemologies and ontologies while harnessing the vital energy of revolutionary consciousness. Is the present redeemable on its own terms? Or does it need a force outside the present and its geography in order to become new and capable of sustaining the life of a people? Or is the present too far gone, incapable of any redemption whatsoever? V. S. Naipaul puts the terms of this bearing of the past directly and with no small bit of melancholy when he writes in *The Middle Passage*, "How can the history of this West Indian futility be written? What tone shall the historian adopt? . . . The history of the islands can never be satisfactorily told. Brutality is not the only difficulty. History is built around achievement and creation; and nothing was created in the West Indies."[16] If there was nothing created in the New World, but instead the world was, for subaltern subjects, destroyed and created only as an alien and alienating space, then what could the Americas be for those born in the horizon of forced migration? Abjection. Landscape is abject—nothing was created here, there can be no home for you here—and so too all that falls alongside it: language, identity, world, place, memory, history, knowing, and being. The endgame differences between Césaire, Fanon, and Naipaul are enormous; they do not share anything like a politics or even a broadly postcolonial sensibility aside from anticolonial diagnostics that center on the intractable character of abjection. Césaire's surge of hypermasculinity in his poetry and the muscular rhetoric of *Discourse on Colonialism* alter the landscape of the Black Atlantic and reinvest alienated space with a virile word that speaks new life into being, drawing on the old. But the present is always something to be surmounted, precisely because it is outside any logic of redemption. Fanon's militancy, realized first in North Africa in the Algerian struggle, gives way to a vision of new postcolonial space carved out initially through purposeful anticolonial violence and a subsequent commitment to the creation of the new. But the present is always surmounted, because it is outside any logic of redemption. Naipaul does not surmount the present at all, for it is always too much for words or militancy and leaves him awash in melancholy. Mr. Biswas's house decays and his debt never goes away. Thus, the melancholy of Naipaul's early work is never upended or subverted in nostalgic evocations of old worlds of India or, most powerfully for him, the forever deferred promise of England. In every return, Césaire, Fanon, and Naipaul see abject landscape as not only the condition but also the fate of the Americas *as* American space. Something from *elsewhere* is needed: the old, the future, or just that something that will never come. Time organizes this thinking. The present and its discontents produces a thinking that either retrieves the promise of the past (Césaire), immerses in the immiserating present (Naipaul), or eschews all connections to place and the time of the known in the interest of the unknowable and the unprecedented future

(Fanon). How does time unmake and make home? This is the deeper existential question animating this mid-century Black Atlantic moment.

And this is also Baldwin's Black Atlantic moment. It is Baldwin's Black Atlantic moment in the sense that it is the reckoning with history and memory in the Americas and in the sense that Baldwin begins to write, both in exile and in the United States, in the midst of this retheorizing of the Black experience. How does Baldwin's engagement with time and home situate him in this debate about the temporality of Black being and being in place?

Machineries of Pain

Baldwin inherits this post–World War II Black Atlantic moment, one in which the meaning of the history of slavery and colonialism is brought to bear on the present. The past is always barely past, of course, even when one theorizes in the intervals of history. What is the interval? And how does the past fold itself, or get folded into, the present, then future? For African and Afro-Caribbean theorists in this period, the present is the moment of decolonization, which has its rough parallel in the United States in desegregation and the slow, often violent, dismantling of the racial state. In this moment, in this folding of the past into the present, Black Atlantic theory asks a shared set of questions: What is the meaning of that history of suffering? And what does a reckoning with that history of suffering have to say about the meaning of diasporic identity?

These questions are central to a number of Baldwin's early essays, but the problem is put in particularly direct terms in "Princes and Powers," the 1956 essay reporting on the Paris Congress of Negro Writers and Artists. Baldwin's report is full of vivid physical descriptions of participants and captures in genuinely complex terms the excited debates at the Congress. But he also pauses at key points to remark on the place (or lack thereof) of African American experience in those debates, parsing out key differences that, in theorizing the question of home, make a difference. In those key points, the essay is an exemplary Baldwin piece that blends self-reportage and description with musings on the meaning of memory and history in the Americas. It is also where Baldwin's argument for the distinctiveness of African Americans emerges, not as a correction of, but as a countertelling and alternative memory to, the cultural and political theorization of diaspora at the Paris Congress. What marks this countertelling and alternative memory? What does Baldwin identify as "that gulf which yawns between the American Negro and all other men of color," and how does the gulf shift our understanding of the postcolonial and desegregation moment?

Baldwin's description of the encounter between the African American delegation to the Congress and delegations from the Caribbean and Africa is particularly telling in this context. The encounter is part physical description;

the Caribbean and African delegations have a difficult time sorting out on the basis of skin color who in the delegation from the United States is Black and who is not. Of course, the entire delegation from the United States *is* African American—and therein lies part of the difference that makes a difference. The meaning of race and blackness is already fraught at the Congress in the moment of perception (one does wonder how much of that "confusion" was a put-on, but that is beside the point). But there is more. What makes the encounter compelling at a deeper level (although skin-based, cross-national racial perception is plenty interesting) is that Baldwin stages it on the grounds of a fundamental disconnect, one initially brought about in a dissenting letter sent by Du Bois. Having had his passport revoked by the United States government, Du Bois wrote an open letter to the Congress that was read aloud at the event, in which he claimed that "any American Negro traveling abroad today must either not care about Negroes or say what the State Department wishes him to say."[17] A wild commentary and broadside against the attendees. Baldwin of course cared deeply about Black people and was hardly a tool of the United States government,[18] but Du Bois's remark does set the rhetorical stage for Baldwin's complication of the very terms of the 1956 Congress. It may be the case that Baldwin would not and could not say what Du Bois, in his pan-African moment, would hope an American delegate and delegation would say: that African Americans share the identity "Black" with all other groups gathered under the heading "the African diaspora." But the difference is not a matter of visas and passport revocations, nor is theorizing in that particular manner, with those cultural and political values, a natural mark of radicalism and authentic blackness. Rather, it is an antechamber philosophical question: What makes an identity and what links, delinks, or mangles the links between that identity and a sense of place?

Articulating this identity was the animating spirit and long cultural program of the Paris Congress.[19] The gathering came about as a response to and extension of the Bandung Conference held one year prior, which was primarily oriented around the *political*—and so not specifically *racial*—question of what it means to live and act in the moment of decolonization and to then undertake militant, realigned anticolonial struggle. The Paris Congress shifts focus away from the Indian Ocean and its histories, away from a generalized theory of the colonized and Global South identity, and asks the cultural question as a racial unity question: What makes the diaspora a unity across difference, and how does that unity begin to give shape to Black Atlantic identity? The existential and cultural consequences of this question are enormous, and Baldwin's concern with the fate of Black life in the United States, at issue from his earliest essays on, sits right alongside the Congress's guiding motif. Whatever differences emerge, they are differences born of a common concern for Black life at the end of white and European domination. For the participants and for Baldwin, liberation desires set in motion a search for Black life.

The central figure of "Princes and Powers" is Aimé Césaire, and in his essay Baldwin registers the full force of the Négritude movement. It is no mystery why Césaire cast such a special and powerful spell over the proceedings. The Négritude movement, on Césaire's rendering, redeems, or at least promises to redeem, the abject landscape of life in the Americas. Négritude offers a curative thought to the sadness of history and, in that offering, speaks to the pained heart of the diaspora. Baldwin of course also sees the profound limitations of that thought for theorizing African American life. Anecdotally, and for Baldwin somewhat humorously, those limits get expression in the strange and (for Baldwin) indefensible claim by Léopold Senghor that Richard Wright belongs to the history of great African writers. But the limits of Négritude flow first and foremost from the profundity and promise of possibility. Césaire is described by Baldwin as an immense presence, small but commanding, the center of the energy of the gathering, and the essay quickly turns to the massive effect of his lecture "Culture and Colonization." In that lecture, Césaire makes his signature distinction between *culture* and *civilization*, with the former naming the extant and irreducible differences between sites (nations, communities) in the diaspora and the latter naming the terms of identity and sameness. Civilization, and this is the big claim in Césaire's work, is a vital force that survives the machineries of pain called slavery and colonialism. Césaire turns to civilization as a metaphysical principle that functions as the regulative ideal for authentic Black cultural production. In this notion of civilization, Césaire, as Baldwin puts it, "had penetrated into the heart of the great wilderness which was Europe and stolen the sacred fire."[20]

Césaire's Négritude is guided by this principle, this sacred fire, which we could characterize as an atavistic-minded method of thinking with traces. The machine of colonialism produces the pain of alienation, but that estrangement is never total for Césaire. Something of Africa, this civilizational *élan vital*, remains in however diminished and fragmented a form for Black subjects in the Americas. The remainder is just that: a remainder. Contrary to what becomes the caricature (however well-earned) of Négritude, Césaire does not actually seek to fantasize Africa back into being for Afro-Caribbeans—and, by extension, African Americans—but instead identifies the element and fragment of Africanness that remains for thinking. The remnant is enough to spark thought, bearing within it the capacities of a divine-like force of revitalization or even salvation. Césaire's quiet gnosticism, perhaps. Africa is a *civilizational* force of unity in difference, which Césaire distinguishes from *culture* (different in each geographic instantiation), and the *element* of authentic Black thinking in the sense that water is the proper element for a fish. It is in the *proper* element that Black cultural life flourishes and in which the abjection of the past can be, if not redeemed, at least transformed by the spark of Africa into a sense of the new that is fundamentally connected to and drawn from the ancestral past, the past, that is, of the elsewhere called

African civilization. The remnant lives inside the Black psyche and its practices, percolating inside the estranged yet searching cultural practices across the diaspora.

This connection to the past is not a matter of total reactivation. Césaire is not so naive and I think it is crucial to not work with an overly caricatured version of Négritude's most important innovations. In that interest, then, it is important to note that the trace or fragment of Africa is not simply one feature among others in the New World landscape. It is instead a relay or interval that turns culture back toward a root (or in search of a possible root) in nonalienated history before (or outside) History and memory that is not contaminated by colonial hegemonies. A root that restores a sense of home to abject space, carving out an *outside* and *otherwise* that operates inside and against Europeanness and its myriad forms of alienation. Africa thus means everything for Césaire, even if its force is not total and overwhelming of the geographic specificities of historical experience. Africa means everything because it is the name, as element and fragment, of the possibility of an authentic home. *This culture here*—for sure. Civilization is an animating life force, not land or map. Césaire was in that sense never a Garveyite or even a Martinican version of Martin Delany. No more migration, ever. Except, that is, in the sense of an aesthetic migratory of a Négritude-inspired reinvention of cultural sensibility and production. But, and this is key, that culture must be *new* rather than nostalgic and imitative of the precolonial past. Colonialism has so radically transformed the landscape of the Americas that no life is possible inside that landscape; Négritude's life philosophy, to borrow Donna Jones's characterization, makes something *outside* and *otherwise* possible.[21] The poetic footage of "Notebook," as it were, serves as a kind of tracking shot, documenting what has happened, literally and figuratively, to the bodies of the colonized. Bloated, sick, infertile, flaccid, barely able to breathe. And so Césaire poses the foundational diasporic question for the Congress: What possibilities are imaginable in this alienated space? What is home without Africa? And what is home with Africa as the force of cultural production of the new?

For Baldwin in "Princes and Powers," what is striking in this account is not how it draws the diaspora into a metaphysical and epistemological unity, but rather and to the contrary how it underscores the enigma of African American life. To put it bluntly, African Americans are not a colonized people. Rather, African Americans, perhaps like all Americans, are already a *new people* and therefore not animated at the root by the traces and fragments, not lost in search of a new element that is also, for Césaire, always the oldest element. Baldwin writes in "A Question of Identity," published two years prior to "Princes and Powers," that "what is overwhelmingly clear . . . to everyone but ourselves is that this history [of the United States] has created an entirely unprecedented people, with a unique and individual past."[22] A provocative claim. And it is a claim that derives its full resonance and significance from a contrast at the center of the Paris Congress. In contrast to the experience of colonization, that defining event of then-contemporary Caribbean and Black African nations, being Black in the United States means a different relation to possibility—even while sharing, with the rest of the diaspora, the violence of the West's machinery of pain. Baldwin writes:

> For what, at bottom, distinguished the Americans from the Negroes who surrounded us, men from Nigeria, Senegal, Barbados, Martinique—so many names for so many disciplines—was the banal and abruptly quite overwhelming fact that we had been born in a society, which, in a way quite inconceivable for Africans, and no longer real for Europeans, was open, and, in a sense which has nothing to do with justice or injustice, was free. It was a society, in short, in which nothing was fixed and we had therefore been born to a greater number of possibilities, wretched as these possibilities seemed at the instant of our birth.[23]

The key term here is *possibility*. Something about the United States and how its machinery of pain formed—and was re-formed *by* African Americans—memory, history, and culture shifts the existential meaning of how the past folds into the present, then future. Rather than the fold that disables in Césaire's work, the past folds into the present for Baldwin in the mode of possibility.

This sense of possibility, however, cannot be thought apart from its qualifying term: *wretched*. Baldwin is no plain or boring optimist. Wretchedness is natal; "at the instant of our birth" is both individual (every child is initiated into a necropolitical system) and collective (a sense of a people is born in that necropolitical system). Baldwin's insistence on the natality of wretchedness marks his flirtation with or even affirmation of Afropessimism's founding insight. Yet for Baldwin wretchedness is not the same across the diaspora, just as possibility means nothing the same across the color line. The theory of an unprecedented people, a thought quietly threaded through "Princes and Powers," demands specificity and a difference that makes a difference. Baldwin writes:

> This [wretched possibility] results in a psychology very different—at its best and at its worst—from the psychology which is produced by a sense of having been invaded and overrun, the sense of having no recourse whatever against oppression other than overthrowing the machinery of the oppressor. We had been dealing with, had been made and mangled by, another machinery altogether. It had never been in our interest to overthrow it. It had been necessary to make the machinery work for our benefit and the possibility of its doing so had been, so to speak, built in.[24]

The machinery of suffering—this is the appeal Baldwin makes, with good reason, in seeking a shared sense of grievance in the Black Atlantic, what Césaire calls horizontal solidarity. But grievance is neither enough nor sufficiently profound; it is merely political and certainly also moral. Machineries of suffering speak to more than just political and moral outrage, complaint, and demand for redress. In that, there is a shared *something* in the Black diaspora. However, as we see in Baldwin's long reflections on language and memory and tradition, machineries of suffering are also constitutive of communities in the sense that communities resist, refuse, survive, and retain, through pleasures and creativity inside a necropolitical system, their own sense of humanity set in their own terms. When Césaire and the Paris Congress shift the conversation toward Africa and questions of civilization, that shift is premised on a prior characterization of the Americas as irredeemable and one-dimensional abject space. Baldwin hesitates and wonders: What survives *our* machinery? That is, how has the mangling of African American life produced a people in a full sense, a world unto itself made in language, culture, intellect, and body, and therefore a world very different than the abject landscape of Césaire's "Notebook"?

Baldwin's response to this cleavage of difference is set in terms of *home*. The anxiety of Black Atlantic theory around questions of memory and history are gathered around the theme of the Paris Congress, which, for all of its variation, proceeds first and finally from the notion that the Americas cannot be home without the *élan vital* of African civilization as redemption. What prompts Baldwin to refuse the redemptive power of an alternative civilization, an elsewhere of America? What has happened to a Black identity made, forged, and re-formed in the "another machinery altogether," such that it makes a world—a vernacular world that is not just resistance, but home—in the midst of the violence that would destroy it?

That Exilic Glance and Its Land

How does Baldwin come to theorize the specificity of the Black experience in the United States? And how does that theorization arrive at the language of home? Paradoxically, perhaps, it is through the experience of exile—the glance back *and* ahead, the strange ecstatic temporality of exilic thinking—that Baldwin comes to the language of home. Not by chance, but, on Baldwin's telling, almost by necessity.

Baldwin tells the details of exile and its meaning in the Paris essays, a series of pieces that, along with reflections on Harlem, first defined his place as a writer.[25] But exile recurs as both an experience and theme across his nonfiction, as well as the companion theme of Americanness—not as an exception, but as a particular, specific historical experience.[26] After a life of transit back and forth across the Atlantic, Baldwin reflects in the 1977 essay

"Every Good-Bye Ain't Gone": "*Every good-bye ain't gone*: human history reverberates with violent upheaval, uprooting, arrival and departure, hello and good-bye. Yet, I am not certain that anyone ever leaves home. When 'home' drops below the horizon, it rises in one's breast and acquires the overwhelming power of menaced love."[27] What, then, is menaced love? It is a love that is love, the overwhelming affect that forges connections to place and community,[28] but, because it is menaced, it also does not deny the catastrophe of racial violence. Thinking home in relation to this notion of love, love that takes on the tortured geography of the Americas, deepens the question of home from what Douglas Field in his interpretation of home in Baldwin's work identifies as either "the church, or house of prayer" or "the metaphorical house of America where African Americans live in cramped quarters."[29] Menaced love suggests another level of intimacy beyond retreat from the world or an empty, cramped container.

Menaced love also helps us reframe Baldwin's peculiar and unexpected sense of optimism about the United States. I say peculiar and unexpected because Baldwin's starting point for reflection is always the abject landscape of, in the beginning, Harlem, then later the condition of the United States more widely, whether that be the intention to perish evoked in the letter to his nephew or the repulsive violence of white supremacy in the late work *Evidence of Things Not Seen*. Or the unpublished work so intensely documented in Raoul Peck's film *I Am Not Your Negro*. In that sense, Baldwin starts in the same diagnostic space as his contemporaries in mid-century Black Atlantic theory do. Baldwin's survey of the poverty and hopelessness in Harlem maps perfectly well onto Césaire's geography of torpor and despair in "Notebook." The decisive difference lies in the conception of home, but also, in this exact moment when exile reframes abject space in what Michael Snediker's calls *queer* optimism. "*Queer optimism*," Snediker writes, "*can be considered as a form of meta-optimism*: it wants to *think* about feeling good, to make disparate aspects of feeling good *thinkable*."[30] Baldwin's work is so attentive to this dimension of Black life in the United States while also being profoundly attuned to antiblack violence and injustice. If we situate this queer optimism and love in relation to vernacular culture, we can see how the pleasures and ecstasies of cultural formation in the interstices of American life—Black life, outside the white gaze—have epistemological and ontological significance. That is, a queer optimism inside menaced love makes life thinkable by embedding Black subjects in a different time, a time of blackness as blackness. Immanence in that time makes existential conceptions of home possible. These are conceptions that move into a different space than those opened up by flight and retreat (the church) or those closed off by the intractable character of Black abjection in interracial space. Black English is paramount here as a sort of antechamber to more expansive notions of cultural production and nuances in identity formation. The relationship that Negroes bear to one another.

If we theorize love as queer optimism, then the often messianic tone of Baldwin's appeal to love shifts from the meaning of that love—something set in the unprecedented future, something not unlike Fanon's new humanism—to a rhetorical flourish that partly obscures the immediacy of its meaning. I am thinking here of the discussion of love in *The Fire Next Time* and how Baldwin settles that discussion in a future outside the fraught racial dialectic of the civil rights era. That dialectic, set in an unprecedented future, is sublated in the moment of surmounting the very terms of conflict wherein whiteness loses its narcissistic attachment to the myth of power and blackness wrests itself free of the atrocity of the white gaze. This iteration of love is a messianic future in the traditional sense: redemption in what is to come, a future. The optimism that comes from that reading of love renders Black life on a Christological model of suffering that is *promised* redemption but, in lieu of that actualization of the promise, is one that remains suspended between abjection and flourishing. Alas, the burden of being God's chosen people and the meek who will, someday and somehow, inherit the earth. The queering of optimism, however, shifts from the suspension of affect to a meta-optimism about those same affects that embody suffering, flourishing, and redemption. Meta-optimism intersects both the possible affects of (and after) liberation—*hope*, in a word—and the forms of life that are already liberated from the white gaze, forms that are already saturated with the pleasures and pains of fully realized cultural and social life.

Exile makes all of this visible to Baldwin: the queering of optimism, the recasting of love as an interstitial affect, and the transformative force of both. Exile makes this possible for Baldwin because of the rising and falling of home in the breast and on the horizon. But as we have seen, that rising in the breast is no simple nostalgia. To be sure, Baldwin's vision is sharpened by the distance exile affords from the minute-by-minute beleaguerment of white racism as well as the peculiar experiences of seeing Americans in Paris and observing how, despite all the Americanisms about interracial life and white violence, a fraught-but-shared identity emerges. Still, exile is not simply the removal of beleaguerments that by some miracle of insight then allows the truth of African Americanness to be revealed. Instead, the exilic glance back across the Atlantic infuses the love of home, which in exile is manifest as longing for place and forms of belonging, with the troubled and troubling qualifier *menaced*. That is, the love of home in exile is a love that is *threatened*; loving home means loving and yearning for what might destroy you at the very same time that it saves you or welcomes you into whatever kind of belonging it (still) has to offer. Vexation of the highest order.

What is the temporality of exile and love?

Any story of home in Baldwin's work has to come to terms with time. Time is the enigma of enigmas and all the more so when it is thought in relation to the looping repetition of history. We cannot reduce time to history, however, nor can we reduce time to memory. And that is part of time's appeal to Baldwin, for in the small distance time gains from memory and history—the elements of pain's repetition—it holds the possibility or even necessity of a certain kind of edifying and emancipating innocence. Time is disciplined by and subjected to memory and history, which is simultaneously the loss of beauty and the taking on of profound things like tradition and heritage. But before that disciplining and subjection, there is something else that commands Baldwin's attention. I am thinking here of how Baldwin describes the importance of children and time in *The Evidence of Things Not Seen*, in which he imagines the discreteness of generational transition as a glimpse into life outside—an *outside* temporalized as the *before*—"the bargain" struck in American racial politics. Baldwin writes:

> One trembles for the young who have been abandoned to the things that the Republic, their elders, have told them to buy. I am speaking, in the main, of the people who imagine themselves to be White—as the Republic imagines itself to be White—but a plague is no respecter of delusions.
>
> Or, in other words, I am saying . . . that there was something in Black Atlanta's reaction to its prolonged ordeal that made me very proud. . . . They were forced to recognize something that, on the basis of the evidence, is no longer real or vivid for the bulk of the Republic that imagines itself to be White: they could not live without their children any more than their children could live without them. *They had not yet struck the bargain that nullified their birthright.*[31]

Antiblack racism is the nullification of birthright, a late evocation of rights to place that echoes Baldwin's claim to title of the land of the nation in "Princes and Powers." For Baldwin in *The Evidence of Things Not Seen*, this means that the passage from youth to maturity is akin to a restaging, with all of its horrifying violence, of the centuries of attempts to sever the relationship between African Americans and their home—a severing that defines the early history, then after, of the entire Black Americas. It is also the abjection of Black life that in the stalled or negative dialectic of race in the United States makes political life possible for white people, a political life that forges white innocence out of a secular immolation: the killing of Black people. Necropolitics. The sacrifice of Black lives, whether literally burned in the rituals of lynching or figuratively incinerated in the oblivion of white American memory, is a pure loss; nothing remains in white memory and white innocence is not at all compromised. In fact, white innocence is *enhanced* or perhaps even *created* in this moment. And yet the temporal gap of Black childhood that Baldwin describes, one in which we can distinguish between the time of innocence, still full of rights to place, belonging, and the unimaginable debt then gift of a history of suffering, and the time of the memory and history of racial violence, means everything. For, in that gap Baldwin can settle, not the innocence of African Americans but the rights to place that exceed and precede the looping repetition of a history that severs—or always wants to sever—the relationship to home. The Atlanta child murders are therefore not a novel or exceptional disappearance of Black life. They are, rather, the restaging of the right to life and place *in the wake and in the remains of death*. Rest in struggle and survival and world making, not rest in peace.

In a certain way, we see this temporal gap recast in exilic consciousness. Exilic *consciousness* extends time in a stretch into the past, which is spatialized by the expanse of nation and ocean; Baldwin literally and figuratively glances at the Americas from the other side of the Atlantic, situating himself both inside and outside the time of the nation while at significant spatial remove. The inside of the time of the nation is the carriage of pain, of mourning, and of the Bigger Thomas who lives inside the skull. But there is also the outside of the time of the nation, the perspective gathered from distance that sees beleaguerment clearly for what it is precisely because the presence of whites is vitiated by the space of exile. That space, however, is not relief or a line of flight. Rather, exile initiates an instructive longing. In exile, Baldwin claims, the overwhelming power of menaced love rises in the chest; thought and affect turn, perhaps for the first time, to the simultaneity of striving and accomplishment, of the future politics to come and the folkways of humanity and belonging that defined a meaningful past folded into the present. *A meaningful past*, not a simple story of abjection. This is critical because it surfaces Baldwin's commitment to the complexity of life under an antiblack racist regime. That complexity has rage and melancholy, yes, but it also has a sense of love that makes and sustains communities and generational inheritance. Exilic consciousness is therefore animated by a love that is always painful, threatened by the memory and history that cling to it and make love a form of resistance and refusal. Possibility is also always the risk of annihilation, of succumbing to the intent to perish and therefore to submit to the terrible bargain that nullifies what has been earned and bequeathed. Exile, in other words, reveals birthright. In the 1950 essay "Encounter on the Seine," Baldwin doubles this sense of exile when he stages an encounter between an African American and an African, imagining this exchange as saturated with the exilic experience of love, home, and menacing power. But, near the close of the essay, he writes:

> It is difficult to make clear that he [the Black American] is not seeking to forfeit his birthright as a black man, but that, on the contrary, it is precisely this birthright which he is struggling to recognize and make articulate. Perhaps it now occurs to him that in this need to establish himself in relation to his past he is most American, that this depthless alienation from oneself and one's people is, in sum, the American experience.[32]

The American experience is the experience of home as a form of alienation—no unprecedented people appear without traumatic breaks with the past and precarious futures. This is a sense of alienation that estranges from one sense of home and place—perhaps the naturalness of abode and the comforts that come from that—and, yet, still sustains a relation to both in the struggle to "make articulate." Articulation means everything here. For Baldwin, birthright is just that: a right to place as a matter of birth. But that in no way entails *words* for place. In fact, for Baldwin, it is precisely the failure of words to name or make sense of place that marks the peculiar alienation of Americanness *as such* and of which African Americans are a particular and emphatic example. Yet, and this is crucial, the time before the struck bargain that nullifies, there is a wanting to say, a desire for a word and words for connection to land.

But this word "land" is already fraught. It is a word for the pain of African American history. The Middle Passage meant the loss of ancestral land as place and belonging, slavery meant suffering for the cultivation of another's land without remuneration or humanity, and the failure of Reconstruction meant the loss of any legal or political title to the land. And so too the pain of the Great Migration, which, for all of its liberation from the terror of the South, also meant saying a sad good-bye to rich and familiar landscapes, no matter how alienated and alienating they were in history and memory. It was still land left behind. It was land saturated with bitter and beautiful memory. The relationship between land and home, the very relation Césaire had explored in "Notebook" and that guides so much Black Atlantic theory in the middle of the century, is therefore simultaneously impossible pain, irrational beauty and menaced love, and, literally and figuratively, the ground of history. With this question of land and home, "Princes and Powers" offers its most unexpected and profound reflection. I have remarked on this passage in previous chapters, just above in partial form in the present chapter, and it is worth quoting here in full. Baldwin writes:

> At bottom, what distinguished the Americans from the Negroes who surrounded us . . . was the banal and abruptly quite overwhelming fact that we had been born in a society, which, in a way quite inconceivable for Africans, and no longer real for Europeans, was open, and, in a sense which has nothing to do with justice or injustice, was free. . . . It may have been the popular impulse to keep us at the bottom of the perpetually shifting and bewildered populace; but we were, on the other hand, almost personally indispensable to each of them, simply because, without us, they could never have been certain, in such a confusion, where the bottom was; and nothing, in any case, could take away our title to the land which we, too, had purchased with our blood.[33]

In claiming title to land, which is neither a title to come nor a promise redeemed in a yet-unknowable future, Baldwin upsets the story of Black Atlantic history. This claim and its upsetting are rooted in the paradoxical meaning of the unimaginable price. Yes, the pain of the past cannot be fathomed and no present or future can make sense of or expiate the violence of the Middle Passage and slavery. If any traumatic event is unrepresentable and outside redemption, it is this event. But the unimaginable is also a price paid for title to the land. Title deferred and denied, but a right to place nonetheless. "Sing or shout or testify or keep it to yourself," Baldwin writes, "but *know whence you came*."[34] And in this paradox, the knowing whence he came, Baldwin outlines what is the crucial difference in the African American experience: for all the violence, it has never been about the colonial relation. The colonial relation extracts, whereas the American relation, however much extraction of labor and life defined two and a half centuries of slavery, enmeshes the abjection of Black life inside and with the identity of the unprecedented people. What this means for the question of home is in some sense a simple story. Enmeshed in the life of the nation, African Americans, on Baldwin's account, experience a connection to place from the very beginning, a title to the land purchased with blood that is then borne out in the present as the *right to place*—acquired through atrocious labor, bequeathed as an unimaginable debt, suffered at every turn, but also survived, refused, and resisted—and so generative of a sense of tradition and belonging both inside and outside the bewilderment of the populace.

Two decades later, Baldwin closes "Every Good-Bye Ain't Gone" with the very same sentiment, drawing on the experience of exile in order to bundle the question of home with notions of history, memory, and sound. What I find so compelling about this passage, one of the most powerful in his oeuvre in my opinion, is how Baldwin blends a history of refusal with an ethics of relation to ancestors and robust sense of memorial inheritance. The ancestors counsel; the ancestors prepared the grounds for a grounded self and collective belonging. Ancestors lived in a house; they counsel home. This is Baldwin's conscience and motivation but also how his conception of home as a paradoxical belonging and nonbelonging draws on inheritance by way of all the themes treated in previous chapters: origin stories, imagination, resistance, affect, aurality, and vernacular language and culture. Themes articulated and won through so unimaginable a price. He writes:

> Neither do I want anyone to suppose that I think that the gem of the ocean has kept any of its promises, but my ancestors counseled me to *keep the faith*: and I promised, I vowed that I would. If I am a part of the American house, and I am, it is because my ancestors paid—*striving to make it my home*—so unimaginable a price: and I have seen some of the effects of that passion everywhere I have been, all over this world. The music is everywhere, resounds, no sounds:

> and tells me that now is the moment, for me, to return to the eye of the hurricane.[35]

This is the price of the ticket. It is also the muddy but real existential meaning of home. Nothing is resolved in this passage at the level of political transformation or transformative vision. But to seek or want that kind of resolution is to miss the nuance and profundity of Baldwin's claim about home, namely, that home is something fashioned out of vernacular forms of life, lived in the interstices of an antiblack interracial world, and that that is a sense of belonging that grounds a sense of a people and a sense of home. Blackness for Black people. Blackness out of and in the service of the flourishing of Black life. A love, outside or otherwise than menaced love, of the beauty of Black embodiment. All of these elements that comprise *home* are incarnate, vital, and temporally grounded rather than suspended in search of another future and another beginning. Not in a naive or utopian sense. Always for Baldwin, these elements and this world are won through the unimaginable price paid by African American ancestors. To love in that space, to be and know in that space, is to love the ancestors, to say and live the gratitude for inheritances and, evoking Glissant's famous turn of phrase from *Poetics of Relation*, "to honor our boats."[36]

A Final Few Words

I began the present reflections with a note on Balfour's and Miller's characterization of Baldwin's nonfiction as a politics of recognition, oriented in part—if not a large part—toward a dialectical transformation of racial politics. In this political theory frame, the question of home is a question of what is to come, a future not-yet (*avenir, à-venir*) and yet spoken in the mode of promise in the present. In this frame, and with this politics of the future, we can register the messianic dimension of Baldwin's remarks on love in texts like *The Fire Next Time*. It is not a god that can save this Baldwin. It is the strange work of love, negotiated by way of revolutions in affect, cultural production, and political confrontation, then *conciliation*. A first friendship, for there is nothing to reconcile in the interracial history of the Americas, no past models for a future of human decency. There is nothing to reconcile to or with. Baldwin's conception of home, however, negotiated through his experience of exile, tells an importantly different story: The right to place operates and has long operated outside the dialectical relationship—stalled by racism—between white and Black people in the United States. *Purchased with our blood*. This evocation of racially specific memory and history in "Princes and Powers" speaks to an anterior relation in African American life, one that is not just a political claim but an existential claim and, let's be real, a direct description of how African Americans have lived and created for centuries.

The history of African American life is not reducible to abjection and companion narratives of deficiency. Rather, there is also always life and *creation*. Naipaul bemoans the notion that nothing was created in the West Indies and that it was itself only a creation and now it decays. But Baldwin, inheritor of the same kinds of violently racist history and memory, hears sound, sound that reminds him of home not just as a nostalgia for the familiar, but as the deep claim of birthright. Revolution and the resolution, such as it is or will be, of the dialectic of race means for Baldwin a moment to renegotiate the cruel bargain of America. Renegotiating it away, in fact, such that the claim to home can take leave of the terribly haunted geography of this country and settle out the muddiness of belonging and nonbelonging without altering the long, deep, and sustaining story of Black vernacular culture. That ethical moment. That demand for respect. This is the unsublatable in racial dialectics.

In the end, the long, sustained meditation on the question of home brings us back, like so many of Baldwin's important ideas, to the conflict with Richard Wright. Baldwin's critique of Wright is always foregrounded with the motif to which he returns again and again: the worthiness of life and the cruelty of antiblack racism. Bigger Thomas is always a truth, even if he is the sign of Wright's limits as a thinker and writer. We all know the line from Baldwin, that no Black person can miss the truth of Wright's character because it accesses the affective life of so much of Black subjectivity. "No American Negro," he writes, "exists who does not have his private Bigger Thomas living in the skull."[37] Bigger Thomas is the social remainder, the abject body alive with its own death and dying. Orlando Patterson could not have asked for a better affective representation of the lived experience of social death. Rage is the last moment of Bigger Thomas's life, a life only waiting for death, the anticipation of the too familiar. And it is precisely this that prompts Baldwin's deepest criticism. Wright's fiction, Baldwin claims, does not understand the richness of African American life that operates outside of the violence of racism. Racism is in Bigger Thomas's body. His death is no less expected than was his violence, his innocence that must become guilt, and all of those themes. But there is more to the life of that body and how it is produced in an antiblack interracial world, which Baldwin captures when he writes in "Many Thousands Gone":

> What this means for [*Native Son*] is that a necessary dimension has been cut away; this dimension being, *that depth of involvement and unspoken recognition of shared experience which creates a way of life*. . . . [Wright's novel] creates its climate of anarchy and unmotivated and unapprehended disaster; and it is this climate, common to most Negro protest novels, which has led us all to believe that in Negro life there exists no tradition, no field of manners, no possibility of ritual or intercourse. . . . For a tradition expresses, after all, nothing more than the long and painful experience of a people.[38]

This form of life, this diversity of blackness and the beauty of life even under regimes of exploitation and machines of pain, what Baldwin's first essay on Wright simply called "humanity," is already more than political belonging and recognition. It is African American life before or outside or otherwise than that racial dialectic. It is a sense of connection and belonging that is cultural and political, yes, but also, perhaps more, a sense of love *inside* memories and histories of violence. Survival is never the whole story, and resistance is only a beginning. Love makes tradition in the space of refusal, even if it is so often love expressed, mobilized, and lived *as* survival and resistance.

It is difficult to reckon with this relation of love to violence if we theorize the meaning of blackness only as a relationality, coconstituted by the white gaze, always in some sense reactive, and therefore dialectical even before the struggle for recognition (or in the wake of its failure). This is surely Wright's position, and it is also the claim set forth in Césaire, Fanon, and other mid-century Black Atlantic thinkers. Such a position structures a theory of resistance out of the tension produced by rage; affect makes protest possible, which, in turn provokes a total transformation of the terms of racial and political identity. Recognition is then cashed out in terms of citizenship. While this is certainly part of the story of Baldwin's work, the other story of home and of titles to land, birthright, and tradition, pushes against the secular in giving voice and attention to the sacred history of what was purchased with blood. That other story, the story of the belonging of African Americans with other African Americans, is, I would argue, the central meaning of Baldwin's nonfiction.[39] It is his ethical sensibility that respects tradition and, more widely, reflects his writerly courage in theorizing what can never be neatly resolved. Baldwin's writing is in many ways animated by four fundamental spirits, and they bear on the question of home with such transformative force: a vernacular sense of Americanness, exilic consciousness, his books, and the music of Bessie Smith. The sound of tradition. "Armed with two Bessie Smith records and a typewriter," Baldwin writes, "I began to try to recreate the life that I had first known as a child and from which I had spent so many years in flight."[40]

Let me close with Smith, then, whose voice and presence show up everywhere in Baldwin's fiction and nonfiction and whose own vision of home is, like Baldwin's, always muddy—yet still home. Her song "Muddy Water" is sung in downriver glance, looking, one imagines, from a club on Beale in Memphis down across South Memphis through, if you take the 51, the terrifyingly named Tennessee border town Whitehaven, or maybe you take the 61 and it is just the memory space of the Great Flood, flat and vast and full of ghostly memory. Either route, you get into the open space of the Delta. Close to the river, which means close to the traffic routes and roots of Black people's pain. Muddied, but home. Muddied because it is home.

Chapter 6

The Racial Double Session

"What, one can't but wonder, can be waiting for him in that house," Baldwin writes in a review of the television series *Roots*. The review is a meditation on the enigma of the very idea of Black humanity. Yet another search for Black life, this time on the televisual screen and in a novel. Baldwin writes that as viewers we lived our own iteration of that enigma. In that horizon, watching and reading, "We had to face whatever was in there, and, while we might call each other nigger, we knew that a man was not a thing."[1] How does Black humanity come into representation? What is repressed in that representation? And what does that representation upend, contest, and at long last, perhaps, make impossible?

We have seen in some detail above how Baldwin's work as a critical theorist gathers together origin stories, imagination, resistance, affect, language, and aurality in order to signal both the conditions for the possibility and the cultural production of a robust conception of home. That conception places Baldwin's thinking in the interstices of interracial life in the United States, cleaving that place on the margins from the hegemony of what beleaguers Black life. In those interstices, Baldwin finds all the elements that make home and identity possible and also joyful: words for things, unmediated bodies, and the place in which to say yes to life. Distinctive. Abundant possibilities. A sort of deep, spiritual marronage that, like Ralph Ellison's lower frequencies, works in a kind of invisibility and lives in the midst of what cannot see or touch it. The relationship that Negroes bear to one another.

In the remarks that follow, I want to explore the meaning, significance, or even just plausibility of a certain optimism in Baldwin's work. That is, I want to ask what kind of optimism operates in Baldwin's nonfiction and especially how that optimism is informed by the particularities of the African American experience and the Black experience more broadly. Those experiences, and they are always plural for Baldwin, intertwine political economy, existential conceptions of the person, and exploratory theories of memory, history, and identity. Part of theorizing an *Afro*-optimism means disentangling some of those features of African American experience in his work so that we might begin to think hard about and take seriously the complex relationship between pessimism, optimism, and the vicissitudes of affect under regimes of antiblack racism.

Life under such regimes is always central to Baldwin's fiction and nonfiction. Indeed, Baldwin will always write close to the nihilistic lessons of Black history, a history in which white violence and terror is the companion to every moment of struggle, articulation, and enunciation. Whatever claims one might make about Baldwin's moments of optimism (which is importantly different than hope), we have to begin with the fact that he was a deeply nihilistic thinker. As a writer, he is varied because themes vary, of course. But the tone of his work up through *Evidence of Things Not Seen* is profoundly nihilistic in ways that land concretely and land in the most morally difficult space of cultural and political theory. The early essays on Harlem are a particularly pointed example. Baldwin writes close to that despair, engaging and evoking all of the senses in his account of the abject space of Harlem.[2] That part of the story is uncomplicated and draws us into Baldwin's work as a kind of pessimism. This pessimism is not at all ideological or metaphysical, but merely descriptive. The world tells a pessimist's story. At the same time, whatever the story Baldwin tells, his writerly voice is attuned not just to forms of resistance amidst the pessimist's story but also to how forms of life live alongside, against, or even wholly outside the sorts of abjection white America is able to produce for Black people. And therein lies the beginning of a theory of Afro-optimism. So, my questions here are, How is an optimism possible in the horizon of Baldwin's thought? And what sorts of modification does that optimism undergo in the context of his work on antiblack racism and the violence and terror of history? In short, How is an optimism possible *inside* pessimism rather than in opposition to it?

Those are the questions I want to address here, and part of the task is to put Baldwin's work in critical conversation with what our contemporary moment calls "Afropessimism." Afropessimism is itself a varied movement, but it shares some common claims that root pessimistic thinking in an ontology of the world; being itself is entwined with antiblackness. But before I turn to all of that, let me make a few notes to set the context.

On the one hand, it is a risky bit of historical rewriting to export a contemporary question like that of Afropessimism to Baldwin's work, which wrestled in such important ways and on its own terms with Richard Wright's nihilism, the nihilism of Harlem, Atlanta after the child murders, and so many other sites of antiblack violence, despair, and mourning. Those sites of nihilism, as we have seen across the preceding chapters, are set in juxtaposition to vernacular cultural forms and critical appropriations of African American origin stories. So, any sense of pessimism in Baldwin has to be mediated by this important, decisive ethical and conceptual intervention. On the other hand, we always read backward, don't we? In fact, reading through a contemporary frame is arguably as responsible a readerly practice as literary historical approaches, if not more so. Sharply framing a reading of

Baldwin has a hermeneutic honesty on the part of us as interpretative readers and Baldwin's quirky engagement with matters of nihilism, social death, and Black life already conceptually embeds his thinking inside questions and prerogatives of Afropessimism. So, the question does not come from nowhere. It is inside the text of Baldwin and also, of course, inside the textuality of our world. If Baldwin moves through Afropessimist prerogatives and conceptual innovations but emerges in a critical contrast to those, then we can say that reading Baldwin with Afropessimism as an interpretative frame offers at least the possibility of immanent critique, which is the most compelling form of critique.

My interest in reading Baldwin in comparative relation to Afropessimism begins with the title and motif of the present project. What is the shadow cast by the unimaginable price of the Black Americas? And what obligations—epistemological, ontological, ethical, aesthetic—issue from that price? How do we live and think and breathe in the horizon of the unimaginable price? The title and motif of *unimaginable price* comes from a passage in Baldwin's "Every Good-Bye Ain't Gone," an essay in which the past—comprised as it is of struggle, survival, resistance, and refusal, and thus a profound, abiding, and demanding inheritance—functions as imperative for the present. Namely, an insistence on a right to place. Baldwin's insistence on a right to place and refusal to concede American history and memory to white conquest and violence is already part way down the road of an Afro-optimism. Indeed, the work of refusal alters the structure of being. To claim *home* inside the house that has hosted unspeakable pain for centuries suggests forms of life that exceed mere survival, quasi-assimilation, or social life of social death. And that excess proves to be everything in Baldwin's work. He writes, and I quote this passage again, "If I am a part of the American house, and I am, it is because my ancestors paid—*striving to make it my home*—so unimaginable a price: and I have seen some of the effects of that passion everywhere I have been, all over this world. The music is everywhere, resounds, no sounds: and tells me that now is the moment, for me, to return to the eye of the hurricane."[3] This passage is written from the position of exile; quite literally, Baldwin is imagining himself back across the Atlantic. As we know from any quick perusal of the early nonfiction, exilic writing is Baldwin's writerly game and mode of serious contemplation, underscoring always the impossibility of Black freedom in the United States, the immensity of suffering, and that *something more* that will always distinguish his reflections from nihilistic rage.

This *something more* begins the story of liberated blackness in Baldwin's work, a problematic that shows up most vividly and first in terms of dialectics of race and identity. Baldwin's work on whiteness is well-known as critique and, to put it in rather boring language, a kind of "social analysis," but whiteness plays an important role in the dialectical resolution of the problem of African American identity. Blackness, as such, is no counterpoint to whiteness. It does not function as a negation of whiteness, it does not start dialectical movement, it is not pre-formed and re-formed in the work of interracial life but is instead *produced by whiteness itself*. Blackness, as the early essays on Harlem tell us, is understood by Baldwin as a site of and name for abjection. The early fiction and nonfiction is a repeating citation of melancholic suffering, nihilism, and despair. The suffering is melancholic because Baldwin does not see in that form of life—a sense of blackness and its life constructed by the white gaze, structured at every level by the figure of blackness produced, then conjured by that gaze—anything like a redemptive power or possibility of resistance. Thus, nihilism and despair follow as both a logical and existential consequence. "All over Harlem," Baldwin writes in the opening paragraph of the 1948 essay "The Harlem Ghetto," "now there is felt the same bitter expectancy with which, in my childhood, we awaited winter: it is coming and it will be hard; there is nothing anyone can do about it."[4] Childhood is simply waiting for what comes, what is hard, and what is inevitable. Recall, too, Baldwin's letter to his nephew in which he says, with such regret and sadness and rage, that the world into which the child is born intends for him to perish. Period. A death world. Necropolitics. All of that nihilistic stuff is built into Baldwin's stunning phrase from "The Harlem Ghetto": *the same bitter expectancy*. This moment of resignation, a resignation to what is and has always been unspeakably difficult, being Black in America, alters the affective landscape of the entirety of Baldwin's work. His exploration of shame and fear maps on to the early work of Frantz Fanon in such interesting ways, as we have seen, and this is crucial for understanding Baldwin's relation to the motifs in Afropessimist thinking. What Fanon in *Black Skin, White Masks* calls the inferiority complex—the affective life of the colonized living under the epidermal schema of antiblack racism—can be found in Baldwin's own treatment of what he calls in "Many Thousands Gone" the "myths we perpetuate about . . . the Negro in America,"[5] namely, that the lifeworld constructed by the white gaze renders transformative affective life impossible for Black people.

The affective life of race and racial identification traverses the interior and intersubjective life of Fanon's and Baldwin's subject. Fanon's famous report in *Black Skin, White Masks* of the white child on the subway, who points at him and says "Maman, look, a Negro; I'm scared!" indexes just this traversal. "Now they were beginning to be scared of me," Fanon writes, "I wanted to kill myself laughing, but laughter had become out of the question."[6] Baldwin indexes the same, writing in "Many Thousands Gone," published just months before *Black Skin, White Masks*, about the double structure of terror and race. "Wherever the Negro face appears," Baldwin writes, "a tension is created, the tension of a silence filled with things unutterable."[7] This is Baldwin's moment of Afropessimism, that moment in which the truth of Wright's fiction becomes as obstinate as it is limiting. And that is one of the complexities of Baldwin's relation to Wright. At a certain level, there was never a deep disagreement about Wright's depiction of African American life under the white gaze. Bigger Thomas is produced by the white gaze as an abject, violent threat and all of the consequences follow: poverty, criminality, death. And this is where Wright appears in Fanon's text, where something very much like Baldwin's sympathetic assessment of Bigger—the figure who lives inside the skull—is articulated. Bigger "acts to put an end to the tension," Fanon writes in *Black Skin, White Masks*. "He answers the world's expectations."[8] Produced like so much Black life under the white gaze, life which is a kind of death or living as dead, there is no other fate. The world has its expectations, antiblack through and through, and on Fanon's rendering Bigger embodies that with spasms of violence. Not quite resistance. More like confirmation of the hopelessness of Black life, lived as nihilistic subjectivity in an antiblack interracial world. Pessimism here appears, not as part of subjectivity, but as subjectivity itself. Like Fanon, Baldwin's work bears plenty of testimony to the specter of an irreversible pessimism and the apocalyptic consequences that issue from that pessimism. If the world is made by the white gaze, then that which is in and of that world cannot ground liberation. Destroy the world in order to make life possible for the first time? Yes, this is the only possibility, if antiblackness is being itself. But that takes us two steps ahead of ourselves.

Wright's work, at least the early fiction with which Baldwin concerns himself, is a pessimism that ends in nihilism. What seems to be hopeless grounds itself in the meaninglessness of a certain condition of existence, being Black. This makes an interesting frame for understanding not only Wright's fiction, but also his life. Exilic life for Wright is about escape and forging—at least in fantasy, which is not nothing—another destiny. Paris, then disappointment in Gold Coast, then Bandung, then an imagined England. Fanon's work sees these same abject possibilities, these same nihilisms that conclude pessimistic sentiment and ontology. Fanon calls for the end of the world. Fanon's conception of a new humanism, the imagined "post" in the postcolonial, is an apocalyptic vision through and through. This is no optimism amidst a pessimistic world, but rather only the last possibility for Black life that lives as social death. Baldwin's work, too, has its apocalyptic moment and here is where the problem of dialectics is so very crucial. If the white gaze has constructed an imaginary, existential, and material idea of blackness that makes Black life impossible, then any contradiction of racial dialectics in the name of that blackness is already fated to failure. The infusion of the antithesis—blackness, guilt, death, negation, impossibility—with the foundational elements of the thesis—whiteness, innocence, life, affirmation, possibility—proscribes the resolution as the terror and silence of the appearance of what Baldwin simply calls "the Negro face." This leads Baldwin in a text like *The Fire Next Time* to generate a messianic figure—Love, in my textual example—that intervenes in this negative dialectic in order to make, largely at the level of vision or metaphysical fantasy, a radically different world.

And yet there is always this other Baldwin, the Baldwin who insists upon home, the writer who, from the position of exile, sees in history and memory the conditions for making a claim to place and identity. It is precisely this tension between apocalyptic and small place registers that produces the possibility of an Afro-optimism. Not an optimism in the world of pessimism and nihilism, not an optimism built into Black subjectivity subjected to the white gaze, but rather an optimism *otherwise*. Between bitter expectancy and the unimaginable price, there is an other and another sense of home and belonging in which some kind of optimism is possible.

Between Abjection and Pessimism

Baldwin's early work is famous for his treatment of exile, but also just as much for his depiction of Harlem. That depiction makes for difficult reading at times; the child is always at stake, both as a site of memory—Baldwin remembering his own childhood and its terror—and as an interval to a future that reproduces the abjection of the past and present. This reproduction works at the affective level; "bitterness" is so often the companion to "survival," which is Baldwin's way of saying that Black life is inseparable from the persistent threat, scent, and ghost of dying too soon. For Baldwin, this is Harlem's life as a concentration or distilled version of African American life more broadly. Harlem is "inarticulate, hungry" and "defeated," producing "a furious, bewildered rage, the rage of people who cannot find solid ground beneath their feet."[9] Searching for and not finding solid ground is how Baldwin characterizes the problem of root, of place, and of home. And this is why his claim to title of the land is so important: a response to bewildered rage, drawing on the same history, and marking the legitimacy of rights to place. Herein lies the righteousness of Baldwin's early fiction and nonfiction both, drawing our sight to this site of despair, then, as he does so deftly in "Princes and Powers," underscoring how that site of despair is central to the logic of the nation—a negative dialectic that creates and sustains whiteness and its sense of supremacy. "It may have been the popular impulse," Baldwin writes in 1956, "to keep us at the bottom of the perpetually shifting and bewildered populace; but we were, on the other hand, almost personally indispensable to each of them, simply because, without us, they could never have been certain . . . where the bottom was."[10] At the bottom of the well and grounded in it, the security and securing of American identities. Subjection as political and cultural economy. At the bottom of the well, a space of thinking life otherwise than the antiblack death world. Resistance and refusal as cultural production and world making.

Baldwin's description of Harlem in many ways mimics the *logic* of and the *account* of racialized space in Fanon's early work, especially *Black Skin, White Masks* and the 1956 essay "Racism and Culture." Both of those works from Fanon describe how deeply embedded the language of race and the violence of antiblack racism are in the lifeworld. At first glance, Fanon simply notes the obvious: Antiblack racism is more than the willfulness and belief structure of racist white people and thus functions across cultural institutions, formations, habits, and the political subconscious. We call this, often rather too casually, "institutional racism." Fanon's critical eye was fixed on this logic and functioning from the beginning and could not have been more plain than when he wrote in "Racism and Culture" that "to study the relations of racism and culture is to raise the question of their reciprocal action," and further that racism, across cultural shifts and changes, "has had to renew itself, to adapt itself, to change its appearance."[11] The persistence of racism, and so also the terms in which we might begin thinking an antiracist theory and politics, is the persistence of time through culture; history moves time without altering the fundamental fixity of antiblack racist ideological forms, even when the practices are changed and political relations are transformed or abolished. Here is Fanon's *decolonial*, rather than *postcolonial* resonance. The distinction between ideological forms and practices and political relations is paramount, which is a distinction between elements of ontology and ontic playfulness with ideological forms. Antiblack racism's most nefarious operation is in this space, finding ways to reproduce atrocity amidst shifting social realities. The lash and the gaze are massively different practices, but they are symptoms of a deeper structure of being itself. Where do we locate antiblack racism in relation to being, beings, and the difference between them? What is antiblackness to ontological difference?

There is something profoundly dispiriting at work here in both Fanon's work and Baldwin's companion meditations. If antiblack racism works at the level of the political unconscious and through the passive operations of a whole constellation of institutional habits and mechanisms, reproducing antiblackness inside being itself and therefore beings as well, then we cannot locate the efficient cause of atrocity. And of course efficient cause is what matters most. The efficient cause links the formal and material aspects of life, which in this case means the transformation of the idea of blackness into material abjection. What becomes of resistance, and therefore liberation as praxis or even just as dream, when the efficient cause is no longer identifiable? This complexity or despair reminds me of the common experience of reading Louis Althusser's account of ideology in his famous "Ideology and Ideological State Apparatuses." Althusser delinks ideology from belief structures, will, and political imposition. There is no life outside ideology for Althusser, but ideology itself only shows up in signals and symptoms, never as something that can be beheld, seized, and either embellished, reshaped, or eliminated. Understanding resistance in this context is complicated, if not nearly impossible. For Althusser and other theory radicals, this is where the hope and promise (and even fantasy) of apocalyptic thinking proves to be a political salve. Antiblack racism functions in Fanon's and Baldwin's work much like ideology in Althusser: invisible, hypervisible, unavoidable, and unidentifiable, glimpsed and seen and felt by its effects and affects. The effects of antiblack racism are clear, from mass incarceration to premature death, and that is plenty urgent for revolutionary feelings and demands. Effects induce rage that finds no expiation outside of radical social and political change, something that is indispensable for political mobilization. The affects are every bit as deeply troubling. Fanon and Baldwin both document, in painful detail, the life of the inferiority complex under regimes of antiblackness. That complex and its cognates debilitate Black life from inside the individual and inside the collective psyche, which, in the cruelest of twists, sets no small part of the labor of reproducing antiblack racism in the bodies of its victims. The epistemological and ontological consequences of this operation are also clear. Self-knowledge and knowledge of the world are always already mediated by the structures of racial interpellation, which means degradation, humiliation, and material abjection. To know is to know under antiblack conditions. For Fanon especially, this shows up as an overwhelming skepticism around popular cultural and social forms in Black life. An ontology follows from these distributions of antiblackness as ideology. Fanon's work gives us as moving testimony to this as we will find anywhere in his *Black Skin, White Masks*, which documents the movement from common utterances to dialectical interventions against the white gaze to language to desire, exploring how the totality of subjectivity is conditioned by this condition. The conclusion toward which we are being drawn is bleak and unrelenting: there is no saving power in blackness as such. Produced out of various interpellations and through the intersection of antiblack racist ideology, its habits, and its mechanisms, *to be* is not *to be Black*, but instead *to be Black* is to *not be*. The zone of nonbeing. Radical abjection. Nothingness. What Calvin Warren simply calls *ontological terror.*

And where does that leave us?

This short reflection draws us into the purview of the contemporary Afropessimist movement, Frank Wilderson's work in particular, but also Jared Sexton's and Warren's various extensions and defenses of the movement. Fanon's and Baldwin's pessimism is rooted in the repetition of subjection of blackness, not just as a social practice or economic reality, but as a total production of the Black subject. *Total production* links the ideological function of antiblack racism to fundamental ontology—a function that Warren has tracked in detail. That link is expressed in Baldwin's exploration of the pathological effects and affects of "the ghetto" (an epistemological and ontological critical term) as well as, of course, Fanon's early treatment of *sociogeny*. The *words* and *ontologizing work* of racial opticality—the white gaze, the epidermalization of race and racism, and the affective life of antiblackness—have phenomenological meaning here: Descriptions are not reportage, but instead identification and elaboration of fundamental, essential structures of lived experience.

The innovation of the Afropessimist movement is to layer this traced impression in Fanon, Baldwin, and others with political economy and a rigorous account of discursive formation. Political economy helps us see how being as antiblackness externalizes itself in ideological sites of reproduction—institutions, broadly conceived. Discursive formation helps us see how the language of race and racism, whether insult, characterization, or threat, is central to the project of abjection and social death. This is an important shift. Afropessimism's obsessive focus on the relation between being, language, institutions, and social death captures the genesis of the subject out of an intensity of political and cultural forces, all of which converge to make the social life of blackness akin to death. Because the subject is produced through the ways in which we speak, act, and think (discursive and political), both subjectivity and intersubjectivity are bound to and by this moment of production. In that way, Afropessimism is for everyone: Blackness and whiteness are surfaced as identity categories, and cultural-political efficient causes, in an antiblack world. The pessimism of Afropessimism derives from this claim, and the "Afro" of Afropessimism derives from the targeting of not just Black people, but the figure of blackness itself. This leads Wilderson to an apocalyptic vision, one that draws explicitly on the later Fanon and his account of radical negation or nonbeing. Wilderson notes in a conversation with Saidiya Hartman:

> I'm not saying that in this space of negation, which is blackness, there is no life. We have tremendous life. But this life is not analogous to those touchstones of cohesion that hold civil society together. In fact, the trajectory of our life (within our terrain of civil death) is bound up in claiming—sometimes individually, sometimes collectively—the violence which Fanon writes about in *The Wretched of the Earth*, that trajectory which, as he says, is "a splinter to the heart of the world" and "puts the settler out of the picture."[12]

I like this qualification here, as it allows Wilderson to say something that, frankly, Fanon cannot. Fanon's account of the world is so saturated with antiblack racism that life itself is impossible; this is part of why the conclusion to *Black Skin, White Masks* sounds so much like a prayer. Or why the rhetorical structure of *The Wretched of the Earth* so importantly revels in fantasies of revenge and vengeance. It is not simply the case that atrocity makes being. For Fanon it is a matter of the most radical and expansive sense of social death: There is no life. Aimé Césaire's opening motifs in "Notebook of a Return to the Native Land" survive Fanon's critique of Négritude and come to characterize being itself. And yet for Wilderson *tremendous life* is still possible, however much that life labors in the shadow of and is overwhelmed by civil-political death. This is a precarious balance. In fact, in proposing this seemingly unnavigable simultaneity, Wilderson might be suggesting something that exceeds the Afropessimist horizon and its prerogatives. But let us pause that question for a moment.

It is important to note that the significance of Black life under the Afropessimist rubric is bound by negation. The elements of Black life on this account are, in the end, more akin to a form of death than any sense of resistance or counternarrative. Sexton makes this clear in a piece on social death, writing,

> To speak of black social life *and* black social death, black social life *against* black social death, black social life *as* black social death, black social life in black social death—all of this is to find oneself in the midst of an argument that is also a profound agreement, an agreement that takes shape in (between) *meconnaissance* and (dis) belief. Black optimism is not the negation of the negation that is afro-pessimism, just as black social life does not negate black social death by inhabiting it and vitalizing it. A living death is as much a death as it is a living. Nothing in afro-pessimism suggests that there is no black (social) life, only that black life is not social life in the universe formed by the codes of state and civil society, of citizen and subject, of nation and culture, of people and place, of history and heritage, of all the things that colonial society has in common with the colonized, of all that capital has in common with labor—the modern world system.[13]

Sexton here relinks the question of Afropessimism to political economy, which, in a certain sense, presses political subjectivity and antisubjectivity more deeply into an everyday notion of necropolitics. It is the political that makes life into death, and so the social life of blackness lives as political death—it is no life at all, in the end. The systematic forestructuring of the shared, interracial world makes this death and life into living death, which means that blackness itself is nothing like a participant in its own abjection. That blackness dies *because of* the world. "Blackness" Sexton writes, "is not the pathogen in afro-pessimism, the world is."[14] This is the apocalyptic moment, the moment in which the world as we know it can never be said to sustain Black life, and so the world itself must die in order for blackness to live. The Afropessimist program, then, eventually has to turn to a targeted diagnostic that eliminates the pathogen in order to make life possible. To eliminate the political order as we know it, an order that is not simply politics but instead being writ large as the politics of life, death, social death, and social life. In other words, to write this politics into the conditions for the possibility of all our imaginable (and then, oriented toward a radical future, unimaginable) identities of subjection *and* revolution.

The motif of the pathogen of the world cannot but recall Baldwin's letter to his nephew. Pathogens create conditions in subjects in Baldwin's letter; illness, here a metaphor, is *caused* by the pathogen, but the subject does not live at any distance from that pathogen. To the contrary, the subject lives in a world that is full of pathogens, many of which can be avoided or embraced, but also many that are obdurate and function as transcendental conditions of living and dying itself. The inexorable character of antiblackness as pathogen thereby translates subjectivity into a relation *to* and *from* the pathogenic world. We are in and of the world. This is a condition of beings in relation to being itself. When being is antiblackness, the condition of being a being is generated from antiblackness. Afropessimism is for everyone. But it means a very specific kind of relation to death for Black people, Black bodies, and Black life. Obviously. It is *Afro*pessimism. Baldwin's letter to his nephew makes this plain when he writes:

> This innocent country set you down in a ghetto in which, in fact, it intended that you should perish. Let me spell out precisely what I mean by that, for the heart of the matter is here, and the root of my dispute with my country. You were born where you were born and faced the future that you faced because you were black and *for no other reason*. The limits of your ambition were, thus, expected to be set forever. You were born into a society which spelled out with brutal clarity, and in as many ways as possible, that you were a worthless human being.[15]

What is there to say after these words? Baldwin documents for his nephew and his reader what Fanon articulated in his most difficult conceptual moments: born into an antiblack world, destined for the zone of nonbeing, fully embodied as social death, and anticipating premature, even extrajudicial, death. Total loss of a sense of place in shared interracial space. In this moment of loss, where no words come to mind, we catch sight of Afropessimism's fundamental truth: When the world is revealed to us as it truly is, this antiblack racist world, no words that come from that world that can heal. This is what it means to be speechless.

Toward an Afro-Optimism

Sexton's revision and nuance of Wilderson's account of negation underscores a crucial element in Afropessimist thinking: an entwining of life and death that defines survival and cultural production under antiblack racist regimes. With this element, Afropessimism incorporates the salient objection to pessimistic theory, namely, that there is *life* in the midst of death and abjection. This life is little more than the zombification of subjectivity; death and life coexist, even cohabitate, under the exploitative logic of white supremacy. Orlando Patterson's conception of social death shows its legacy here, shifting from a generalized theory of enslavement in his *Slavery and Social Death* to an incisive theory of antiblackness and being in Afropessimism. It is not enough to simply say that life goes on. Social life does not neutralize or negate the negation we call social death. Afropessimism is instead a nondialectical intervention in theorizing death and life, which in this context means, per Wilderson's remarks, that the fact of Black social life cannot function as a disruptive negation. Dialectics, after all, begin with disruption. After disruption, the thesis and its negation are never the same, and something new and incomparable—if dialectics are radical and transformative—emerges. Afropessimism is ontology, not dialectics, and fundamental ontology at that. Being is obstinate and produces beings without moving from the founding condition of antiblackness.

To be sure, Baldwin's relation to this kind of pessimism is fraught and complicated. The pathogen of the world nicely describes the abjection Baldwin documents in Harlem, then elsewhere. Abjection is unavoidable, baked into the institutions and habits of *being American* from the beginning. So, the question is not of the illusion of abjection but of the fate of nihilisms and pessimisms that issue from abjection. But, at the same time, Baldwin is nothing like Richard Wright; this old debate about the meaning of literature, politics, and racialized experience remains relevant and lies at the heart of both how Afropessimism *wants* to mark its comprehensive reach and the possibilities of immanent critique. One can think here of Wright's appeal to the underground in both the short story "The Man Who Lived Underground" and the long existential novel *The Outsider*, in which, for both pieces, the only condition of Black life as *possible* life, a condition imposed upon his characters by the social death depicted above ground, is life with or amidst white people. Interracial life, something we have seen described by Baldwin as invariably a death world for Black people. And that is no life at all, only a living death. Baldwin's long criticism of Wright, however, circles around this very issue: Does Wright and do his characters understand and engage with the *complexity* of Black life? Or is the pessimism of Wright and his characters derived from a misunderstanding of the fundamental personhood of Black people in relation to history, memory, and interstitial sites of living, thinking, and making? And if there is this misunderstanding, a misunderstanding that oversubscribes death to Black life, then how might a revised and proper understanding of this complexity in Baldwin's work function as a kind of critical reply to Afropessimism? This zigzag across figures and moments in intellectual history opens up some of the most urgent questions in critical Black studies.

In theorizing this reply to Afropessimism in Baldwin's work, and what the significance of that response might be for thinking blackness and identity, I want to turn briefly to Michael Snediker's account of queer optimism in his book by that same title. In particular, I am interested in how Snediker's account moves against what he calls the "intense absorption into the category of melancholia"[16] as a precondition of theorizing subject formation in the context of violence, trauma, and loss. This context and the broader theoretical frame of melancholia is critical for addressing the terms of Afropessimism. The abjection of the world produces, for Wilderson and Sexton, a sense of melancholic subjectivity that cannot be overcome by or through the terms of the world. Melancholy's power, of course, draws from the inability of the melancholic to name and identify the object of their beleaguerment, which, in turn, makes it impossible to work through the pain of the past and present. The future is nothing but repetition of horror and disgust. Afropessimism, in this sense, is a theory of melancholy in the very same moment that it entwines being and antiblackness with a named source: whiteness. Or is whiteness even an object to be named? A complicated question. The affective work of melancholy is both a sign of the condition of antiblack being and a reproduction of its violence inside the psyche of the oppressed. That is, antiblack racism, as the totality of being, renders such overcoming impossible as a matter of principle. Antiblackness is neither an object nor a possession of a group or demographic but rather a transcendental condition that makes groups, demographics, and possession itself possible. *Being* not beings. Subjects produced in that totality, including subjects with a compulsion to resist, are compromised by the available terms; the world is the pathogen and cannot cure itself, for it is the agent of its own disease. Melancholia, the affective aftereffect of the pathogen, as it were, offers no promise of liberation and pervades the psychological and embodied life of everything from the inferiority complex to efforts at resistance inside the antiblack world. Liberation, as we have seen, can only come through the destruction of the being of the world that produces violence, trauma, and loss, and all of their companion affects.

In pushing against the dominance of melancholia in theories of pessimism, Snediker proposes the alternative of *taking positive affects seriously*. This strikes me as interesting and exceptionally suggestive, for in taking affect seriously we are committed to neither the inherent true *nor* false consciousness of positive affect. Instead, we are committed to seeing something compelling, something suggestive of another modality of being—a modality that moves thinking out of the stalled or impeded dialectic of opposition and domination, which leads us to theorize the urgency of resistance, and toward something like the life and world of refusal. Refusal is its own kind of optimism. How does Snediker help us think about this? Two aspects of Snediker's queer optimism are of particular importance here. First, he describes queer optimism as *meta*-optimism, an epistemologically prior sense of *interest in* rather than the ontologically prior condition of *being optimistic*. The time structure difference here is a difference that makes a difference. Meta-optimism is not invested in rewriting the pessimism of the past and its fold into the present, nor is it a vision of future possibility. Rather, it is a dispositional question. Snediker writes:

> Queer optimism, immanently rather than futurally oriented, does not entail predisposition in the way that conventional optimism entails predisposition. It presents a critical field and asks that this field be taken seriously. . . . Queer optimism doesn't aspire toward happiness, but instead finds happiness *interesting*. Queer optimism, in this sense, can be considered a form of meta-optimism: it wants to *think* about feeling good, to make disparate aspects of feeling good thinkable.[17]

The nonfixity and nondeclarative sense of affective life is crucial, as the turn toward finding happiness—or any other affect that labors *apart* from (and so not necessarily *against*) pessimism—*interesting* and *thinkable* opens up a particularly compelling theoretical field. The theoretical field of interested affect, of thinkable affect, depersonalizes affective life and opens up the possibility of bringing that life to bear intimately and immanently on the structure of being. Perhaps not being itself, but, if we work this queer optimism back into Baldwin's texts, perhaps something like the otherwise or outside of being. Why is being a closed field? And what happens to thinking affect and world if we take the nonclosure of being seriously? Snediker's shift toward this field, the field of the interesting and the thinkable, allows us to suspend the time of being optimistic in order to glimpse refusal at the affective level and in tension with pessimism's darkening sun. This affective level operates in excess of what we properly call the subject or the self. It operates otherwise than being but also as its own sense of being and possibility.

There is an important second aspect of queer optimism. Snediker shifts theorizing optimism from a theory of the subject or self to a theory of the *person*. This is a crucial shift, as it suggests that, if we creolize the concept with racialized experience, there is a field of Black thinkability, affect, and (to put it metaphysically) *life* that functions otherwise than what is produced by a discursive field. Discourse and being have such an intimate relation; language is the house of being (Heidegger was right about that), and social-political realities are produced and reproduced in discursive formations, re-formations, and counter-formations. The space of refusal, occupied by what Snediker calls personhood, bears a very different relation to desire and knowledge. Those different relations open up the possibilities of outsides, interstices, and worlds thought otherwise. Snediker writes, "Queer optimism insists on thinking about personhood—as opposed to subjectivity—in terms of a durability neither immediately nor proleptically subject to structuralist or poststructuralist scrutiny. . . . [Subjects and selves] inhabit (*and sometimes unknowingly curate*) particular discursive labyrinths . . . of discipline, desire, and knowledge to which examinations of personhood at best only obliquely speak."[18] I find this note on the *curation* of discursivity to be of particular interest, as it speaks to what is not just an epistemological position—a theory of how we know ourselves as a chiasma of interiority and political economy—but also the reproduction of being in cultural and political theory.

Such an observation raises the difficult, troubling question of how a theory might be said to curate its own epistemological conditions and thereby curate and reproduce its own production of subjects and selves. This is a particularly interesting question to raise in critical relation to Afropessimist ontology, the persistent question about the closure of being and also how, if at all, a theory can account for not just the object of theory—melancholic, abject social death—but also the subject of theorizing—the one who is able to see necessity and also possibility. Whence *that* subjectivity?

Snediker's shift from subject to person recalls, for me, Baldwin's oldest dispute: the meaning of the protest novel and Richard Wright's fiction. Baldwin's long argument with Wright has straightforward contours. He acknowledges the fundamental truth of Wright's character Bigger Thomas, a character who, for better or worse, stands in for the entirety of Wright's literary production. (Baldwin's refusal to engage Wright's fiction after *Black Boy* or Wright's nonfiction is a separate and perplexing issue.) Bigger is Baldwin's Afropessimist and a precursor to the movement, the character who embodies the affects of life lived under regimes of antiblack racism; the abjection of Harlem, the suffocating political economy of race in the United States, and the failure of exile to offer alternative forms of life place Bigger, for Baldwin, inside the skull of every African American. The truth of Bigger, the profundity and importance of Wright's earliest fiction, is also troubled and troubling from the outset. Baldwin's worry, famously, is that Wright plays on the innocence of white Americans—"since no American has the knowledge or authority to contest it and no Negro has the voice,"[19] as Baldwin puts it in "Many Thousands Gone"—and in so doing speaks blackness into existence inside what we would now call a discursive economy. The discursive construction of abject blackness, the social death figure of Afropessimism, implicates white people in such interesting ways, dialectical implication, to be precise, insofar as white identity needs its other. But it needs that other without the guilt or shame of having made an identity out of abjection. The evasion of responsibility is as constitutive of whiteness as the relation to abject Black life. Wright's *innovation* is his witness to Black suffering. Wright's *complicity*, for Baldwin, lies in his reification of white innocence and the muting of both Black resistance and the worlds made by generations of refusal. This last part, the countereconomy of refusal, is utterly crucial.

Are we fated to this discursive economy? Snediker is right that the language of subjects and selves is caught in this economy and that such an economy, dedicated as it is to the production of subaltern creatures, produces subjects and selves of abjection, melancholia, and the unredeemable. Queer pessimists and Afropessimists share this fundamental theoretical structure: The language of abjection is constitutive of a world of immense suffering and incapacitation. But what do we make of Snediker's appeal to the person, and how can this appeal be worked through the racial schema we find in Baldwin's thinking?

The logic of antiblackness in Afropessimism, especially in Calvin Warren's engagement with fundamental ontology in *Ontological Terror*, locates blackness both inside being as necessity and outside being as possibility. That is, blackness is radical nothingness—a Heideggerian retooling of Fanon's zone of nonbeing. Yet, that blackness is subjected to and subjugated by the play of being. Warren argues that "black incarnate nothing [is] in a metaphysical world and that the world is both fascinated with this nothing and terrified of it."[20] This is both cruelly ironic and an articulation of the impossibility of Black life. Incapacitated by discursive formations of subjectivity, Black life is necessarily subjected to being's violence against nothingness while also separated from all that being makes possible. The relation of blackness to being is peculiar but also trapped inside a closed system. Ontology is not just fundamental, but total.

How might a notion of *the person* shift this sense of being and relation? In his critique of Wright in "Many Thousands Gone," Baldwin appeals to two senses of relation, both of which, in interesting ways, extend what Snediker calls the person into the question of memory, history, and identity. Baldwin writes, and it is worth quoting again in full:

> What this means for [*Native Son*] is that a necessary dimension has been cut away; this dimension being the relationship that Negroes bear to one another, *that depth of involvement and unspoken recognition of shared experience which creates a way of life*. . . . [Wright's novel] creates its climate of anarchy and unmotivated and unapprehended disaster; and it is this climate, common to most Negro protest novels, which has led us all to believe that in Negro life there exists no tradition, no field of manners, no possibility of ritual or intercourse. . . . For a tradition expresses, after all, nothing more than the long and painful experience of a people.[21]

This is a remarkable passage for a number of reasons. To begin, Baldwin's critique of Wright takes on real substance outside negation—moving away from quick negative characterizations and toward an alternative vision of sociality and being—and is therefore genuinely transformative. The amputation, the cutting away of "a necessary dimension," disables Wright; he cannot see the complexity of Black life because he only allows that life to be spoken into existence inside the discursive forms of white supremacy, inside the closed system of being. So, of course Wright's Black people must die, go underground, dismember, and generally reflect, in literary hyperbole but also in a kind of sociology, life under antiblack racism. But this second bit from Baldwin is just so important. His invocation of "the relationship that Negroes bear to one another" establishes a schematic of intimacy that is also communal, collective, and perhaps in its own way political. Whatever we call it, it is a whole world and does not need more than what it already is. A relationship with its own civitas, perhaps. This relationship between Black people is a relationship that, at least programmatically but also in world-making practice and praxis, takes place outside the white gaze. Perhaps being is *not* a closed system. Perhaps the relation Black people bear to one another, on their own terms and in their own ritually constructed and reproduced worlds, disputes all claims to a closed system of being. This double session, reading and then rereading ontology, disrupts closure with the simple gesture of relation. Relation that is not one inside being as antiblackness but relation that makes its own kind of relational meaning. Ethical. Political. Cultural. Existential. Folkways. Pathways. Worldways. Knowledge. Origins. Being. Acting. Judging. Gesture. Language. Affect. Home. All of which are the event of a people in interstitial relation, at the edge of being, disruptive and interruptive but also fully outside the relations of "being." A counterrelation to social death.

An Afro-optimism takes root in exactly this space: the space of tradition, the space of relationship, a space in which exist manners, rituals, folkways, dispute, identification, and all those other ways of creating *a people* that make a future possible. This future is never forgetful or utopian in the sense of a dreamscape disburdened of the past. It is not Fanon's new humanism or concluding political dream in *Black Skin, White Masks*. In fact, very much to the contrary, it is rooted in a tradition that expresses "the long and painful experience of a people." Therein lies Baldwin's most complicated moment. How do we render that long, painful experience such that tradition is not merely or exclusively a tradition of lament, plea, and testimony to the unspeakable? That is, how is tradition not wholly or largely embedded in conceptions, political praxes, and material realities of the abjection of blackness? Or, maybe I can put it this way: How can we think the African American tradition as something like the blues? That tradition of community and sound that is full of history's sadness and terror, but also dance music, shit-talking music, music for fucking, music for laughing, music for work, music for after work, music for not finding work, drunk music, theorizing music, friendship music, controversy sounds and drop beats that move a people together, and so just plain music for all of what we would simply call *life*? We can think here again of Ralph Ellison, who in his essay "Blues People" calls Bessie Smith a *priestess*,[22] a being who, through performance, conjures worlds, memories, histories, and identities. All of that conjuring is at the juke joint. The juke is no urban club. It is not the jazz lounge in uptown or the village between interracial walkways and pathways. The juke is located outside of the town, of the plantation, of the city, and therefore of being itself. The juke joint as the opening of closure.[23]

I am also thinking here of Baldwin's account of what I explored previously in the opening and fourth chapter: his notion of "black English." In particular, I have in mind that pair of essays from the late 1970s, where, much like Du Bois in *Souls of Black Folk*, Baldwin traces the origin of African American language back to the Sorrow Songs. This example plays a twofold role here.

First, by linking his account rhetorically and in a grand historical gesture to Du Bois's final chapter in *Souls*, as well as Alain Locke's rewrite of the same in the 1920s, Baldwin marks tradition with an origin—the pain of the Auction Block, the cry of resistance and mourning—but also with sublimity. This last part is so critical. For Baldwin, the origin story of the Auction Block does not set in motion a total system of social death but instead doubles the world. One moment of that world is the closure of being. Another moment, simultaneous and also wholly other than the time of closure, is the opening of the system. Crack. Fissure. Break. Fracture. Space and place thought and lived *otherwise*—an ontological path underpinning what Kevin Quashie calls an interest in "an aesthetic imaginary founded on black worldness."[24] The trick is transforming the negative sublime into something other than abject memory, which the African American tradition has done with such transcendent beauty. Recall how Frederick Douglass hears the song of enslaved people working in the distance and is moved by the pain, but also the gorgeousness of its philosophical expression. Or, one can recall Locke's remark at the beginning of "The Negro Spirituals," in which he describes the Sorrow Songs as "the most characteristic product of the race genius yet in America."[25] Second, the focus on the question of language and the cultural politics surrounding speech, diction, and the intellect, in which Baldwin intervenes at the level of the *person*—the expressive totality, full of nuance, and the texture of "the relationship that Negroes bear to one another"—and also in the discursive formation of more than just abject subjects. Black English interpellates, creates, and grounds subjectivity first and foremost through that subject's grounding in tradition, belonging, and its complexities—and even contradiction. In other words, language, issuing from tradition and the experience of a people, mixes discursive formation with the property and propriety of the person. The relation Negroes bear to one another is Black self-possession *in a world thought and lived otherwise*. For Baldwin, this mixture is expressed in the musicality of speech, how cadence, tone, and expressive culture offer a full counternarrative to the coloniality typically attributed to diglossic political contexts. Baldwin writes, and it is worth quoting this passage again in full:

> It is out of this, and much more than this, that black American music springs. This music begins on the auction block.
>
> Now, whoever is unable to face this—the auction block; whoever cannot see that that auction block is the demolition, by Europe, of all human standards: a demolition accomplished, furthermore, at that hour of the world's history, in the name of "civilization"; whoever pretends that the slave mother does not weep, until this hour, for her slaughtered son, that the son does not weep for his slaughtered father; or whoever pretends that the white father did not, literally, and knowing what he was doing, hand, and burn, and castrate, his black son—whoever cannot face this can never pay the price for the "beat" which is the key to music, and the key to life.

> Music is our witness, and our ally. The "beat" is the confession which recognizes, changes, and conquers time.
>
> Then, history becomes a garment we can wear, and share, and not a cloak in which to hide; and time becomes a friend.[26]

The key issue here for theorizing an Afro-optimism is time. Discursive formations that produce abject subjects, subjects who wail and plead and remember too much pain, are not subject to time. Or if they are subject to it, like Fanon's evocation of the culture that reshapes itself in order to maintain the racial order in "Racism and Culture," discursive formations keep paradoxical time, blending the slow retreat of old ideas with the fixity of eternal racial order. This is the reciprocal action of racialized, racist time.

What, then, converts time into the element of an Afro-optimism, a blackness interested in its own happiness and thinking its own affects, queered in order to exit the merely discursive order, and so simultaneously immanent to the political economy of Afropessimism yet otherwise than its epistemological and ontological constraints? That is a lot. Let me spell out these terms. The epistemological conditions articulated in or as an Afropessimism are particularly powerful, allowing Wilderson, Hartman, Warren, and others to identify both the possibility and actuality of reproducing the logic of subjection across time. Formations of knowledge carry this racialized ideology with them, such that expressions of life—something Sexton is right to emphasize as possible within pessimistic theory—are neither exclusive of nor contrary to the diagnostic claims of Afropessimism. When those epistemological conditions are flipped into an account of discursivity, knowledge and language produce being; what it means to *be* Black is inseparable from what it means to know the world, how the world knows you, how you speak of the world, how to have the world speak to you, and therefore how blackness is doubled as an object of public and private knowledge. Histories of subjection are akin to epistemologies and ontologies of the present. An eternal present, if the abjection of blackness and maintenance of Black being works.

Baldwin converts that same history in this notion of *conquering* time, a relation to the temporality of memory, haunting, and specters of the future that is simultaneously committed to witness and to combat. To witness time, the history of subjection, is to register its passage through the time of the life/death world of African Americans, of white supremacy, and of all of those crucial points of intersection. And that's just it: These are points of *intersection*. The Afropessimist graph of discursive formation flattens the world such that *subjects* are produced, not *persons* for whom inheritance is at once the threat (and reality) of subjection, the honoring of struggle and its unimaginable price, *and* the conquest of a certain kind of time that opens the putatively closed system with histories of refusal. Conquest, strangely enough, is characterized by Baldwin as a *confession*, suggesting that in speaking the past—or, better, hearing how it has already been spoken—a recognition that also transforms is manifest in the *person* and collective *persons* who comprise tradition, interstitial worlds, and the being otherwise of vernacular culture's soul work. That transformation of history, making it into what Baldwin calls "a garment we can wear," conquers time, not as a repetition and reversal of subjection, but instead as a condition of friendship.

What, then, is this time as friendship? Time is friendship in that moment when life exceeds what the confession confronts—the terms of Afropessimism, which, in a certain (and perhaps decisive) sense, are the terms that white supremacy proscribes and prescribes for a pathogenic world that creates blackness. But there is also this excess, what Baldwin calls tradition, created in the movement of sound, image, and concept between Black people. This is also the work of refusal, the withdrawal of interest and struggle in the interracial world and the movement toward thinking and being otherwise. Thinking and being in the borderlands of the shared world, inside the opening of the closed system on which Afropessimism depends. This dependency is critical; in many ways, Afropessimist approaches to ontology work in a pre-deconstructive space, deploying notions of closure as the *foundation* of theory as if poststructuralist thinkers had not put closure into such profound question. That questioning of closure in the European philosophical context is translated as the work of refusal in the Black Americas and the Black United States in particular. The work of refusal is neither insurgent nor resistance labor proper. It is, rather, a different sort of economy, one that cannot be reduced to a discursive formation, even as it is plenty of that. That different sort of economy is one in which we find the pleasures of the blues, not just the melancholia of its lament. *Change the joke, slip the yoke.* What would it mean to find those pleasures *interesting* and to have them provoke us to *think hard* about them?

The person is alive in excess of death, and perhaps that is enough to begin theorizing outside pessimism. That is my single suggestion here, put in rather blunt terms. Let me conclude with Baldwin's own words, words that recall my initial characterization of Afro-optimism as between bitter expectation and belonging. From an interview with Kenneth Clarke: "I can't be a pessimist because I'm alive. To be a pessimist means that you have agreed that human life is an academic matter, so I'm forced to be an optimist. I'm forced to believe that we can survive whatever we must survive. But the future of the Negro in this country is precisely as bright or as dark as the future of the country."[27] For any writer on Baldwin who raises the question of optimism, this is the first quotation that comes to mind. It invites what so much of Baldwin's writing invites: a quick sound bite to summarize a different kind of feeling. But it is more than that. For that reason, I waited until almost ten thousand words on pessimism and optimism to quote it, because it is anything but a sound bite. Baldwin plays on an irony here and it is compelling. The fragility of white identity is revealed by the dialectical structure of its formation, a formation that produces the illusion of innocence and the material reality of immense guilt and shame. White people *need* the abjection of blackness, and so much labor—interpersonal and institutional and everything else in between—is dedicated to the reproduction of an illusory closed system of being. Afropessimism exposes the atrocity of this ontology and, in response, calls for what Aimé Césaire, Fanon, and so many others called for: the end of the world. Apocalypse? Perhaps that is emancipation. Perhaps liberation means the destruction of the world as we know it. But there is another question to be asked, one that Baldwin asks of his fellow African Americans: Have we in some ways always been free, when we are together and apart from these other people? Ontology as a closed system is an academic matter because the souls of Black folk have lived otherwise. Lived where? In the opening, not just in the wake. In the borderlands, not just in the ghetto. In the vernacular, not just in the alienated space of white language hegemony.

This is Baldwin's optimism. The optimism of small places. Small places are entire worlds. To inherit them is to inherit the cry of the Auction Block made into the sound of Ray Charles, made into the sorcery of Bessie Smith, and all those other ways that small places make space for the person. Every good-bye ain't gone.

Afterword

✦

On the Ethics of Inheritance

I began *So Unimaginable a Price: Baldwin and the Black Atlantic* with the observation that James Baldwin's work, especially his nonfiction and interviews, is ready-made for our age. He has a word for everything. He is quotable. His insights are pithy and direct. He mixes hope with outrage, which is forever needed. His observations have proven to exceed his moment, something both tragic (the world has not changed that much) and testimony to his genius as a thinker (he understood race and nation at a depth few achieve in writing). But for all the meme-able sound bites and compelling, relatable remarks, what remains to be understood is how Baldwin works as a *thinker*. What do I mean by that? Plainly put: How did he understand knowledge production? How did he understand being? How did he understand language, embodiment, and affect? How did he understand Black identity in an Atlantic world context, as a theoretical achievement embedded in all those ways of knowing and being we call "African American"? In the end, that last bit is the cornerstone toward which all of his arguments lead: What does it mean to be African American? Baldwin's pursuit of this question has nothing to do with prescriptive, normative, or authenticity claims. Rather, the question is just that—a question. What sets the interrogative in motion is a simple observation from "Many Thousands Gone" that carries with it such consequences: the relation that Negroes bear to one another. Baldwin takes that relation and unfolds it. Not embellishes it or gasses it up but just unfolds it and describes what it is: "that depth of involvement and unspoken recognition of shared experience which creates a way of life."[1] How does a "way of life" register in critical theory? And how might that change the sound-bite character of so much of Baldwin's presence in our popular and intellectual worlds?

The public portrait of Baldwin as eminent commentator on America's race problem is immensely important and even indispensable. I am always so happy to see him show up in my social media with incisive words and his iconic facial expressions. There are so many facial expressions. Baldwin was so photogenic; his face was the feature of an entire exhibition at the National Portrait Gallery.[2] That never hurts one's historical reputation, if we are honest. But really thinking about and with Baldwin is ultimately about his words and his insights and how they remake our conscience and then illuminate aspects of our shared and unshared worlds. My work in this book does not add much to *that* element of Baldwin, although that was never my aim. What I have wanted to achieve is pretty straightforward: embed Baldwin in his mid-century moment, allow his work to critically resonate across the Atlantic in comparative study, and situate his thinking inside contemporary discussions of affect and related critical problems. For me, this is crucial work because Baldwin was an observer and witness, yes, but both observing and witnessing implicate deep and abiding theoretical issues. Observation is mediated. Let us excavate the structures of that mediation. Witnessing is intertwined with who and what we are. Let us disclose structures of subjectivity that draw out our conscience and how conscience both does and does not transform us and our moral consciousness. In other words, let us read Baldwin phenomenologically and see, from inside the lived experience he documents with clarity and precision, the sedimentations of history and memory in the imagination, in our senses of necessity, and in our senses of possibility. This last part is his push against the nihilism of his moment, of our moment, of the long Black Atlantic moment, and of what seems like the future of all our moments. The necessity of *this* life is a limit, but like all limits, it is also an occasion for refusal and resistance. The closure of life in a nihilistic system of antiblackness is leaky, fractured, and open to thinking and being otherwise. Baldwin's treatment of everything from the double meaning of pain to the promise and realities of love to interstitial cultural and social formation steps into this opening at the limit. Therein lies his hearty and challenging contribution to critical theory.

That is what I hope to have brought to the surface across this book: Baldwin the thinker and theorist. Very little work has been done on this aspect of Baldwin's writing, and perhaps there is good reason for that. This is also why my work here has not engaged in close debate with existing literatures. So little is written in a theoretical register that there are not genuine, expansive critical theory debates around Baldwin's work. I hope I have changed that a bit and initiated a different modality of reading his nonfiction. But the light citation touch of this book is intentional. I want the hermeneutic event—the simultaneous revelation of the text and revelation of my own interests as a reader—to say its piece without burdensome interference. Revealing the theoretical Baldwin requires purposive reading and philosophical treatment that is both attentive to the primary source and honest about the interests of me the interpreter. The ideas are there in the primary texts, of course. This book is nothing like a series of fabrications. But those ideas often lay hidden in how Baldwin writes and articulates himself; the smart public for whom he wrote asks for a style, and that style is nothing like what we imagine when we say the word "philosophy" or the phrase "critical theory." The latter two characterizations are very much the opposite of how Baldwin writes—at least on first glance. Baldwin writes in a conversational, autopoetic style suited to the magazines that asked for his contributions. Philosophy and critical theory have well-earned reputations as writing that holds opacity as a value, obscurant expression as constitutive of moments of theorizing. But we are readers when we write, framing and drawing out insight like a stain applied to wood draws out hidden grains—grains that were there, but needed specific, targeted treatment in order to make them visible, vibrant, and compelling. That stain, so to speak, is the broad mid-century Atlantic world moment.

Reading Baldwin as a *thinker* expands our appreciation of his work as a nonfiction writer and, for me, offers important insights into thinking about the place of race—blackness in particular, of course, but also race more broadly—in critical theory. Professional philosophy has only just begun the process of taking race seriously as a theoretical issue, and for the most part that taking seriously has meant a genealogy of the concept and initial readings of important figures in the Black intellectual tradition. Baldwin has not been a part of that movement and shift in philosophy in any significant way. I hope this book does a bit of work toward making Baldwin philosophically relevant. And I would say the same about critical theoretical work more widely, work that has taken blackness and race seriously for a few generations but in which Baldwin has barely factored as a voice and source of compelling insight. In contemporary philosophy of race, a subfield in which I have only the smallest bit of participation, Baldwin is completely absent as a critic and thinker (so are most from the Black intellectual tradition, which makes some sense given how committed that area of study is to genealogies of the concept of race). In global Black critical theory circles, Baldwin is often too literary and too autopoetic for consistent engagement. If the text is not theoretically *toned*, then it seems fated to be a latecomer to the field. Even in a number of key texts, like Paul Gilroy's paradigm-shifting *The Black Atlantic*, Baldwin garners barely a mention—even though in that case he confounds so many of Gilroy's claims. But as I hope to have shown, Baldwin is absolutely a critical theory figure whose work yields incredible insights when framed properly and read with a creative, expansive eye. The hermeneutic event *produces* insight.

In this way, I hope that *So Unimaginable a Price: Baldwin and the Black Atlantic* is a compelling alternative frame for reading Baldwin outside of literary history. My highest aspiration in this book—books should always have a big vision and hope—has been to reframe Baldwin scholarship and entirely shift models of interpretation. I know that will not be the case, which means my more modest and realistic aim is to suggest some new paths. And new paths are definitely desirable, if not outright needed. So much of the commentary on his work consists of literary-historical reading, linking him to his moment in the United States and to key figures and movements of his time. Who were his mentors? Who were his foils? Where did he travel and why? Who were his interlocutors and partners in crime? That kind of reading is particularly well-suited to Baldwin's fiction and nonfiction. He himself wrote to his moment in the United States and to that strange between space of long and short histories of Black presence—sometimes the Auction Block, sometimes a bar in Paris. And I think we all deeply value that kind of reading and accounting. It gives Baldwin's writerly and cultural life contour and shape in important ways. But, and I have repeated this across the book, that is very different than an excavation of Baldwin the *thinker*, whose work is animated by shifting yet stable conceptual constellations that organize his fiction and nonfiction work. Reading with and for critical theory lays out that constellation and, when put in a comparative context, distinguishes Baldwin the thinker from many of his peers inside and outside the United States. As well, it resituates Baldwin in our own moment, something I hope to have shown in my engagement with elements of Afropessimism. Both literary history and critical theory locate figures and texts in specific, different senses of time and the history of ideas. I want Baldwin to exist in all of these times. He is that interesting and important. What comes next? In the end, that is what I want from this book, to provoke responses and rewritings of theoretical and comparative motifs. There is always and rightly so much more to be said than what I have said here.

With the preceding chapters in place, I think one of the more interesting insights to be drawn from Baldwin's linking of vernacular cultural formation to the Auction Block as critical concept surrounds what we can call an ethics of inheritance. This is a crucial question in the Black Americas, and Baldwin's work speaks directly to it, so let me conclude with some words.

It is plenty to take note of inheritance, to see how it bears down on the everydayness of existence in ways both destructive and liberatory, sometimes at the same time, and to understand at the level of being's relation to memory how subjectivity is the sedimentation of the past, folded into the present, and reconfigured in anticipation of a future. Such thinking is at the root of theories of refusal as well as theories of resistance. Baldwin's account of time's folds, of the memorial structure of inheritance, recalls for me what Édouard Glissant writes in *Poetics of Relation* while reflecting on the abyssal structure of the Middle Passage: "For us, and without exception, and no matter how much distance we may keep, the abyss is also a projection of and a perspective into the unknown. Beyond its chasm we gamble on the unknown. We take sides in this game of the world. We hail a renewed Indies; we are for it. And for this Relation made of storms and profound moments of peace in which we may honor our boats."[3] There is so much worth reflecting on in this passage. Glissant notes something incredibly important here about inheritance, namely, that inheritance in the Black Americas brings with it harrowing pain and also a sense of adriftness, dissociation from origins, and struggle to identify and love a sense of place. Inheritance often means absence, abyss. Or at least begins there. Pain is not solely visceral or the cry. Pain is also the nothingness that gives to thinking what thinking cannot handle: a projection of the unknown. What does it mean to inherit the unknown? What does it mean to inherit the known that is known only because of the unknown that gave it life? This is Glissant's question in thinking after the Middle Passage, but it is also the question of the Black Americas when Africa, what Fanon called "the great black mirage,"[4] is not an anchor and is instead a fragment, a sliver, and a hint. To begin *here*, in this place, is to begin with the unknown and the subordinate relation of the known to the unknown.

How does one approach such precarious memory and history? The abyss and its absences call us to responsibility. That is why Glissant ends this passage with the phrase "in which we may honor our boats." To honor the boats is to refuse to remember them as unmediated abjection, and so also to remember them in their capacity to birth new forms of life, perhaps new senses and experiences of *a people*. "No place in the world," Glissant writes, "can accommodate itself to the slightest forgetting of a crime, of the slightest shadow cast. We ask that the unspoken parts of our histories be conjured, so that we enter, all together and free, into the *tout-monde*. Together again, let us name the Slave Trade and slavery perpetrated in the Americas, a crime against humanity."[5] A stunning bit from Glissant here. Conjuring the pain of the past, naming it for what it is—a crime against humanity—and then linking conjuring to participation in *tout-monde* (his notion of a globalized cultural space) is an ethical intervention in history and memory. This is an ethical intervention that understands the link between both inheritance and ontology (our very being is at stake in this conjuring) and inheritance and responsibility (the past demands care). Memory is forever troubled in the Americas. It is, after all, a synonym for conquest and enslavement, the founding wounds of the hemisphere. Troubled memory is forever precarious. Thus, the need for care, cultivation, ethics, and honoring the boats. Honor the pain of the boats. Honor what it meant to have said yes to life in a death world in and after the boats.

This question of an ethics of memory and critical theory is where Baldwin is at his best. Baldwin's work spends so much time with children, in love with how they play and how they manifest the future in its most profound sense, but also in crisis because the world they inherit, the world he already inhabits, is one in which those children are meant to perish. He is never naive about the potential of antiblack violence. That much we know. Every Black child inherits the boats and the auction blocks and the necropolitical world of interracial life. This is the melancholy that permeates so much of Baldwin's writing. Often quiet, always moody, and forever his toughest words. I am thinking here not just of his letter to his nephew, but also age in the other direction, namely, his long meditation on his father, race, and death in "Notes of a Native Son." That early essay is so troubled and troubling and in that voice it is able to express something endemic to the African American condition in this godforsaken country. "He had lived and died in an intolerable bitterness of spirit," Baldwin writes of his father, "and it frightened me, as we drove him to the graveyard through those unquiet, ruined streets, to see how powerful and overflowing this bitterness could be and to realize that this bitterness now was mine."[6] This is part of inheritance. The ethics of this inheritance is peculiar and complicated, but I think "Notes of a Native Son" is an exemplary case of how to care for bitter and embittering memory: witness, testimony, honest words, and a recognition of how one is implicated even in those moments one might find revolting, angering, and dispiriting. Baldwin's articulation of himself into his father's life and death lays bare the most difficult of intimacies. Intimacies that exceed the father and the son and become ancestral. "I saw that this had been for my ancestors," he writes, "and now would be for me an awful thing to live with and that the bitterness which had helped to kill my father could also kill me."[7]

But Baldwin's commitment to the complexity of Black life, and not just Black death, is the other and perhaps most significant moment of this ethics of inheritance. What does it mean to inherit black English? Or to inherit the righteous claim to home against all worldly forces asserting the opposite? Or to remember the cry on the auction block and honor the yes to life that lay buried in that cry? Or to think against abjection without erasing abjection from the facts of our shared world? I am thinking here in particular about Baldwin's treatment of Uncle Tom and Aunt Jemima in a number of essays, and specifically his remarks in "Many Thousands Gone." Tom and Jemima are our inheritance. What would it mean to *encounter* them, perhaps even to welcome them? They are literary figures, yes, but they are also figures who express something about the facts of our shared world. They are, in Baldwin's words, "the national joke." That joke, precisely because it is national and the nation invites—if not insists upon—aspiration to belonging on the nation's own terms, puts Uncle Tom and Aunt Jemima into a kind of limbo. An undecidable place. They are in an undecidable place because they raise a question: What would it mean to remember them? What does it mean to inherit their names?

One mode of inheritance, the mode of shame and rejection, is described by Baldwin as that of "a group of amazingly well-adjusted young men and women, almost as dark, but ferociously literate, well-dressed and scrubbed, who are never laughed at, who are not likely ever to set foot in a cotton or tobacco field or in anything but the most modern of kitchens."[8] For this group, Tom and Jemima are inherited as shame and the effort against that shame condemns Uncle and Aunt to oblivion. Let's forget that era; we are different now. This deeply troubles Baldwin precisely because it approaches inheritance without *care* and *generous concern*. What would it mean to care for this inheritance, to see and hear and read and think Tom and Jemima as heritage and birthright, constitutive of who and what is an African American? It means commitment to the claim, or just the remembrance, that abjection is never the closure of our world. Baldwin writes:

> Aunt Jemima and Uncle Tom, our creations, at the last evaded us; they had a life—their own, perhaps a better life than ours—and they would never tell us what it was. At the point where we were driven most privately and painfully to conjecture what depths of contempt, what heights of indifference, what prodigies of resilience, what untamable superiority allowed them so vividly to endure, neither perishing nor rising up in a body to wipe us from the earth, the image perpetually shattered and the word failed.[9]

Endurance. Privacy. Pain. But, in the end and most importantly, a life that was their own and evades us when we see them as abject, shameful, and the source of our unease. To care for inheritance is to contemplate with generosity what is given as shameful, not out of indulgence or pleasure in shame but in search of Black life. Uncle Tom and Aunt Jemima *lived*. They had a life. What do we know about that? We actually do not know. So, we imagine, and we imagine with generosity. When we imagine with generosity, the obstinacy of being itself appears as a gift. Untamable and resilient? To care for the past is to care for how the secrets of history's Tom and Jemima secrete their meaning to African American life, expressive culture, the politics of refusal and resistance, and all those other things that lay at the center of Baldwin's love for Black people. And that is a love that begins and ends with what Baldwin describes as the counsel of his ancestors: *to keep the faith*.

ACKNOWLEDGMENTS

I can't lie: I don't know quite how to write this set of acknowledgments. Writing this book has easily been my loneliest writing process. I spent so much time writing in the cracks of my day, whether while the morning coffee steeped and before I pressed it and began my day or while sitting in the car waiting for my kid's bus to arrive or in that hour or so with me downstairs while my family people sat in bed upstairs winding down their night watching anime and laughing. Or all those other cracks. My first acknowledgement is therefore to myself. It was hard to write this, nothing made it easy, but I did it anyway. Good job, John! All I can say is that I hope it is a decent read for anyone who picks it up. I think it has some stuff for learning.

The book project started when I had my one and thus far only sabbatical leave as a fellow at Harvard University, in what was then called the Du Bois Institute. I appreciate all the folks there so much. Everyone was smart and generous in conversation, but I am mostly appreciative for the mood of intelligence, fun, friendship, and respect: Mark Anthony Neal, Bryan Sinche, Achille Mbembe, Christopher Lee, Henry Louis Gates for funding the whole thing, Chris Emdin, Shose Kęssi, and Lauren Coyle. Also to Abby Wolf and most especially to Krishna Lewis. I appreciate all the friendship so much. It is the only reason why I want to do this thing called reading, writing, and thinking. To talk and have friends.

No small part of this project was worked out in a small seminar on Baldwin's nonfiction at the University of Maryland. Our conversations regenerated my affection for the book idea, and, in many ways, it is the only reason why it ever got done. So, my students: Adesubomi Adewole, Kelsey Coleman (especially you!), Leilani Kieti, Crystina Martinez, Christina McPhail, Iyana Moore, Javan Scott, and Katelin Ten (especially you too!). This class was the beginning of a few fantastic student-teacher relationships, which is extra special to me, but it was also a one-time amazing seminar with others. Grateful to all of you for it. You can't know what it meant to meet and talk Baldwin twice per week, to hear your enthusiasm, to get your pushback when I had too bold ideas, to see you get bored when the ideas weren't bold enough. I learned that semester. This book is better because of you folks. Thank you.

As a formal book project, a thanks to three editors at Northwestern University Press. Faith Wilson Stein for the check-ins and not revoking the contract when I forgot to reply, and also for the kind critiques that made this a much better book. Trevor Perri for his interest way back when, giving me a contract that let me write to completion with confidence. And in the very beginning of this project, thank you Jane Bunker—the editor for my first book two and a half decades ago, and then the initial advisor for this one—for telling me to write up a proposal, then putting me in contact with Trevor. Human touches in this professional transaction in each stage. You people are the best.

I also want to single out my dear friend and now long-time collaborator Grant Farred. I know you, Grant, and I know you prefer fewer words than more, so let me just say this: our collaborations on Baldwin and related projects have been the best professional experiences of my career and your friendship means more than you probably understand. Or maybe you do understand. This stuff sustains a person. It sustains me. Thank you.

I offer this book in memory of Jeffrey B. Ferguson, who left us way too young and too early; we will forever miss his presence. Jeff, I learned so much from you. You're the reason I took Baldwin seriously in the first place. We shared an office for those years in Cooper House at Amherst College and I absolutely loved it. We'd sit and talk about Ellison, Wright, Baldwin. You'd try to convince me I need to read more Albert Murray and George Schuyler; I'd try to convince you that you need to read some West Indian writers, and we'd both get yelled at by Rowland Abíọdún for not reading enough Africans. I miss those conversations all the time. Just as much, I miss your three-piece suits, your Mercedes, and your swag. It made my day every day. More than anything I miss how fucking funny you always were and also how you were deadly serious about everything that matters. When Marisa and I got married, you hugged me and said, "You did right, but you also got real lucky. Don't mess it up." I won't. When you met Miles Henry, you said he was "too pretty" and launched into a story about how your father loved Muhammad Ali because he was also too pretty, how you already loved this kid Miles. When you met Satchel Bee you stopped short of breath and said, "Goddamn that is a great name." It meant something real that you loved these moments for me. All of this is a way of rambling into saying something really simple: I miss you, man. So much. And I won't stop missing you, ever.

Lastly, of course, thank you to Marisa, Miles Henry, and Satchel Bee. My life is unimaginable without you. I am a philosophical person by nature and practice, and the first imperative is to know thyself. The Oracle at Delphi was right. I have only come to know myself through the life we live together. It is a good life. It makes all things possible. It makes the world go around. It also made a tiny space in my life to write this book. Thank you. I love you three so much, you don't even know.

Part of chapter 2 originally appeared as "Baldwin's Three Africans," *CR: The New Centennial Review* 16, no. 2 (2016), published by Michigan State University Press. A version of chapter 4 originally appeared as "Vernaculars of Home," *Critical Philosophy of Race* 3, no. 2 (2015): https://doi.org/10.5325/critphilrace.3.2.0203, used with permission from Penn State University Press.

NOTES

Prefatory Notes

1. See an interesting essay on Baldwin, social media, and the contemporary moment by Melanie Walsh, "Tweets of a Native Son," *American Quarterly* 70, no. 3 (2018): 531–59.

2. Justin A. Joyce has written an insightful and compelling piece on Baldwin and contemporary movements, with special attention to social media and witnessing work, that is well worth anyone's reading time. See, "The Matter of Black Lives: Baldwin Today," in *James Baldwin in Context,* ed. Quentin Miller (Cambridge University Press, 2019).

3. On Baldwin and his pressing relevance in the contemporary moment, see also Eddie Glaude, *Begin Again: James Baldwin's American and Its Urgent Lessons for Our Own* (Penguin Books, 2020).

4. On this question of Baldwin's style and voice, see the excellent piece by William E. Dow, "Journeys of the 'I' in James Baldwin's Literary-Journalistic Essays," in *Of Latitudes Unknown: James Baldwin's Radical Imagination,* ed. Alice Mikal Craven and William E. Dow (Bloomsbury Publishing, 2020).

5. See Michele Elam, ed., *The Cambridge Companion to James Baldwin* (Cambridge University Press, 2015), and Quentin Miller, ed., *James Baldwin in Context* (Cambridge University Press, 2019). The one exception is my own essay on Baldwin and the Négritude movement in the *James Baldwin in Context* volume.

Introduction

1. James Baldwin, "Stranger in the Village," in *The Price of the Ticket* (Beacon Press, 2021), 101.

2. James Baldwin, "White Man's Guilt," in *The Price of the Ticket*, 414.

3. Enrique Dussel, "The 'World-System': Europe as 'Center' and Its 'Periphery' Beyond Eurocentrism," in *Beyond Philosophy: Ethics, History, Marxism, and Liberation Theology,* ed. and trans. Eduardo Mendieta (Rowman and Littlefield, 2003).

4. Antonio Benítez-Rojo, *The Repeating Island: The Caribbean and the Postmodern Perspective,* trans. James Maraniss (Duke University Press, 1996), 8–9.

5. Baldwin, "The Fire Next Time," in *The Price of the Ticket*, 385.

6. Baldwin, "The Fire Next Time," 383.

7. Baldwin, "The Fire Next Time," 383.

8. For an excellent introduction to the problematic of the protest novel, with constant reference to Baldwin and Wright, see Brian Norman, "The Protest Essay Tradition," in *James Baldwin in Context,* ed. Quentin Miller (Cambridge University Press, 2019). Also, Briallen Hopper's essay "'Over and Over and Over Again': James Baldwin, *Uncle Tom's Cabin,* and the Afterlife of an American Story," in

James Baldwin: America and Beyond, ed. Cora Kaplan and Bill Schwarz (University of Michigan Press, 2011), tracks with real insight Baldwin's return to this story and its motifs.

9. James Baldwin, "Everybody's Protest Novel," in *The Price of the Ticket*, 39.

10. Baldwin, "Everybody's Protest Novel," 40.

11. Baldwin, "Princes and Powers," 49–50.

12. Aimé Césaire, "Culture and Colonization," trans. Brent Hayes Edwards, *Social Text* 103 (Summer 2010): 129–30.

13. For an example, and one of the only ones, of this kind of comparative work with Baldwin, see Begüm Adalet, "Tensions, Terrors, Tenderness: James Baldwin's Politics of Comparison," *Comparative Studies of South Asia, Africa, and the Middle East* 38, no. 3 (2018): 508–25. See also the really interesting conversation published in 2020 between Jovita dos Santos Pinto, Noémi Michel, Patricia Purtschert, Paola Bacchetta, and Vanessa Naef, "Baldwin's Transatlantic Reverberations: Between 'Stranger in the Village' and *I Am Not Your Negro,*" *James Baldwin Review* 6, no. 1 (2020): 176–98.

Chapter 1

1. James Baldwin, "Many Thousands Gone," in *The Price of the Ticket* (Beacon Press, 2021), 76.

2. Baldwin, "Many Thousands Gone," 76.

3. On the theme of beautiful blackness and the Black Atlantic moment, see also my "The Poetics of Beautiful Blackness: On Baldwin and Négritude," in *James Baldwin in Context,* ed. Quentin Miller (Cambridge University Press, 2019), 223–33.

4. On sound in Douglass and its relation to the Black Americas, see my "Orality and the Slave Sublime," in *The Caribbean Oral Tradition: Literature, Performance, and Practice* (Palgrave, 2016), 109–27.

5. W. E. B. Du Bois, *Souls of Black Folk* (Oxford University Press, 2007), 121.

6. Du Bois, *Souls of Black Folk,* 121–22.

7. Ralph Ellison, "Blues People," in *Shadow and Act* (Vintage Books, 1995), 257.

8. Alain Locke, "The Negro Spirituals," in *The Works of Alain Locke,* ed. Charles Molesworth (Oxford University Press, 2012), 105.

9. On the place of vitalist thought in Négritude and mid-century Black Atlantic thought, see Donna V. Jones, *The Racial Discourses of Life Philosophy: Négritude, Vitalism, and Modernity* (Columbia University Press, 2010).

10. "I say to the ancestor who sold me, and to the ancestor who bought me, I have no father, I want no such father, although I can understand you, black ghost, white ghost, when you both whisper 'history . . .' " Derek Walcott, "The Muse of History," in *What the Twilight Says* (Farrar, Straus, and Giroux, 1998), 64.

11. Édouard Glissant, *Poetics of Relation,* trans. Betsy Wing (University of Michigan Press, 1997), 7.

12. Glissant, *Poetics of Relation,* 11.

13. Glissant, *Poetics of Relation,* 8–9.

14. Édouard Glissant, *Introduction to a Poetics of Diversity,* trans. Celia Britton (Liverpool University Press, 2020), 87.

15. On the persistent theme of children and childhood in Baldwin's work, see Marisa Parham, "17, or Tough, Dark, Vulnerable, Moody," *New Centennial*

Review 16, no. 2 (2016): 65–80, and also from the same issue, Michele Elam, "Baldwin's Boys," 17–30.

16. James Baldwin, "On Language, Race, and the Black Writer," in *The Cross of Redemption: Uncollected Writings* (Knopf Doubleday, 2011), 140.

17. Patrick Chamoiseau, *School Days* (University of Nebraska Press, 1997), 21.

18. James Baldwin, "Of the Sorrow Songs: The Cross of Redemption," in *The Cross of Redemption: Uncollected Writings,* 152–53.

19. Joseph Weiss has written on trauma in Baldwin's work with reference to Jean Améry's description of the same, but Weiss's focus is on how fantasies of revenge operate as healing and therapeutic interventions. Weiss does fantastic work with both thinkers and offers a compelling interpretation, although it takes the question of history's pain in a very different direction than I am here—and that I would say is Baldwin's own direction. He puts revenge and rage under such critical scrutiny, and yet, as Weiss demonstrates, it has its own kind of reparative work. See, Joseph Weiss, "Tortuous Time," *James Baldwin Review* 8, no. 1 (2022): 86–107.

20. Michelle Wright's linking of Baldwin and what she calls Middle Passage epistemology is particularly instructive here, especially because she places that notion in relation to questions of quantum physics, undecidability, and a very Glissantian notion of chaos. See Michelle Wright, *Physics of Blackness* (University of Minnesota Press, 2015), 109–40.

21. Clarence E. Hardy makes an interesting argument for the Spirituals and the carriage of pain as central for understanding religion in Baldwin's work, in particular in *Go Tell It on the Mountain.* That concern with Baldwin's religious thinking is not central to the question of origin story *as such,* but it does take up other dimensions of the afterlives of origins. See Clarence E. Hardy, *James Baldwin's God: Sex, Hope, and Crisis in Black Holiness* (University of Tennessee Press, 2009).

22. Du Bois, *Souls of Black Folk,* 121.

23. Du Bois, *Souls of Black Folk,* 123.

Chapter 2

1. James Baldwin, "*A Lonely Rage,* by Bobby Seale," in *The Cross of Redemption: Uncollected Writings* (Vintage, 2011), 287.

2. James Baldwin, "Princes and Powers," in *The Price of the Ticket* (Beacon Press, 2021), 55.

3. The relationship between Wright and Baldwin is a key part of most work on Baldwin. For a particularly good and interesting overview of that critical relationship, see Alice Mikal Craven, "Responding to Richard Wright," in *James Baldwin in Context* (Cambridge University Press, 2019).

4. Dagmawi Woubshet outlines a compelling and convincing account of Baldwin's development of an idea of Africa, one that is attentive to shifts and turns in his thinking—a different approach than I am taking here, but an immensely important one. See his "James Baldwin's Late Encounters with Africa," *Nka: Journal of Contemporary African Art* 42–43 (2018): 222–32.

5. I am working here from Baldwin's primary nonfiction texts, but for a detailed and generous treatment of Baldwin on Africa, rooted in an interview from 1960, see Douglas Field, "What Is Africa to Baldwin? Cultural Illegitimacy and the

Step-Fatherland," in *James Baldwin: America and Beyond,* ed. Cora Kaplan and Bill Schwarz (University of Michigan Press, 2011).

6. James Baldwin, "The Price of the Ticket," in *The Price of the Ticket*, 12.

7. James Baldwin, "In Search of a Majority," in *The Price of the Ticket,* 239.

8. I cannot take up the question of Baldwin and psychoanalysis with any rigor here, and mostly I am deploying a term for interpretative purposes. But there are important questions to ask about Baldwin's own reckoning with psychoanalysis, which get both overview and depth treatment in Dorothy Stringer's "James Baldwin's Psychoanalysis," *James Baldwin Review* 10, no. 1 (2024): 105–26.

9. James Baldwin, "East River, Downtown," in *The Price of the Ticket,* 275.

10. Baldwin, "East River, Downtown," 275.

11. Baldwin, "East River, Downtown," 275.

12. James Baldwin, "They Can't Turn Back," in *The Price of the Ticket*, 234.

13. James Baldwin, "The Harlem Ghetto," in *The Price of the Ticket,* 20.

14. Baldwin, "Princes and Powers," 55.

15. Léopold Senghor, "The Spirit of Civilization," *Presence Africaine*, nos. 8–10 (1956): 58.

16. Baldwin, "Princes and Powers," 60.

17. Baldwin, "Princes and Powers," 61.

18. Baldwin, "Princes and Powers," 54.

19. James Baldwin, "From Nationalism, Colonialism, and the United States: One Minute to Twelve—a Forum," in *The Cross of Redemption,* 12.

20. James Baldwin, "The Fire Next Time," in *The Price of the Ticket,* 381.

21. See, James T. Campbell, *Middle Passages: African American Journeys to Africa, 1797–2005* (Penguin Books, 2007).

22. On Wright in Ghana, see the excellent treatment of his cultural politics of diaspora—much of which resonates with Baldwin's own—in Kevin Gaines, "Revisiting Richard Wright in Ghana: Black Radicalism and the Dialectics of Diaspora," *Social Text* 19, no. 2 (Summer 2001): 75–101.

23. James Baldwin, "They Can't Turn Back," in *The Price of the Ticket*, 234.

24. James Baldwin, "Many Thousands Gone," in *The Price of the Ticket,* 82.

25. James Baldwin, "The Uses of the Blues," in *The Cross of Redemption,* 75.

26. James Baldwin, "Alas, Poor Richard," in *The Price of the Ticket,* 294.

27. Édouard Glissant, *Poetics of Relation,* trans. Betsy Wing (University of Michigan Press, 1999), 11.

28. Baldwin, "Princes and Powers," 55.

29. James Baldwin, "Faulkner and Desegregation," in *The Price of the Ticket,* 157.

30. Baldwin, "Faulkner and Desegregation," 158.

31. On the question of Baldwin and the strategic question of "going slow," see Tyler Williams, "How Faulkner Means Everything He Says: An Essay on James Baldwin's Politics of Intentionality," *New Centennial Review* 15, no. 3 (Winter 2015): 49–64.

32. Baldwin, "Faulkner and Desegregation," 160.

33. Baldwin, "Faulkner and Desegregation," 160.

34. William Faulkner, *Requiem for a Nun* (Vintage, 2012), 73.

35. James Baldwin, "Black English: A Dishonest Argument," in *The Cross of Redemption,* 154.

36. Baldwin, "Faulkner and Desegregation," 162.

37. Baldwin, "Faulkner and Desegregation," 162.

38. Richard Wright, "Richard Wright Tells Us: The White Problem in the United States, an Interview with Raphaël Tardon," trans. Kenneth Kinnamon, in *Conversations with Richard Wright*, ed. Kenneth Kinnamon and Michel Fabre (University of Mississippi Press, 1993), 99.

39. Although not specifically concerned with Faulkner and instead the civil rights movement broadly, the question of whiteness and its crisis moment gets excellent treatment in Kathy Roberts Forde, "'To End the Racial Nightmare and Achieve Our Country': James Baldwin and the U.S. Civil Rights Movement," in *Of Latitudes Unknown: James Baldwin's Radical Imagination* (Bloomsbury Publishing, 2020), 74ff.

40. Norman Mailer, "The White Negro," in *Mind of an Outlaw: Selected Essays,* ed. Phillip Sipiora (Random House Publishing, 2014), 45.

41. On narcissism, one of my favorite bits from Mailer is his remark on Baldwin in "An Evening with Jackie Kennedy," where he writes, "Jimmy Baldwin once entertained the readers of *Esquire* with a sweet and generously written piece called *The Black Boy Looks at the White Boy* in which he talked a great deal about himself and a little bit about me, a proportion I thought well taken since he is on the best of terms with Baldwin and digs next to nothing about this white boy. As a method, I think it has its merits." "An Evening with Jackie Kennedy," in *Mind of an Outlaw,* 150.

A stunning bit of irony or perhaps self-parody, but it underscores Mailer's need of proximity to some form of blackness, including Baldwin's blackness, which Mailer had assailed as too thin and weak to write great literature. And yet, the compulsion to speak back to Baldwin is strong. By any blackness necessary, apparently.

42. On Mailer, blackness, and sexuality, see George Schulman's excellent treatment in *American Prophecy: Race and Redemption in American Political Culture* (University of Minnesota Press, 2008), 160ff.

43. Mailer, "The White Negro," 62.

44. James Baldwin, "The Black Boy Looks at the White Boy," in *The Price of the Ticket,* 305.

45. Baldwin, "From Nationalism, Colonialism, and the United States," 15.

46. Theodor Adorno, *Negative Dialectics* (Continuum, 1981), xix.

47. James Baldwin, "The White Problem," in *The Cross of Redemption*, 78.

48. Baldwin, "The White Problem," 78.

49. Baldwin, "From Nationalism, Colonialism, and the United States," 14–15.

50. James Baldwin, "Princes and Powers," in *The Price of the Ticket,* 45.

51. James Baldwin, "Alas, Poor Richard," in *The Price of the Ticket,* 280.

52. Baldwin, "Alas, Poor Richard," 280.

53. James Baldwin, "Many Thousands Gone," 87.

54. Baldwin, "Many Thousands Gone," 84.

55. Baldwin, "Many Thousands Gone," 84–85.

Chapter 3

1. Aimé Césaire, "Interview with René Depestre," in *Discourse on Colonialism,* trans. Joan Pinkham (Monthly Review Press, 2001), 89.

2. I will set aside the question of Baldwin as activist here and just note my characterization of him as witness rather than political actor and that I hold strong to this portrait of Baldwin. This is a disputed characterization, of course, and worthy of its own independent treatment. On the issue of Baldwin the activist, see the particularly interesting section in *James Baldwin Review* 10, no. 1 (2024), "The Witness as Activist: James Baldwin and the Congress of Racial Equality (CORE) in 1963." On the other side of my own portrait of Baldwin, see Ed Pavlić's exemplary and challenging reflection in that same volume on Baldwin as political actor in an essay titled "'The Confrontation': James Baldwin's Tour for CORE, May 1963," 62–77.

3. While few commentators have taken up Fanon and Baldwin together, it is a striking intellectual site of comparison. My interests here are around questions of affect, but for a short yet compelling treatment of Fanon and Baldwin—framed by the question of radical politics—see James Miller, "James Baldwin's Black Power: *No Name in the Street,* Fanon, Camus, and the Black Panthers," in *Of Latitudes Unknown: James Baldwin's Radical Imagination,* ed. Alice Mikal Craven and William E. Dow (Bloomsbury, 2022).

4. For a treatment of shame and sexuality, focused on Baldwin's novel *Giovanni's Room*, see the excellent work in Monica Pearl, "*Chagrin d'amour:* Intimacy, Shame, and the Closet in James Baldwin's *Giovanni's Room,*" *James Baldwin Review* 6, no. 1 (2020): 64–84.

5. Frantz Fanon, "The 'North African Syndrome,'" in *Toward the African Revolution,* trans. Haakon Chevalier (Grove Press, 1994), 3–4.

6. Fanon, "The 'North African Syndrome,'" 3.

7. See for example Martin Heidegger, *Being and Time,* trans. John Macquarrie and Edward Robinson (Harper & Row, 1962), section 29, which elaborates the *there* of Dasein in terms of state of mind.

8. Louis Althusser, "Ideology and Ideological State Apparatuses," in *Lenin and Philosophy* (Monthly Review Press, 2001).

9. Frantz Fanon, *Black Skin, White Masks*, trans. Richard Philcox (Grove Press, 2008), 1–2.

10. Fanon, *Black Skin, White Masks*, 4.

11. Fanon, *Black Skin, White Masks,* 170.

12. Fanon, *Black Skin, White Masks,* 94.

13. James Baldwin, "The Fire Next Time," in *The Price of the Ticket* (Beacon Press, 2004), 354.

14. Tommie Shelby's work on community nationalism in *We Who Are Dark* (Harvard University Press, 2003) is helpful here. Even though Shelby is critical of the ultimate scope of such nationalism, seeing important limits in the political strategy, his treatment of Black Power and its promise can be nicely mapped on to this reading of Baldwin.

15. Baldwin, "The Fire Next Time," 349.

16. James Baldwin, "Everybody's Protest Novel," in *The Price of the Ticket*, 43.

17. Baldwin, "Everybody's Protest Novel," 44.

18. Fanon, "The 'North African Syndrome,'" 7.

19. On the importance of rage as revolutionary affect in Fanon, see my "Fanon's Two Memories," *South Atlantic Quarterly* 112, no. 1 (2013): 5–22.

20. It is precisely this mode of thinking that raises the question of the *necessity* and *restorative power* of rage as an affect. See Myisha Cherry, "On Baldwin

and Black Rage," *Critical Philosophy of Race* 10, no. 1 (2022): 1–21, as well as the link between rage and trauma in Joseph Weiss, "Tortuous Time: Undoing the Past in Jean Améry and James Baldwin," *James Baldwin Review* 8, no. 1 (2022): 86–107. I remain unconvinced by these parallel arguments about the centrality of rage in Baldwin's work; neither essay, to my mind, takes the criticisms of Richard Wright to heart and instead instrumentalize Baldwin a bit in order to make the author's broader theoretical claim work. Baldwin had no real taste for rage even in his moments of outrage. The criticisms of Wright make the reasons for that quite clear. That said, both essays are excellent and add dimensionality to the question of affect in Baldwin's nonfiction.

21. Baldwin, "The Fire Next Time," 364.

22. See Donna V. Jones's fantastic book *The Racial Discourses of Life Philosophy* (Columbia University Press, 2010), which demonstrates the deep and abiding debt the foundational figures of Négritude owe to the life philosophy of various European thinkers—in particular, Henri Bergson, Pierre Teilhard de Chardin, and Friedrich Nietzsche, as well as the (often racist) anthropological work of the late nineteenth century in Africa.

23. Aimé Césaire, "Culture and Colonization," trans. Brent Hayes Edwards, *Social Text* 28, no. 2 (2010): 127–44.

24. James Baldwin, "Princes and Powers," in *The Price of the Ticket,* 45.

25. It is worth noting here that Baldwin's assertion of title and right to land, and therefore home, calls us to a comparative, critical study of the relation of theorizing conquest and place from an African American perspective to theorization of indigeneity and the same. This is a massive and important study, to be sure, and cannot be done responsibly here. But I wanted to note this abyss at the heart of Baldwin's reclamation of psychic and cultural space. While it is won through the impossible price of the Middle Passage, slavery, and the Auction Block, it is also (quietly in Baldwin's text) won through the impossible price of the mass displacement and genocide of indigenous peoples. What would it mean to think both resonances of impossible price?

In addition to posing a critical question to Baldwin's work, this raises a broad and incredibly complex question of how to theorize the Black experience in settler colonies outside of the continent—a sense of place that entwines enslavement and settler status in such complicated ways. This is not a question of solidarity or shared senses of suffering white violence, but instead a question of belonging, place, and the irrevocably fucked-up epistemology and ontology of the settled Americas. What is the meaning of home in *this* horizon? A question for another project, but also a question raised as immanent to this moment of thinking affect, home, and place and most emphatically chapter 5 below.

26. Fanon, *Black Skin, White Masks*, xvi–xvii.

27. Fanon, *Black Skin, White Masks,* xii.

28. Fanon, *Black Skin, White Masks,* xviii.

29. Fanon, *Black Skin, White Masks,* 179.

30. Baldwin, "The Fire Next Time," 375.

31. For a detailed account of the function of grievance in Fanon's *Wretched of the Earth*, see my "Fanon's Two Memories," where I argue that Fanon works with two memories, one of which he retains as necessary for revolutionary consciousness (grievance against colonialism) and the other suppressed as necessary for

the same (grievance against internal slave trade in Africa), but he never justifies the distinction. This double-handed gesture undercuts the project of *Wretched of the Earth* for a handful of reasons, the most prominent being the occlusion of memory's anarchic power to form and deform political consciousness.

32. Baldwin, "The Fire Next Time," 386.

33. James Baldwin, "Encounter on the Seine: Black Meets Brown," in *The Price of the Ticket,* 50.

34. James Baldwin, "Everybody's Protest Novel," in *The Price of the Ticket,* 45.

35. James Baldwin, "If Black English Isn't a Language, Then Tell Me, What Is?," in *The Price of the Ticket,* 659.

36. On the relation of creole language formation and painful memory, see my "Orality and the Slave Sublime," in *The Caribbean Oral Tradition: Literature, Performance, and Practice,* ed. Hanétha Vété-Congolo (Palgrave Books, 2016).

Chapter 4

1. James Baldwin, "On Language, Race, and the Black Writer," in *The Cross of Redemption: Uncollected Writings,* ed. Randall Keenan (Pantheon, 2010), 114.

2. This raises a broader and important question about the place of music and musicality in Baldwin's work more widely. On that question, the really brilliant commentary that is both smarter than my thinking on the issue and more comprehensively engaged with Baldwin's archive is Ed Pavlić's *Who Can Affort to Improvise? James Baldwin and Black Music, the Lyric and the Listeners* (Fordham University Press, 2016).

3. Martin Heidegger, "Letter on Humanism," trans. David F. Krell, in *Basic Writings* (Harper Perennial, 1993), 217.

4. On this question of love as a paradoxical, gratuitous gesture, see Grant Farred, "Love Is Asymmetrical: James Baldwin's *The Fire Next Time,*" *Critical Philosophy of Race* 3, no. 2 (2015): 284–303.

5. Baldwin, "On Language, Race, and the Black Writer," 116. Emphasis mine.

6. Alain Locke, "The Negro Spirituals," in *The New Negro,* ed. Alain Locke (Atheneum, 1968), 199.

7. Kamau Brathwaite, *History of the Voice* (University of Michigan Press, 1993), 263.

8. Frederick Douglass, *Narrative of the Life of Frederick Douglass, An American Slave, Written by Himself* (City Lights Books, 2010), 120.

9. Douglass, *Narrative,* 120–21.

10. W. E. B. Du Bois, *The Souls of Black Folk* (Oxford University Press, 2007), 129.

11. Du Bois, *Souls,* 170.

12. Du Bois, *Souls,* 169. My emphasis.

13. James Baldwin, "Of the Sorrow Songs: The Cross of Redemption," in *The Cross of Redemption: Uncollected Writings,* 124.

14. Heidegger, "Letter on Humanism," 217.

15. Frantz Fanon, *Black Skin, White Masks,* trans. Richard Philcox (Grove Press, 2004), 1–2.

16. Fanon, *Black Skin, White Masks,* 21.

17. James Baldwin, "If Black English Isn't a Language, Then Tell Me, What Is?," in *The Price of the Ticket* (St. Martin's Press, 1986), 649.

18. Baldwin, "If Black English Isn't a Language, Then Tell Me, What Is?," 649.

19. This is the thesis of Calvin Warren's book *Ontological Terror* (Duke University Press, 2018), which expands the notion of being as antiblackness into Heidegger's difficult meditation on "the nothing." Warren's novel twist on nihilism—which becomes, in his hands, an iteration of pessimism—is an imposing thought. Baldwin's theorization of vernacular language as what keeps Black life from submersion serves as something of a response to Warren's claim, to the extent that Baldwin links vernacular language to the question of being. I revisit this theme in the final chapter of this project.

20. Baldwin, "If Black English Isn't a Language, Then Tell Me, What Is?," 660.

21. Frantz Fanon, "Racism and Culture," in *Toward the African Revolution*, trans. Haakon Chevalier (Grove Press, 1994), 37.

22. James Baldwin, "Black English: A Dishonest Argument," in *The Cross of Redemption*, 128.

23. James Baldwin, "Many Thousands Gone," in *The Price of the Ticket*, 75.

24. Baldwin, "Black English: A Dishonest Argument," 126–27.

25. The relationship of sound to life, especially in this context of theorizing vernacular language, raises the question of how Baldwin's work employs (or does not employ) his theory of language. I will say this much: Baldwin regularly appeals to turns of phrase, sayings, and tropes from blues, jazz, and folk life more generally. That said, he is not a vernacular stylist in any serious way, whether in his fiction or nonfiction.

For me, this does not compromise his reflections any more than, say, Édouard Glissant's defense of creolization and language is compromised by his writing in French. Rather, it opens up the wider question, one warranting extensive elaboration and exploration, of how vernacular forms function at the level of explicit practice *and* as subtle transformations of medium. The subtle transformations of the medium would show up in Baldwin's often messianic voice, which calls upon many of the very forms of African American preacherly practice that "The Fire Next Time" critiques, while simultaneously enacting. Or how a phrase from a Bessie Smith song might appear as a kind of proof or argument all unto itself at a key moment in an essay. In any case, the argument in defense of black English is to my mind best understood as clearing space for more radical experimentation and innovation; Baldwin, like most theorists clearing such space, is, in this sense, writing toward a time he does not yet inhabit.

26. Marisa Parham, *Haunting and Displacement in African-American Literature and Culture* (Routledge, 2009), 128.

27. James Baldwin, "On Language, Race, and the Black Writer," 114.

28. Ralph Ellison, *Invisible Man* (Vintage Books 1980), 8.

Chapter 5

1. James Baldwin, "The Price of the Ticket," in *The Price of the Ticket* (Beacon Press, 2021), 7.

2. James Baldwin, "The Fire Next Time," in *The Price of the Ticket* (Beacon Press, 2021), 340.

3. James Baldwin, "Of the Sorrow Songs: The Cross of Redemption," in *The Cross of Redemption: The Uncollected Essays of James Baldwin* (Knopf Doubleday, 2011), 152.

4. Marisa Parham, *Haunting and Displacement in African-American Literature and Culture* (Routledge, 2009), 109.

5. As I hope to show, in asking the question of home I am moving to an existential, affective, and critically theoretical sense of home and not continuing the painstaking, incredibly interesting scholarship of Magdalena Zaborowska in her books *James Baldwin's Turkish Decade: Erotics of Exile* (Duke University Press, 2009) and *Me and My House: James Baldwin's Last Decade in France* (Duke University Press, 2018), as well as her concise and sharp essay, of which I am a real fan, "East Meets West: Baldwin in Istanbul in the 1960s," in *James Baldwin in Context,* ed. Quentin Miller (Cambridge University Press, 2019). Every reader owes Zaborowska a huge debt for her careful research and clear, generous presentation of Baldwin's life in exile.

6. Lawrie Balfour, *The Evidence of Things Not Said: James Baldwin and the Promise of American Democracy* (Cornell University Press, 2000), 62.

7. James Baldwin, "Princes and Powers," in *The Price of the Ticket,* 55.

8. For an extensive and diverse set of reflections on Baldwin and US politics, see the great collection *A Political Companion to James Baldwin,* ed. Susan J. McWilliams (University of Kentucky Press, 2017).

9. On this theme, with specific reference to Baldwin and Césaire, see my "The Poetics of Beautiful Blackness: On Baldwin and Négritude," in *James Baldwin in Context,* ed. Quentin Miller (Cambridge University Press, 2019), 233–43.

10. Aimé Césaire, "Notebook of a Return to the Native Land," in *Aimé Césaire: The Collected Poetry*, trans. Clayton Eshleman and Annette Smith (University of California Press, 1998), 35.

11. Aimé Césaire, *Discourse on Colonialism,* trans. Joan Pinkham (Monthly Review Press, 2000), 73.

12. Césaire, "Notebook," 55.

13. On this reading of Césaire, see my "Césaire's Apocalyptic Word," *South Atlantic Quarterly* 115, no. 3 (2016): 567–84.

14. On Fanon and the abjection of Caribbean landscape and history, see my "Martinique Between Fanon and Naipaul," *Journal of French and Francophone Philosophy* 30, no. 2 (2022): 128–45.

15. Frantz Fanon, *The Wretched of the Earth*, trans. Richard Philcox (Grove Press, 2004), 239. Emphasis mine.

16. V. S. Naipaul, *The Middle Passage* (Vintage, 1981), 28–29. For the proximity of Naipaul's theorization of Caribbean abjection to that of Fanon, see my "Martinique Between Fanon and Naipaul."

17. Baldwin, "Princes and Powers," 54.

18. On Baldwin and FBI surveillance and intelligence gathering, see the stunning collection of documents published in William J. Maxwell, ed., *James Baldwin: The FBI File* (Arcade Publishing, 2017).

19. It is noteworthy that the program had two figures speaking in very different directions—Richard Wright, who took the occasion to revisit questions of Marxism and industrialization in Africa, and George Lamming, who took the

occasion to muse on the meaning of the writer (something his other nonfiction treats in real detail). On the place of Lamming and the congress in Baldwin's essay "Princes and Powers," see Kevin Gaines, "Exile and the Private Life of James Baldwin, George Lamming, and the First World Congress of Negro Writers and Artists," in *James Baldwin: America and Beyond,* ed. Cora Kaplan and Bill Schwarz (University of Michigan Press, 2011).

20. Baldwin, "Princes and Powers," 64.

21. Donna V. Jones, *The Racial Discourses of Life Philosophy: Négritude, Vitalism, and Modernity* (New York: Columbia University Press, 2011).

22. James Baldwin, "A Question of Identity," in *The Price of the Ticket*, 110.

23. Baldwin, "Princes and Powers," 64.

24. Baldwin, "Princes and Powers," 55.

25. For a broad and insightful interpretation of this cluster of works, see James Miller's excellent essay "What Does It Mean to Be an American? The Dialectics of Self-Discovery in Baldwin's Paris Essays (1950–1961)," *Journal of American Studies* 42, no. 1 (2008): 51–66.

26. The theme of exile and Americanness receives excellent treatment in Cheryl Wall, "Stranger at Home: James Baldwin on What It Means to Be an American," in *James Baldwin: America and Beyond.*

27. James Baldwin, "Every Good-Bye Ain't Gone," in *The Price of the Ticket,* 655.

28. On the relation between Baldwin's fiction and his understanding of love as community making, see Christopher Freeburg, "Baldwin and the Occasion of Love," in *The Cambridge Companion to James Baldwin,* ed. Michele Elam (Cambridge University Press, 2015). Freeburg's focus on Baldwin's fiction allows him to account for the *surprise* and *shock* of a love that disorients and reorders community. In many ways, this dramatizes the meaning of menaced love, but it also personalizes it in a way that Baldwin's nonfiction does not—and the nonfiction, in this way, allows us to see how theoretically and ontologically the term "love" resonates across his thinking.

29. Douglas Field, "'Perhaps home is not a place but simply an irrevocable condition': At Home in the Life and Work of James Baldwin," *James Baldwin Review* 4, no. 1 (2018): 2.

30. Michael Snediker, "Queer Optimism," *Postmodern Culture* 16, no. 3 (May 2006): 13.

31. James Baldwin, *The Evidence of Things Not Seen* (Henry Holt, 1985), 17–18. On the theme of childhood and violence in this late work, see Jonathan Eburne, "The Terror of Being Destroyed," *Critical Philosophy of Race* 3, no. 2 (2015): 259–83.

32. James Baldwin, "Encounter on the Seine: Black Meets Brown," in *The Price of the Ticket,* 50.

33. Baldwin, "Princes and Powers," 56.

34. James Baldwin, "The Price of the Ticket," in *The Price of the Ticket,* 11.

35. Baldwin, "Every Good-Bye Ain't Gone," 656.

36. Édouard Glissant, *Poetics of Relation,* trans. Betsy Wing (University of Michigan Press, 1977), 9.

37. James Baldwin, "Many Thousands Gone," in *The Price of the Ticket*, 87.

38. Baldwin, "Many Thousands Gone," 83.

39. This relation between African Americans, constitutive of both interstitial life and tradition, sits alongside what Ernest L. Gibson III has so importantly articulated as Baldwin's search for fraternity in *Salvific Manhood: James Baldwin's Novelization of Male Intimacy* (University of Nebraska Press, 2019). I say it sits alongside because Gibson is correct to note and explore how Baldwin's fiction wrestles with the disconnect between Black men and Black men of difference—sexuality, class, region, and so on—and forges paths of possibility rather than proposing another world or recalling us to a world before. For me, what I am saying here about Baldwin and home is precisely the context in which the search for salvific manhood is urgent and a crisis: It strikes at the heart of what makes Black life livable and joyful. What would it mean to call men into another form of intimacy inside the home? This is Baldwin's question and Gibson's question, one we absolutely must ask. Forever grateful for Gibson's book for that reason alone.

40. James Baldwin, "The Discovery of What It Means to Be an American," in *The Price of the Ticket,* 180.

Chapter 6

1. James Baldwin, "A Review of *Roots,*" in *The Price of the Ticket* (Beacon Press, 2021), 562.

2. See also Herb Boyd's treatment of the meaning and condition of Harlem from the Harlem Renaissance up to Baldwin's death in "Harlem During and After the Renaissance," in *James Baldwin in Context,* ed. Quentin Miller (Cambridge University Press, 2019), 7–16.

3. James Baldwin, "Every Good-Bye Ain't Gone," in *The Price of the Ticket,* 657.

4. James Baldwin, "The Harlem Ghetto," in *The Price of the Ticket,* 13.

5. James Baldwin, "Many Thousands Gone," in *The Price of the Ticket,* 77.

6. Frantz Fanon, *Black Skin, White Masks*, trans. Richard Philcox (Grove Press, 2008), 90.

7. Baldwin, "Many Thousands Gone," 78.

8. Fanon, *Black Skin, White Masks*, 118.

9. Baldwin, "The Harlem Ghetto," 22.

10. Baldwin, "Princes and Powers," in *The Price of the Ticket,* 55.

11. Frantz Fanon, "Racism and Culture," in *Toward the African Revolution,* trans. Haakon Chevalier (Grove Press, 1967), 37.

12. Frank Wilderson, "The Position of the Unthought: An Interview with Saidiya Hartman," *Qui Parle* 13, no. 2 (Spring/Summer 2003): 187.

13. Jared Sexton, "The Social Life of Social Death," *Intensions* 5 (Fall/Winter 2011): 28.

14. Sexton, "The Social Life of Social Death," 31.

15. Baldwin, "The Fire Next Time," in *The Price of the Ticket,* 340.

16. Michael Snediker, *Queer Optimism: Lyric Personhood and other Felicitous Persuasions* (Johns Hopkins University Press, 2009), 14.

17. Snediker, *Queer Optimism*, 3.

18. Snediker, *Queer Optimism,* 3–4.

19. Baldwin, "Many Thousands Gone," 87.

20. Calvin Warren, *Ontological Terror: Blackness, Nihilism, and Emancipation* (Duke University Press, 2018), 21.

21. Baldwin, "Many Thousands Gone," 83.

22. Ralph Ellison, "Blues People," in *Shadow and Act* (Knopf Doubleday, 2011), 257.

23. Music as opening of closure is a companion discourse with music and existential freedom, an issue that is explored in such interesting ways in Radiclani Clytus, "Paying Dues and Playing the Blues: Baldwin's Existential Jazz," in *The Cambridge Companion to James Baldwin,* ed. Michele Elam (Cambridge University Press, 2015), 70–84.

24. Kevin Quashie, *Black Aliveness, or a Poetics of Being* (Duke University Press, 2021), 9. Although Quashie's book places "being" in the title, his project is very different than the kind of ontological inquiry I have done in this chapter and those preceding. For Quashie, the interest is in aesthetics as a space of liberated or *alive* expressiveness—something that exceeds the merely aesthetic and addresses questions of identity, which is itself an inquiry into being. But it does not pose the question of being as such and how being is thought as a closed system but opens in acts of refusal and resistance. I think that, in the end, Quashie's text and what I am doing here end up being parallel, companion projects toward the same end.

25. Alain Locke, "The Negro Spirituals," in *The Works of Alain Locke,* ed. Charles Molesworth (Oxford University Press, 2012), 105.

26. James Baldwin, "Of the Sorrow Songs: The Cross of Redemption," in *The Cross of Redemption: The Uncollected Essays of James Baldwin* (Knopf Doubleday, 2011), 124.

27. James Baldwin and Raoul Peck, *I Am Not Your Negro* (New York: Vintage Books, 2017), 108.

Afterword

1. James Baldwin, "Many Thousands Gone," in *The Price of the Ticket* (Beacon Press, 2021), 83.

2. The images from this stunning exhibit are collected in *This Morning, This Evening, So Soon: James Baldwin and the Voices of Queer Resistance,* ed. Hilton Als and Rhea L. Combs (Delmonico Books/National Portrait Gallery, Smithsonian Institution, 2024).

3. Édouard Glissant, *Poetics of Relation,* trans. Betsy Wing (University of Michigan Press, 1999), 8–9.

4. Frantz Fanon, "West Indians and Africans," in *Toward the African Revolution,* trans. Haakon Chevalier (Grove Press, 1967), 27.

5. Édouard Glissant, *A New Region of the World: Aesthetics I,* trans. Martin Munro (Liverpool University Press, 2023), 122.

6. James Baldwin, "Notes of a Native Son," in *The Price of the Ticket,* 139.

7. Baldwin, "Notes of a Native Son."

8. Baldwin, "Many Thousands Gone," 77.

9. Baldwin, "Many Thousands Gone," 78.

INDEX